FROM CRONKITE TO COLBERT

FROM CRONKITE TO COLBERT

The Evolution of Broadcast News

♦ ♦ ♦

Geoffrey Baym

OXFORD
UNIVERSITY PRESS

OXFORD
UNIVERSITY PRESS

Oxford University Press, Inc., publishes works that further
Oxford University's objective of excellence in research, scholarship,
and education.

Oxford New York
Auckland Cape Town Dar es Salaam Hong Kong Karachi
Kuala Lumpur Madrid Melbourne Mexico City Nairobi
New Delhi Shanghai Taipei Toronto

With offices in
Argentina Austria Brazil Chile Czech Republic France Greece
Guatemala Hungary Italy Japan Poland Portugal Singapore
South Korea Switzerland Thailand Turkey Ukraine Vietnam

First published by Paradigm Publishers
Published by Oxford University Press,
198 Madison Avenue, New York, New York 10016
http://www.oup.com

Library of Congress Cataloging-in-Publication Data available

ISBN 978-0-19-994583-2 (hardback)
ISBN 978-0-19-994584-9 (paperback)

For Jennifer

CONTENTS

ACKNOWLEDGMENTS

As the renowned English scholar Jack Stillinger has rightly noted, despite the name on the cover, every book is a product of multiple authors. This one is no exception. It represents the culmination of a process that has unfolded over several years, and to which many people have contributed. Among those, David Paletz stands at the forefront. Both as the editor of the series within which this book has found a home, and in his previous position at the helm of *Political Communication*, he has enthusiastically offered me his support and his critical eye, even taking time out from his holiday on the French Riviera to help make my work better. For that, I am grateful. I am likewise grateful for my teachers at the University of Utah—Jim Anderson, Mary Strine, and Bob Avery—under whose tutelage the foundations of this book were laid. In the years since then, I have received invaluable encouragement and insight from Michael Delli Carpini, Kevin Barnhurst, Jeffrey Jones, and Dannagal Young, among others. Traces of these fine scholars run throughout the following pages. Of course, those pages would not exist at all if not for the labor of Jennifer Knerr and her fine team at Paradigm Publishers. I am thankful for their help and their patience. Finally, I could never have written this book if not for the extraordinary examples and constant motivation I find in my parents and my elder sister, whose own books have long lined my shelves. Nor could I have accomplished a task such as this without my wife Jennifer's boundless love and energy, which always sustain me.

1

♦ ♦ ♦

JON STEWART, BRIAN WILLIAMS, AND TED KOPPEL'S GIANT HEAD

Real News/Fake News

On an ordinary Thursday night during an uneventful time of the year, Jon Stewart was starting off his "fake news" program, *The Daily Show,* as he usually does. "We've got a great show for you," he began, but before he could continue, he was interrupted by the looming image of newsman Ted Koppel's head, projected in giant proportions on the video screen behind him. Speaking in the voice of an authoritative newscaster of a bygone era, the giant head of Ted Koppel proclaimed to Stewart: "I have unconfirmed reports coming in that say, quote, 'you suck.'" After a brief pause for the audience to laugh, the giant head put a finger to its ear and continued. "I'm now getting confirmed reports. At 11:05 Eastern Standard Time, it is now official that you, in fact, do suck."[1]

The moment was over quickly, but it was as remarkable as it was brief. Here was Koppel, whose departure from ABC's *Nightline* in 2005 was taken by many as more evidence of the demise of serious broadcast journalism, appearing on Comedy Central to jokingly lambaste the comedian who somehow has become one of the more trusted newscasters on television. The humor was complex, with Koppel's charge that Stewart "sucks" evoking his own concerns, made a few years earlier, that young people were abandoning traditional sources of news (such as his), and instead turning to *The Daily Show* and late-night comedy for news about government and politics. Indeed, as he was rising to a position of national prominence, Stewart himself appeared on Koppel's *Nightline* to discuss the shifting landscape of news, politics, and truth in American life. Koppel, who had anchored *Nightline* at that point for twenty-four years, bemoaned the fact that "a lot of television viewers, more, quite frankly, than I'm comfortable with, [now] get their news from the comedy channel." Despite Stewart's reassurances that *The Daily Show* hardly was a serious source of information, Koppel insisted otherwise. "It's no joke anymore," he lamented. "The reality of it is that there are a lot of people out there" who turn to you, he told Stewart, "to be informed. They actually think that they're coming closer to the truth," he worried, than they do by watching network news and public affairs programs such as *Nightline*.

Whether or not Koppel's worries were justified, he was accurately identifying the profound transformation we have been watching in the domain of news, public affairs media, and national political discourse. Increasing numbers of people—especially, but not only, the younger ones—have abandoned the so-called mainstream media outlets for alternative news sources, and an even larger number simply have "tuned out" from the world of news and politics altogether. As recently as the summer of 2008, in the heat of the historical presidential campaign between Barack Obama and the Republican John McCain, 34 percent of eighteen- to twenty-four-year-olds reported paying no attention to news on an ordinary day. That was an increase of 9 percent in just the past decade. Older people likewise have become increasingly less interested in news, with as many as 22 percent of people ages thirty to thirty-four also saying they go "newsless" most days. At the same time, and certainly not coincidentally, people have become deeply skeptical about "the news" itself. A recent survey found that the most trusted source of news is CNN, but only 30 percent of respondents said they believed all or most of what that network reported, a decline from 42 percent ten years earlier. Only 24 percent of Americans said they believe all or most of the information on Koppel's old show, the ABC nightly news, while Americans appear even more distrustful of print news. Only 22 percent said they believe all or most of the news in their local papers, 18 percent for the venerable *New York Times*, and just 16 percent for *USA Today*.[2]

Perhaps one could see this stark reality underlying the brief appearance of Ted Koppel's giant head on *The Daily Show* that night. But one also might be able to see the equally valid concern that the news media in general have devolved into a kind of infotainment—of corporate-produced entertainment masquerading as worthwhile information. For several years now, scholars and journalists alike have been warning about the worldwide spread of a "ratings-driven television journalism," one that provides happy talk, news-you-can-use, and stories about celebrity, sports, and crime at the expense of news about politics, public affairs, and civic culture.[3] Such commercialized infotainment, the critics argue, has undermined the public-service ethos of broadcast journalism—the assumption, to quote from Bill Kovach and Tom Rosenstiel, that the purpose of news is "to provide people with the information they need to be free and self governing."[4]

Appearing as a giant head on *The Daily Show,* however, Koppel appeared to have moved from being concerned about the decline of serious news to complicit in the ascendancy of entertainment. He playfully invokes that earlier, and increasingly rare kind of "real" news, the one in which the trusted newscaster would speak dispassionately of official facts and confirmed reports. His giant head becomes a caricature of the old insistence that news was, or could be, *disembodied*—"news from nowhere," the scholar Edward J. Epstein once called it[5]—the ostensibly objective effort to record the occurrence of the actual and verify its location in place and time. Koppel references that vanishing form of authoritative broadcast journalism to poke equal fun at Stewart and his style of "fake" news—a new kind of informational programming punctuated by laughter, sarcasm, and irony: remarkable for its nonliteral language and its subjective point of view.

This strange mixture of old and new offers a small window of insight into the changing nature of broadcast journalism and public affairs media, a window that opened a bit further later that same night, when NBC's Brian Williams, the anchor of the most-watched news program on television, appeared as Stewart's interview guest. Williams, of course, was the first "real" newscaster to have appeared as a giant head looking over Stewart's shoulder, a bit of self-reflexive humor on the part of *The Daily Show* highlighting Stewart's unlikely importance in the world of television news and American politics. Williams began his interview that night by referencing his role as the original giant head, making a series of crude jokes that played on the sexual connotations of the word "head." He then revealed that although he had agreed to be the giant head, he had refused Stewart's request that his giant head say the monster-like line "Williams hungry!" That, he explained, because he needed to preserve the "dignity" expected from the anchor of a network newscast. At that point, however, Koppel's giant head reappeared on the screen, and in beast-like fashion growled, "Koppel hungry!" Agreeing that Koppel is a television news "legend," Williams simply shrugged his shoulders and suggested that Koppel's departure from network news "frees him up" to be more playful and perhaps less dignified. It remains unclear, though, whether Williams thought that making crude "head" jokes was indeed behavior becoming the serious anchor, or if his claim of dignity was itself a tongue-in-cheek reference to an obsolete ideal.

From there, however, Williams reverted to a far more dignified posture, discussing his recent trip to Iraq. He returned to the traditional role of anchor, authoritatively describing his firsthand impressions of the war and trying to objectively summarize the complexities of the situation. Recognizing the shift, Stewart remarked that "it's amazing that you have the ability to talk so eloquently about that, and still do the really stupid shit we ask you to do." Williams's versatility—his ability to speak eloquently *and* "do stupid shit," to move, that is, between the serious and the silly, the playful and the professional—may indicate his "amazing" talent as a performer. It also, however, indicates the complicated nature of television news in an age marked by the profound conflation of journalism and entertainment. Williams's shifting performance on *The Daily Show* is emblematic of the current identity crisis in television news, a scattered profession that increasingly has become part informational resource, part circus sideshow, and entirely (and often crassly) self-promotional. In turn, it has become difficult to distinguish the informative from the distracting, the valuable from the manipulative, and indeed the real news from the fake.

Such may be the contrast drawn, not between Stewart, the fake anchor, and Williams, the real one, but between *Koppel* and Williams, who together represent two rather different paradigms of television news. Borrowing the concept from Thomas Kuhn, scholars argue that one can define a "journalistic paradigm"—a set of assumptions about the proper boundaries of theory and method, about how one does work that can be considered, at that moment, to be "journalism," and about why one does it in the first place.[6] The history of news reveals that journalism has never been a singular entity; rather, one can define a number of different paradigms that have taken shape over time. One of the last of his breed, Koppel, who began his career at ABC in 1963, is a remnant of a professionalized approach to news, the kind of public service journalism epitomized by Edward R. Murrow, Walter Cronkite, and the golden age of network television. Koppel is a product of the network age, a time when the anchors of the nightly network newscast were among the most trusted people in America and their programs were taken as the news of record, the authoritative summary of the day's events. Broadcast news then was assumed to be a democratic resource that would hold the government accountable for its actions and provide citizens with the information they needed to be active participants in the political process. If Koppel represents this residual paradigm of news, Williams, by contrast, represents the dominant paradigm of television news today. Two generations removed from Cronkite, he is the network anchor for the multichannel era, a time in which multibillion-dollar conglomerates compete through a variety of media platforms for attention from an increasingly fragmented audience. News has become a corporate product, focus-grouped and advertiser-approved, a kind of commercial journalism that blurs the line between news and entertainment in the name of profit, not democratic service.

This narrative of decline, of paradigm shift from the professional to the commercial, is by now a familiar one. We have long heard the worry that soft news has replaced hard news, entertainment has obscured information, and public service has been drowned out by the pursuit of private gain. The "sword" of journalism has been blunted, its former practitioners complain, the once-impenetrable wall between news and marketing breached, and the mission of informing the public abandoned for the much baser endeavor of selling eyeballs to advertisers.[7] The political theorist Jürgen Habermas influentially suggested that the public sphere—the imagined arena of open, rational-critical debate he argued was both essential for citizen engagement and enacted in early newspapers—had been colonized by a commodified mass media and, with it, the democratic conversation had been transformed into a commercial product packaged to sell.[8] Others have argued that we have been "amusing ourselves to death": that infotainment has "dumbed down" the populous and at the same time masked the real exercise of political-economic power.[9]

The brief exchange among Stewart, Williams, and Koppel's giant head, however, hints at a more complex picture. Compared to the dominant and the residual, Jon Stewart represents something altogether different, an emergent paradigm of hybrid media that blends news and entertainment in unprecedented ways. Although critics are quick to dismiss *The Daily Show* as a legitimate source of news (as is Stewart himself), it is clear that *The Daily Show* and its spin-off *The Colbert Report* have become central sites for news and political discussion in an increasingly complicated media environment. In early 2008, 28 percent of survey respondents reported learning at least something about the presidential campaign from comedy shows such as *The Daily Show*. Among eighteen- to twenty-nine-year-olds, that figure climbed to nearly 40 percent.[10] Stewart himself has been ranked as high as number 4 on a list of the country's most admired journalists (tied, perhaps not coincidentally, with Brian Williams).[11] And despite the accusation that the audience is largely made up of "stoned slackers," both *The Daily Show* and *The Colbert Report* reach viewers diverse in age and political affiliation, and high in education and political knowledge.[12] For those reasons, the interview segments on both shows have become near-mandatory bookings for authors selling works of political nonfiction as well as for politicians hoping to influence the national conversation. Senator John McCain, for example, used multiple visits to *The Daily Show* to revive his flagging campaign for the 2008 Republican presidential nomination. Hillary Clinton likewise appeared on the show for a ten-minute interview the night before the critical Ohio and Texas Democratic primaries, and Barack Obama appeared less than a week before he would win the presidency. For his part, Stephen Colbert insisted he gave Republican Mike Huckabee the "Colbert Bump," helping lift him from political obscurity. One empirical study has documented such a "bump," at least in fundraising by Democratic congressional representatives who have appeared on Colbert's "Better Know a District."[13]

Perhaps with some of that in mind, longtime political journalist Maureen Dowd, in a cover article in *Rolling Stone* magazine, declared Stewart and Colbert to be "America's anchors," the twenty-first-century equivalent of Cronkite and Murrow.[14] Although the specifics of that particular comparison may not stand up to close scrutiny, it does identify the current paradigm shift occurring in news and public affairs media. Stewart and Colbert have emerged as important sources of information, discussion, and, as we will see, critical inquiry—indications that what counts as journalism, both in practice and in the public imagination, is shifting again. This book, then, is about these multiple paradigm shifts—from the residual to the dominant, and from the dominant to the emergent—that are radically changing the nature of broadcast journalism and public affairs media. In the pages that follow, I trace a historical trajectory that begins with Cronkite and the broadcast journalism of the network age and ends, but for the moment, with Stewart and Colbert, who now sit at the vanguard of today's fragmented, post-network moment of journalistic instability and exploration.

To make sense of the evolution of news from Cronkite to Colbert is to confront the popular but misleading conceptual opposition between real news and fake news. The guiding premise here is that the dividing line between real and fake is not, and perhaps never was, as clear as many might hope or assume. It is difficult, if not impossible, to distinguish between news and entertainment with any true measure of precision.[15] The theorist Michel Foucault would further suggest that one cannot easily identify the line between politics and literature.[16] For Mikhail Bakhtin, the demarcation between nonfiction and fiction might be equally hard to pin down.[17] Upon closer inspection, these sets of opposites obscure far more than they reveal, hiding from view the elaborate conventions—historical, institutional, and cultural—that both enable and constrain our efforts to speak about and make sense of the world.

Ultimately, that is the real terrain the journey from Cronkite to Colbert takes us through, for it is, after all, the work of journalism—to represent the world, or to produce, as one journalism textbook explains, the "best obtainable version of the truth."[18] As such, this book is a study of genre: of journalistic forms and language, of the ways in which television news is assembled and the things it is in turn able to say. It also, however, is a study of authority, of the kinds of people who hold the power to appear on television and in whom (and for what reasons) we are asked to put our trust. It necessarily is also a consideration of truth, or more specifically, of the relationship between different kinds of journalism and the age-old need to speak truth to power. And in that, this book is about the democratic process, that great political experiment whose success or failure has come so largely to depend on the nature of its news media.

News Discourse and Political Culture

It is axiomatic that the vitality of democracy depends on an informed citizenry. As James Madison famously proclaimed, a "popular government" demands "popular information or the means of acquiring it," lest it devolve into a "farce or a tragedy."[19] Today, more than ever, news media serve as a primary link connecting individuals to the political process. Arguing that they overwhelmingly fail to provide the kind of information that is a necessary resource for citizenship and democratic participation, critics such as John Nichols and Robert McChesney worry that American politics has, as Madison warned, become both tragedy and farce.[20] I share their normative expectation that broadcast journalism and public affairs media should provide accurate, meaningful, and—most important of all—critical information to the citizenry. And indeed, the evolution of news reveals profound shifts in the quantity, quality, and character of the information made readily available to the public.

A focus on information alone, however, fails to acknowledge the broader role that "news" plays in a society. The journalism scholar Robert Park many years ago suggested that news could be understood as a form of knowledge, something more than just information. "News performs somewhat the same function for the public that perception does for the individual," he wrote. "It does not so much inform as *orient the public*." For Park, news contributed "not only to history and to sociology, but to folklore and literature . . . not merely to the social sciences, but to the humanities."[21] To put the point slightly differently, news is not simply the transmission of content from a sender to a receiver, but rather a form of communication, one that helps to shape the boundaries of community and the contours of culture.[22]

The inquiry that follows here builds on the insight that broadcast news is less transmission than it is communication—less information than discourse, a way of speaking about and thus making sense of politics, governance, and public life. Never simply a window to the world, television news disseminates information about politics, but more importantly it helps constitute the very parameters of political culture itself. It informs the popularly shared "imagination, values, and dispositions" that in turn constitute "the character of political processes and political behavior."[23] Political culture precedes individual citizens' knowledge, attitudes, and beliefs—the kind of political traits that media researchers are usually interested in measuring. It forms the ground from which people subsequently can think and act politically, and is inseparable from the ways in which people understand their own identities as citizens. The political force of news, therefore, ultimately lies in its ability to influence what Foucault once described as "the spontaneous philosophy of those who [do] not philosophize."[24] To consider the evolution of news from Cronkite to Colbert thus is to think not just about what we know but about how we know—about the shifting ways in which we conceptualize the political system, the nature of political authority, and the shape of social knowledge.

Evolutions

When Ted Koppel's giant head proclaims that Jon Stewart sucks, or when political scientists worry about the rise of infotainment, they are invoking a set of expectations about the nature of the political system and the media's proper role within it that is an inheritance from an earlier age. Our assumptions about what real news is, or should be, largely stem from the ideals of the public-service approach that characterized what NBC News pioneer Reuven Frank once celebrated as "the brief, wonderful life of network news."[25] As I will argue, it may be wise to avoid Frank's nostalgia for an earlier time, one that contained its own wealth of contradictions. More importantly, though, we must recognize that our expectations of news—our assumptions about the "real" and the "fake"—are the product of a bygone era.

In the years since Walter Cronkite could be America's anchor, television itself—which we can understand both as an institution and as a cultural practice—has undergone a series of fundamental transformations. Scholars have identified three distinct periods in the evolution of television, three historical moments of various lengths shaped by differing constellations of political, economic, technological, and cultural factors.[26] The period that has had the greatest hold on the popular imagination and still informs our basic assumptions about what television news is, or should be, is the network age, the time frame stretching from the widespread adoption of television in the 1950s to the rise of cable in the 1980s. During those three decades, "television" was synonymous with CBS, NBC, and ABC. Simply put, the institutional conventions of the "Big Three" determined what television was. Beginning in the mid-1980s, however, developing technologies would lead to a dramatic expansion of viewing options and the end of network hegemony during what we can call the multichannel era. Finally, in just the past few years, the multichannel era has been giving way to the truly post-network age, an unstable time of technological convergence and rapidly changing media forms and practices. As we will see, each of these historical moments has engendered contrasting paradigms of broadcast news.

The Network Age

The paradigm of broadcast journalism that we take as "real" was a product of the early- to mid-twentieth century and tied to the development of a national system of communication. The communication scholar James Carey argued that "modern media" such as film, radio, and finally television created the very possibility of the mass audience.[27] The mass media reached their full ascendancy with the network age of TV, when, in a time before cable, satellite, the VCR, and even the remote control, the average American home received only three or four television channels. CBS, NBC, and ABC together commanded some 90 percent of the prime-time viewing audience and the annual profits that came with their dominance of the airwaves.[28] Such truly national media "represented a centripetal force in social organization," Carey suggested, one that produced the "remarkable potential for the centralization of power and authority."[29] Indeed, the network news divisions both facilitated and inordinately influenced American political life. If, in the 1950s, Americans brought television into their homes, by the end of the next decade it had become their favorite source of news. In the late-1960s, as many as one out of four people in the country watched the network news each evening, and twice as many as that said they believed the news on television more than they trusted the news in print.[30]

The most watched, and most trusted, news on television was provided by CBS. Beginning with Edward R. Murrow's radio reports from London during World War II, the so-called Tiffany Network was the leading force in broadcast journalism during the network age. Following the war, Murrow and the team of reporters he had assembled—including Eric Sevareid and Howard K. Smith, whose voices we will hear in subsequent chapters—returned to the States to develop the new craft of television news. Murrow himself would quickly become the stuff of legend with his 1954 confrontation with right-wing demagogue Senator Joseph McCarthy (a Republican from Wisconsin) on the public affairs program *See It Now.*

In 1948, CBS had launched the network's first nightly news program, a fifteen-minute summary of the top national stories of the day. Less than a decade later, more than 14 million people were tuning in to *The CBS-TV News* each night, giving the short program a greater "circulation" than any single newspaper or magazine in the world. In 1963, CBS would again establish journalism precedent, expanding its evening news program to a full half-hour. The anchor of that show was Walter Cronkite, who had been working for CBS News as a reporter and then anchor since 1950, six years after Murrow first offered him a job. As anchor and managing editor of the *Evening News*, Cronkite quickly became a fixture in millions of American homes. In 1972, a public opinion survey found that Cronkite—or "Uncle Walter" as many thought of him—was the most trusted man in the country. He would continue to anchor the *Evening News* until his retirement in 1981, at which point President Jimmy Carter awarded him the Medal of Freedom, the highest civilian honor in the United States.[31]

The prestige of CBS and the wider authority of network news were enabled by a federal regulatory posture that defined broadcasting as an "infrastructure industry" essential for national economic development.[32]

Beginning with the federal Communications Act of 1934, the government protected the networks from the uncertainties of competition by erecting steep barriers to entry that, among other things, limited the development of cable television for years after the advent of the technology. At the same time, federal regulation was built on the principle of trusteeship, the insistence that in order to profit from the use of the public airwaves, broadcasters were obliged to act as trustees of the air and serve the "public interest, convenience, and necessity." Arguing that "the foundation stone of the American system of broadcasting . . . is the right of the public to be informed," the Federal Communications Commission mandated that broadcasters air public affairs programming. For many local television stations, that requirement was easily met by broadcasting the nightly network news.[33]

For their part, Americans were assumed to have met their civic responsibility by watching the nightly news. And as scholars have noted, the implicit agreement in the television business to air news on every channel at the same time each day—and particularly during television's dinner hour—effectively forced people who wanted to watch TV at that time to watch news. Because of that, network news may have played a particularly important role in reaching less-educated people, those who did not get news from other sources.[34] By most accounts, the networks understood that with such influence came responsibility. Richard Salant, while he was president of CBS News, saw the news as "something that CBS owed to the public and to its conscience,"[35] while network president Frank Stanton argued that network news played a "critical" function in the formation of public opinion and therefore in the "very survival of democracy itself."[36] Insisting on an "impenetrable wall" between "the newsroom and the boardroom," between "church and state, cathedral and cash register," network newsworkers saw themselves in the business of public information, a distinct enterprise from the networks' wider profit-seeking strategies.[37]

Journalism scholar Daniel Hallin describes Salant's and the other networks' approach to news as "high-modern" journalism, a paradigm that was steeped in the logic of the American progressive movement.[38] Itself an offshoot of the wider historical age generally referred to as "modernity," the progressive era was marked by the twin forces of rationalization and professionalization—the dividing of social life into distinct domains and the reliance on professional expertise to identify and solve problems within those domains. Ascending hand in hand with the scientific enterprise, high-modern journalists were assumed to be informational professionals, value-free experts committed to the ideals of an objective public interest and the rational pursuit of social order. Thus Salant could confidently insist that "our job is to give people not what they want but what they *ought* to have."[39]

Drawing clear distinctions between the stories the people might want and the news they most certainly would need, Salant asserted a staunch division between "journalism" and "show business," insisting that his employees draw the sharpest of possible lines between the two: sharp, he suggested, "to the point of eccentricity."[40] Salant gave voice to the institutional conventions that divided the television industry into clearly defined news and entertainment divisions. Produced largely in Los Angeles, the latter was the primary business of the networks, earning revenue and filling the majority of the daily schedule. The former, by contrast, was freed from any expectation of commercial gain, headquartered instead in New York, and aired during limited and predictable times: mostly the dinner hour and Sunday mornings, except for those rare instances when it would "interrupt our regularly scheduled programming."

This understanding of the bright line between news and entertainment was firmly grounded in the categorical distinctions modernity assumed between the domains of the political-normative and the aesthetic-expressive. The former was assumed to be the realm of social organization and resource allocation, justice, and the collective good. The latter, by contrast, was seen as the proper domain of art and affect, pleasure and play.[41] To the high-modern newsworkers, it seemed obvious that broadcast journalism was part and parcel of the political-normative domain. News was the rational-critical investigation of matters of assumed public importance and thus not to be mistaken for the aesthetic-expressive content that filled the rest of the networks' schedules, despite—or perhaps because of—the fact, as Salant noted, "it all comes out sequentially on the same point of the dial and on the same tube."[42]

Despite the nostalgia that so many former newsworkers have for this earlier era of news, the high-modern paradigm offered a narrow understanding of the kinds of issues, identities, voices, and values that could be considered properly political. James Carey argues that it reduced the role of the citizens, speaking at and for them but allowing them no role in the conversation except as the audience.[43] News of the network age imposed what Mikhail Bakhtin once called a "unitary language"—a consolidation of the "verbal-ideological world" that occurs hand in hand with wider processes of sociocultural and political-economic centralization.[44] Network news produced a singular worldview that limited the range of understandings about the nature of the political domain and the ways in which it could be represented. Reproduced each day, this worldview was taken as the self-evident expression of common sense. Thus Cronkite could sign off every newscast by insisting that "that's the way it is"—a remarkable claim asserting not just the accuracy of his content, but also the validity and universality of the assumptions upon which the content was based.

Multichannel Transformations

Recent history has demonstrated that the networks' centralized influence and authority were dependent upon their economic dominance and a regulatory posture grounded in the conviction that the airwaves were a limited public good. Both of those pillars of support would disintegrate, however, during the multichannel era. Beginning with the advent of "electronic news gathering" equipment (i.e., video shooting and editing systems), which allowed local stations to compete for news audiences; continuing through the spread of cable, satellite TV, and various video recording systems; and culminating with the advent of the Internet, technological changes in the late-twentieth century produced an expanding multiplicity of channels and fractured the networks' hold on the mass audience.

Encouraged by a landscape in which news had become available on network, local, and twenty-four-hour cable TV, and convinced that broadcasting required no special oversight, that the television was, in the words of Reagan-era FCC Chairman Mark Fowler, a household appliance like any other—a "toaster with a picture"—the federal government abandoned the logic of scarcity and its protection of network news. Beginning during the Reagan presidency and culminating with the Telecommunications Act of 1996, the government dropped most of the regulations that mandated news and public affairs programming.[45] Conceptualizing the public as an assemblage of consumers, not citizens, and the "public interest" as that which consumers want, not need, the act embraced Fowler's vision of "a commercial broadcasting system where the marketplace rather than the myths of a trusteeship approach determines what programming the American people receive on radio and television and who provides it."[46]

If the multiplication of media outlets dislodged the networks and opened the possibility of a competitive information marketplace, the 1996 act also accelerated the consolidation of media ownership, enabling the growth of the multinational, multibillion-dollar conglomerates that today control information and entertainment providers of every variety, from network television to local radio, from newspapers to movie studios, from book publishers to magazines, and more recently, from popular Internet social networking sites to the most frequented online news sources. If an earlier generation of network executives saw themselves as broadcasters who recognized the power of programming to and speaking for the nation, the new breed of media managers were businesspeople, committed only to increasing shareholder values. As early as 1986, when his company took control of NBC, General Electric's CEO Jack Welch dismissed the idea that network news was a "public trust" to be protected from the commercial imperative. His new president of NBC, Robert Wright, insisted that he couldn't even "understand the concept."[47]

Instead, the primary tilt of the new corporate landscape was toward commodification, the reconceptualization of all media as products packaged for maximum profit. A market-driven approach to news replaced an earlier professional model, with news producers now striving to attract, rather than inform, audiences. Salant's insistence that news provide the information the public ought to know was abandoned in the face of the commercial insistence that newscasts appeal to the right demographics and appease the advertisers who want to reach them. In practice, this meant a turn away from hard news focused on governmental policy and foreign affairs and, as CNN President Jonathan Klein would demand of his news staff, toward "emotionally gripping, character-driven narratives."[48] Conceptualized less as a democratic service than as a synergistic resource in an integrated conglomerate structure, television news largely became another style of "reality TV," a narrative-based form of infotainment, blending the aesthetic-expressive with the political-normative in the effort to tell engaging stories about the real.

To put the point differently, the high-modern paradigm of the network age evolved into a postmodern paradigm in the multichannel era. For some critics, NBC's Brian Williams may be the "poster boy" for the paradigm that dominates the news on TV today. "No one understands this NASCAR nation more than Brian," celebrated NBC's president, Jeff Zucker, as Williams prepared to take over the *Nightly News* anchor chair. For his part, Williams promised to get out of the "New York-Washington axis" to tell stories that would resonate in the nation's heartland.[49] Rejecting the residual high-modern logic that professional journalists should, or could, define an objective public interest, he instead insisted that "the American people have a funny way of deciding what their reality is."[50] With that, Williams effectively expressed the assumptions that underlie a postmodern approach to the news—the epistemological relativism that rejects the possibility of objectivity while suspecting that all normative standards are culturally located and historically contingent. No longer striving to tell it "the way it is," the postmodern newscast instead tries to tell it the way the audience most wants to hear it. For critics, the clear danger of such a paradigm is that in the absence of a commitment to truth, news too easily becomes a mouthpiece for feel-good propaganda—for political proclamations such as "mission accomplished" and "heckuva job, Brownie" that bear little resemblance to the reality they claim to represent—in place of the kind of democratic insight the high-modern paradigm promised.

Post-Network Possibilities

For many observers of media, the story would appear to end there: A corporate-dominated media environment reduced news to hollow spectacle, gutting the democratic vitality of mass-mediated journalism. To be sure, the power of the contemporary media conglomerates and their profit agenda is not to be underestimated. At the same time, however, we must recognize that in just the last few years, the context of media has changed drastically. The period of multichannel transition is giving way to the post-network age, a time of instability in which media technologies, institutions, practices, and forms are in a state of flux. Americans remain committed to their television—TV is still the number 1 source of news in the country—but television viewing has grown increasingly more complicated. By the summer of 2008, more than 60 percent of U.S. households reported having cable (and the average cable system now provides access to well over one hundred channels), a third have satellite TV, and slightly more than that have digital recorders that allow a far greater measure of control over the flow of programming. At the same time, though, 71 percent of households have personal computers with broadband Internet connections that enable on-demand streaming of high-resolution video, while 15 percent of Americans now carry so-called smartphones, cellular telephones equipped with full multimedia capabilities.[51]

Because of these ongoing technological developments, media producers have lost the tight control they used to have over where and when viewers watch particular programs. But these changes also have engendered new opportunities. The television scholar Amanda Lotz notes that the post-network age has led to a "vast expansion in economically viable content," as media producers explore new distribution possibilities and alternative models for financing shows and generating revenue from them.[52] Actively pursuing strategies of convergence, media companies have reconceptualized the television show itself. No longer a linear and bounded program to be distributed through a particular medium, the "show" has become digital content—a nonlinear data stream that moves fluidly among and across media platforms. y[53]

In such a landscape, patterns of news consumption are shifting accordingly. Audience attention is spread over more and more outlets, while the very habit of watching news at particular times each day (especially during the dinner hour) is disappearing. More than half of Americans can now be categorized as "news grazers," people who get news "from time to time." Nearly a quarter say that they watch newscasts on the Internet, and a third say they watch individual news videos online. More than two-thirds say they have received news through their e-mail, while more than half of the people who get news online say they follow links to individual stories without ever visiting a news organization's home page.[54]

The major corporate news providers still dominate the online traffic in news. Three of the five most-visited news sites—MSN, CNN, and MSNBC—are produced by or in partnership with the dominant players in the television news business. The other two—Yahoo! and Google—provide convenient access to a range of stories from the Associated Press and other high-profile news operations. But this kind of corporate news now has to coexist alongside an ever-increasing array of web-based sources for political information and conversation that provide global and often instantaneous access to text, images, and video. Ongoing developments in handheld cameras and computer-based editing systems continue to diminish the access barriers to production, while websites such as YouTube provide virtually unlimited capacity for the distribution of user-generated content. The result is an expanding and unconstrainable discursive environment, a "communicative space," suggests one scholar of media and democracy, "of infinite size."[55]

As the new media scholar Henry Jenkins explains, the emerging media environment is driving the spread of "convergence culture." Jenkins describes a "paradigm shift" from "medium-specific content toward content that flows across multiple media channels, toward the increased interdependence of communications systems, toward multiple ways of accessing media content, and toward ever more complex relations between top-down corporate media and bottom-up participatory culture."[56] The defining feature of convergence culture is experimentation—the rethinking of previous assumptions about what media are and how they work. In this unstable environment, television's programming forms—the genres that long functioned to catalogue and classify media content—have themselves become marked by instability, the lines that distinguish one from another harder, if not impossible, to identify. News producers continue to experiment with a range of genres and forms, generating an increasing variety of infotainment approaches that mimic fictional entertainment for the presentation of factual content. Along with this aestheticization of the political-normative sphere, though, we also now are seeing the flip side of infotainment, the politicization of the aesthetic-expressive sphere. In an age when such cross-genre hybridization has become the norm, the producers of entertainment television, both factual and fictional, are mining the world of politics and current events. The result is what Jeffrey Jones has labeled "new political television," an emergent genre that draws equally from informational and entertainment forms and offers new ways of talking about and engaging with politics.[57]

The conflation of techniques and topics speaks to something deeper than the latest trend in programming strategies. The blurring of generic boundaries reflects an underlying recognition of the arbitrary nature of those boundaries and a challenge to the structures of political and social power upon which such differentiation ultimately depends.[58] That is to say, the melding of genres reflects the decentering forces of multiculturalism that simultaneously are constituent and constitutive of the audience fragmentation that defines the post-network age. To borrow from Mikhail Bakhtin, we are experiencing a process of "verbal-ideological decentering," one that inevitably occurs "when a national culture loses its sealed-off and self-sufficient character, when it becomes conscious of itself as only one among *other* cultures and languages."[59]

The kind of "unitary language" imposed by the high-modern paradigm of news and the centralized power of the network age always obscures an unavoidable multiplicity of languages and worldviews. Despite the appearances of uniformity, Bakhtin reminds us that language in any era is always stratified into "social dialects, characteristic group behavior, professional jargons, generic languages, languages of generations and age groups, tendentious languages, languages of the authorities, of various circles and of passing fashions, languages that serve the specific sociopolitical purposes of the day, even of the hour."[60] In the current media landscape, however, when all of these voices are making their way into the public arena and finding expression in a myriad of genres and forms, the "struggle in socio-linguistic points of view" that remains suppressed in times of centralization emerges, and the frameworks for making sense of reality proffered by dominant discourses in turn become open to debate and rearticulation. In a heterogeneous culture in which multiple voices are continually overlapping, the result is a deep hybridization, not just the intentional stylistic manipulation of form, but a more profound melding of the very conceptual systems that shape both media content and public discourse.

Part and parcel with the emergence of convergence culture, therefore, is the phenomenon of discursive integration, in which the styles, standards, and assumptions of multiple and at times incompatible discourses are continuously placed and re-placed in new and often momentary arrangements. In a media era marked by the permeability of form and the fluidity of content, the political-normative has become interwoven with the aesthetic-expressive, while discourses of high-modernism and postmodernism, of rational-critical debate and aesthetic consumption, regularly collide.

This discursively integrated nature of contemporary politics and political media was clearly evident during the 2008 presidential campaign, an election in which entertainment-based television played a more influential role than ever. According to one study, candidates for the presidency appeared on late-night talk shows (including *The Daily Show* and *The Colbert Report*) 110 times during the lengthy campaign—that compared to 25 appearances four years earlier.[61] Barack Obama, Hillary Clinton, and John McCain all paid visits to the sketch comedy show *Saturday Night Live*. Of course, SNL's most significant contribution to the campaign came with comedian Tina Fey's repeated parody of the Republican vice-presidential nominee, Sarah Palin.

Following her unlikely nomination, the little-known governor of Alaska quickly became the target of stinging political humor, nowhere more so than on SNL, where Fey (whose resemblance to Palin was widely noted) mastered her verbal intonations and physical mannerisms. In all, Fey would appear six times as Palin, including skits alongside the *real* Palin and then the actual John McCain. Fey's parody was at its most devastating, though, in her re-creation of Palin's disastrous interview with the CBS anchor Katie Couric. Couric was one of only three national TV personalities whom the Republican campaign had allowed access to Palin. That interview was broadcast in four segments on the *Evening News* in late September 2008. In it, Palin stumbled badly, largely unable to answer most of Couric's questions (including ones as simple as "What newspapers do you read?") and often rambling incoherently when pressed to discuss matters of policy. For her part, Couric was awarded a Walter Cronkite Award for the interview, which

CBS celebrated as a "defining moment" in the campaign.[62] SNL's version of it, however, may have been equally, if not more, significant.

Fey appeared alongside SNL's Amy Poehler, who played the role of Couric and asked several of the same questions the real Couric had asked Palin. At times, Fey's answers directly quoted Palin, re-creating her scattered, meandering, and largely nonsensical replies, all to the delight of the audience and the millions who would later watch the skit online. The news media were quick to get in on the action as well. Both CNN's Wolf Blitzer and MSNBC's Keith Olbermann would replay bits from the CBS interview and the SNL version, focusing largely on Fey's verbatim reciting of Palin's own words. Subsequently, many of the journalists who had been given little access to the real Palin began relying on the Fey impersonation, circulating and amplifying it; using it perhaps to make the kinds of critical claims about Palin's competence to be vice president that the rules of "objectivity" prohibited. Indeed one study has found that Fey's performance became interwoven with journalistic reports on Palin and the Couric interview. As the campaign neared its final days, journalists regularly invoked the inane claim "I can see Russia from my house!" to characterize Palin, that despite the fact that it was Fey—not Palin—who had said it.[63]

John McCain also had his problems with entertainment television in 2008. Although he had long been a recurrent guest on *The Daily Show* and had announced his candidacy on *The Late Show with David Letterman*, his last-minute decision to cancel another appearance with Letterman may have irreparably damaged his campaign. McCain was scheduled to be Letterman's guest in late September (the very same day the Palin interview began running on CBS) but had abruptly canceled, ostensibly because he had decided to "suspend" his campaign and return to Washington to play a role in discussions over the burgeoning financial crisis. Letterman did not respond kindly, instead spending his entire program that night insulting McCain, challenging his choice of Palin as a running mate, mocking his wealth and his age, and questioning his judgment, integrity, and fitness for office. Then when his producers discovered that McCain actually was still in New York at the time and preparing for an interview of his own with Katie Couric, they tapped into the CBS News feed while Letterman continued his assault on McCain. "Hey John, I've got a question," Letterman yelled over live pictures of McCain and Couric. "You need a ride to the airport?"[64]

Even worse for McCain, Letterman's fill-in guest that night was Keith Olbermann, the sportscaster turned entertaining newsman, who was no fan of the McCain campaign. Olbermann delightedly joined in the roasting and then referred to it repeatedly on his own prime-time program on MSNBC in the following days. Finally, after three weeks of bad press, largely emanating from Letterman himself and circulated online, McCain returned to the program with figurative hat in hand. That appearance drew an audience of some six and a half million people, compared to the show's regular viewership of three million. In the twenty-three-minute conversation that followed, Letterman grilled McCain on a number of serious topics, including Palin's qualifications for the vice presidency, the increasingly negative tone of his campaign, and his ever-changing stand on economic policy.[65] Far from being the kind of casual chat that once characterized the late-night interview, this one did indeed resemble a new form of political TV, one in which the comedian had taken on the unlikely role of critical journalist.

As the SNL re-creation of the Couric-Palin interview, its treatment in the political press, and McCain's Letterman debacle illustrate, the boundaries between news and comedy and between politics and entertainment have become fundamentally obscured in a discursively integrated, post-network age. In this emergent landscape, Jon Stewart and Stephen Colbert may indeed be the new breed of anchor—not the stars of fake news but the vanguard of a new kind of public affairs media, a much-needed reimagination of the possibilities of political journalism in a post-network age. As we will see, in comparison to Cronkite's high-modernism or Williams's postmodernism, they represent a still-developing neo-modern paradigm of news, one that uses the style of postmodernism to pursue the high-modern ideals of public information and democratic accountability that motivated news of the network age.

Trajectories

Through a series of case studies, the chapters that follow chart a historical trajectory from Cronkite to Colbert. Offering more than a simple narrative about the breakdown of "real" news or the rise of infotainment, they instead tell a story of shifting paradigms of news and public affairs media that are both symptoms and causes of wider transformations in the surrounding media landscape. The path from Cronkite to Colbert reveals more than just the corruption of a serious informational form by the logic of entertainment, a revolution, to borrow Kuhn's language, in which one paradigm has overrun another. Rather, three different ages have engendered three different paradigms, all of which, as the exchange between Stewart, Williams, and Koppel's giant head illustrates, coexist today in varying degrees, sometimes in cooperation and sometimes in antagonism. Adapted to different environments, the residual high-modern, the dominant postmodern, and the emergent neo-modern paradigms are ultimately of the same species: media forms that bridge the divide between the citizen and the state, between the individual and public life. They provide us, however, with contrasting lenses through which we know about, engage with, and ultimately understand the political domain.

The next chapter begins at the apex of the network age and, in particular, with network coverage of Watergate, the infamous scandal in the early 1970s that led to the only resignation of a sitting president in U.S. history. The work of Walter Cronkite and his colleagues during Watergate exemplifies the ideals and the limitations of the high-modern paradigm and its assumption that news was an authoritative informational resource intended to serve the democratic needs of a rational-critical citizenry. To better understand the contours of the high-modern paradigm, I compare the Watergate coverage to network coverage of a similar yet remarkably different presidential scandal—the impeachment of Bill Clinton twenty-five years later. Itself an indicator of more postmodern times, the Monica Lewinsky scandal of 1998 and its coverage lay bare the transformation in broadcast journalism from the high-modern to the postmodern, from the democratic work of holding power accountable to a corporatized form of reality-based entertainment competing for ratings in a multichannel era.

In chapter 2, "Representing Reality," I specifically look at the form of news in those two eras, at the representational techniques that broadcast journalists use to package reality for the television screen. The power of form is to shape the boundaries of the journalistic imagination; form provides the templates that arrange and constrain journalistic accounts of the real. The coverage of Watergate reveals the high-modern pursuit of realism, its attempt to transparently present the actual and "let the facts speak for themselves." The Clinton coverage, however, demonstrates a postmodern indulgence in artifice, the nightly news' recognition and perhaps celebration of its efforts to use elements of the real to generate televisual spectacle. In chapter 3, "Publicizing Politics," I turn to the language of news—to the different ways the networks spoke about the two presidential scandals. Here the analysis considers the word choices, rhetorical tropes, and conceptual frames used to explain national politics in the two contrasting eras. In particular, I examine the organizing metaphors that structured the coverage and reveal the differing ways the high-modern and postmodern paradigms understand the nature of politics and the purpose of news.

Together, chapters 2 and 3 make the case that our assumptions about what exactly constitutes "real" news reflect the standards and practices of the network age and the high-modern paradigm. In the multichannel era, however, "the news" has become something distinctly more postmodern and less "real." In the next two chapters, I extend the analysis of the postmodern paradigm, examining broadcast news coverage of the bitterly contested 2004 presidential campaign. In many ways, the reelection of George Bush was a pivotal point in the evolution of television news, marking the real breakdown of the nightly news as viable democratic resource. Although they would continued to posture as real news, the networks and the other mainstream producers of daily news found themselves unwilling or unable to counter a postmodern presidential administration that was committed to aggressively manipulating the news media, turning public information into marketing for the purpose of manufacturing public perception. Chapter 4, "The Slow Death of CBS News," examines this dynamic, exploring in particular the collapse of the CBS *Evening News* and its rich legacy as the house of Murrow and Cronkite. The performance of Dan Rather's *Evening News* in 2004 well illustrated the insurmountable problems facing the residual concept of the authoritative newscast in an advanced postmodern, multichannel environment.

If the 2004 campaign tells the story of breakdown, however, it also begins the story of reinvention. That campaign was a truly multichannel affair, as an increasing range of media outlets offered election coverage and audiences embraced a host of alternative sources of political information and conversation. Even as they continued to hemorrhage viewers (and those who remained were older than ever), the networks themselves contributed to this expansion of broadcast news, re-creating themselves across a variety of forms and channels. At CBS, the *Evening News* remained the flagship operation, but having merged with the corporate giant Viacom four years earlier, the CBS News brand was being recrafted in synergistic combinations with a number of its Viacom partners.

In chapter 5, "News from Somewhere," I consider three of these: CBS's *Early Show,* the network's version of "breakfast TV" specifically designed for women; the short-lived BET *Nightly News,* an unlikely cooperative venture between CBS and Black Entertainment Television to produce a national newscast targeting African-Americans; and MTV's *Choose or Lose,* the equally surprising effort by the teen-culture channel to explain presidential politics to young people. Each news form was designed to reach more narrowly defined, culturally differentiated audiences than the network nightly news and experimented with the possibilities of paradigms. Together they offered hybrid blends that complicated the standard approach of contemporary broadcast news and generated multiple frames for understanding journalism, accessing politics, and ultimately making sense of the real.

The different kinds of news examined in chapters 4 and 5 illustrate the problems and possibilities opened up in the multichannel era. The 2004 presidential campaign, however, stood at the dawn of the post-network age, and, not coincidentally, it also was in 2004 that a program produced by Comedy Central, itself another Viacom subsidiary, emerged as a central location for mediated political information, commentary, and conversation. The last thee chapters thus turn to *The Daily Show* and *The Colbert Report,* programs that have been enabled by the centrifugal forces that define the post-network age: the fracturing of a centralized, authoritative model of broadcast journalism and an equal willingness to rethink assumptions about what television news is supposed to look like and how it should work. Unlike the examples of multichannel news considered in chapter 5, which largely sought to rework postmodern network news for more narrowly conceptualized audiences, *The Daily Show* and *The Colbert Report* instead offer something radically different. Never claiming to be news, and consistently denying they share any of the intentions, agenda, or responsibilities of the news, they mimic but ultimately reject the dominant conventions of newscasting. They employ new methods and open unfamiliar spaces for the consideration of politics and public affairs on post-network television.

Chapter 6, "*The Daily Show* and the Reinvention of Political Journalism," explores the ascendance of *The Daily Show,* which largely was a response to the machinations of the Bush administration and its momentary, yet immensely consequential, co-option of the mainstream news media. I examine the novel ways in which *The Daily Show* draws on and reworks generic conventions of both the nightly news and the late-night talk show to create a powerful form of critical journalism, one that uses satire to challenge power, parody to critique the so-called real news, and dialogue to enact a model of deliberative democracy. Chapter 7, "'Nothing I'm Saying Means Anything,'" extends the analysis to *The Colbert Report,* which was launched in the fall of 2005 and is to cable news punditry as *The Daily Show* is to the nightly news. A complex reaction to the kind of opinion talk that has substituted itself for news on so much contemporary TV, *The Colbert Report* represents an ironic counterweight to the postmodern privileging of emotion over logic, volume over fact, and "truthiness" over truth.

Spanning the divide between discursive domains—between the serious and the silly, the informative and the entertaining, and ultimately the modern and the postmodern—*The Daily Show* and *The Colbert Report* are increasingly straddling divisions among media platforms and technologies. In chapter 8, "Networked News: Stewart, Colbert, and the New Public Sphere," I take up the question of convergence, the driving force in public affairs media in the post-network age. Specifically, I follow the two shows as they migrate from television and into an online environment, that continuously morphing space in which the very nature of the journalistic text is undergoing profound changes in its packaging, its dissemination, and, most importantly, its relationship to its audience.

With that, we reach a momentary resting point, the current culmination of the journey from Cronkite to Colbert. The dynamics of change described here are continuing to accelerate as we move further into the post-network age and as the neo-modern paradigm gains wider currency. One can see that clearly in the political and social transformations we've just recently witnessed, including the 2008 election of Barack Obama, who himself might be the first neo-modern president. I consider that point in chapter 9, "Real News, Fake News, and the Conversation of Democracy," which retraces the contours of the dominant, residual, and emergent inclinations in broadcast news, public affairs, and popular political discourse. There I synthesize the differing assumptions the three paradigms make about the nature of democracy, the role of the media, and finally the differing visions of citizenship they articulate—the roles, that is, they tell us we should play in our own political process. I end, finally, on an optimistic note, with the hope, as recent events may suggest, that broadcast news in the post-network era might become more democratically useful and that our shared political culture will be better off for it.

2

♦ ♦ ♦

REPRESENTING REALITY

To hear Jon Stewart and the people at Comedy Central tell it, *The Daily Show* is fake news, a "nightly half-hour series unburdened by objectivity, journalistic integrity or even accuracy." They claim "zero credibility" and insist that watching the show is not a substitute for the news—it's "even better than being informed."[1] They might be right on that last point, but the label of "fake news" so carefully cultivated by the show's creators and readily adopted by most observers is, at heart, misleading. That's because any notion of "fake" depends upon an equal conception of a "real." To suggest *The Daily Show* is fake news is to assume that there is some authentic or legitimate kind of news: a journalism of information and accuracy, integrity and objectivity. Certainly these are the ideals advanced by most journalism schools, but a lap around the dial of contemporary television quickly reveals that this imagined "real" news is hard to find. Rather than insist on some ahistorical, universal notion of News (with a capital *N*), scholars of journalism history have argued that in the absence of any codified set of professional guidelines, a standardized entrance examination, or a supervisory guild, news instead is defined and constrained by a set of cultural practices, informal and often implicit agreements about proper conduct, style, and form.[2] Today, those practices are in flux and increasingly multiple, debatable, and open for reconsideration.

The ideals of "real" news (the ones Comedy Central insists you won't find on *The Daily Show*) are obviously compelling, but we make a mistake if we assume they are synonymous with journalism itself. Instead, they can be better understood as a legacy of the high-modern period in American journalism, which Daniel Hallin dates roughly from the end of World War II until the waning years of the twentieth century.[3] In this chapter and the next, I explore that paradigm of high-modern broadcast news—its conventional practices and discursive assumptions—and examine its dissolution into a more postmodern kind of reality-based television programming. In particular, these chapters compare and contrast network television news coverage of Watergate and the Richard Nixon impeachment process of 1973–74 with similar coverage from the network news of the Monica Lewinsky scandal and the impeachment of Bill Clinton in 1998.

Although the nature of the president's transgressions in the two scandals was quite different—one involved explicit violations of constitutional law and an effort to subvert the democratic process, the other a failed attempt to cover up an extramarital affair—the impeachment of a sitting president itself is by definition one of the most significant moments in a democratic system. It contains fundamental implications for representation and electoral accountability, and calls into question the basic divisions of power between the three official branches of government. At the same time it has much to tell us about that unofficial fourth branch, the news media. That is to say, coverage of impeachment can be understood as a critical incident for journalism, one that offers insight into the styles and standards of journalistic practice dominant at the time.[4] By comparing coverage of two impeachment processes occurring within twenty-five years of one another, we can clearly see some of the ways in which the practice of news evolved as the network age gave way to the multichannel era.

In this chapter, I specifically look at the form of broadcast news during the two presidential impeachment processes. Form is something different from content. If content is the substance of news—its topics, the questions it asks, the information it provides, the stories it tells—its form is its representational techniques, the devices it employs to translate reality onto the TV screen. These include aspects of the news such as production techniques, including camera shots and editing strategies, but also patterns of sourcing and quoting, as well as the ways in which the broadcast journalists present themselves on air.[5] Scholars of news have argued that form is powerful—that it constructs the audience's field of vision, instructing its viewers in both what to attend to and, more importantly, how to attend.[6]

My analysis here is based on more than 270 network news stories drawn from key moments during Watergate and the Clinton Affair.[7] Although in many ways the two presidential scandals were different animals, they followed similar trajectories. In both, there was an initial moment when the president became fully implicated in serious misconduct. In Watergate, that came with John Dean's testimony before the Senate's Ervin Committee in June 1973; for Bill Clinton, it was those first days when the Lewinsky scandal broke in January 1998. Second, in both there came the time when the president's guilt was confirmed, at least in the popular imagination. For Nixon it was the Saturday Night Massacre in October 1973, when he fired the attorney general, the assistant attorney general, and Special Prosecutor Archibald Cox. For Clinton, it was the release of Prosecutor Ken Starr's report in September 1998. Finally, both scandals culminated with congressional debate and votes in favor of impeachment—against Nixon in the House Judiciary Committee in July 1974 (Nixon would resign immediately after) and against Clinton in the House of Representatives in December 1998 (Clinton, of course, would be acquitted in the Senate the next year.)

As we consider the differences in the way the high-modern and postmodern paradigms of news tried to represent the reality of presidential scandal and impeachment, we must recognize that despite its claim to be a "window to the world," news can never represent reality transparently. Television news never gives us *the* world. Rather it always presents a view of the world, one that has been "heightened, telescoped, dramatized, reconstructed, fetishized, miniaturized, or otherwise modified."[8] The view of the world offered through the stories of television news is unavoidably shaped by the formal conventions of representation that enable and constrain its production. In turn, those conventions of form speak to a deeper organizing logic, an often unspoken set of assumptions about what news is, how it can be practiced, and ultimately what it should be.

High-Modern Journalism

Richard Salant, who ran CBS News through the 1960s and 1970s, often gave voice to the assumptions that organized high-modern journalism. As we saw in chapter 1, he regularly insisted that CBS News producers draw "the sharpest possible line" between their side of "the broadcast business, which is dealing with fact," and that in which their "associates on the entertainment side of the business are generally engaged, which is dealing with fiction and drama." Although both entertainment and news came out "sequentially on the same point of the dial and on the same tube," Salant was confident that one could be clearly distinguished from the other.

Entertainment, he recognized, was free to indulge in dramatic license, in "fiction-which-represents-truth rationales." It could manipulate the tools of television in pursuit of the aesthetic and the telling of a good story. In order to maintain their integrity and credibility, however, broadcast journalists were compelled to avoid any "production technique which would give the viewer an impression of any fact other than the actual fact." That might make the CBS *Evening News* "a little less interesting to some," he realized, "but that is the price we pay for dealing with fact and truth."[9]

Underscoring Salant's insistence on the bright line between news and entertainment was a modernist worldview that divided the social world into distinguishable domains of discourse, practice, and expertise. News was assumed to belong within the political-normative arena, its proper subject matter the exploration of governance and the public good. For Salant, it was never to be mistaken for the aesthetic-expressive content that filled the rest of the network programming schedule. The modernist divide between the political-normative and the aesthetic-expressive itself was predicated upon a faith in the unproblematic distinction between artifice and realism, between the capability of the television apparatus to manufacture a fictional reality, and the possibility of representing the world as it actually is.

To the high-modern mind, the purpose of news was to record the actual. Thus it is no coincidence that network coverage of Watergate largely was built around a formal device then referred to as the "actuality"—what today might tellingly be called the "sound bite." The actuality is the televisual equivalent of the direct quote, that small piece of the actually existent, captured by the camera and relayed on the nightly news. It also is the centerpiece of the Watergate stories examined here. Nearly 40 percent of the entire body of coverage—of the total airtime—was comprised of actualities from lawmakers and other central participants in the political process. Perhaps the best known of these came from Presidential Counsel John Dean, who notably testified before the Senate's Ervin Committee that he had told the president that "there was a cancer growing on the presidency," a cancer that was "growing more deadly every day." Although history has come to remember Dean's tight quote warning of a malignant tumor endangering the Oval Office, its original treatment on the nightly news is startling to the contemporary mind. It begins, as some may remember, with Dean speaking his famous words: "I began by telling the president there was a cancer growing on the presidency and if the cancer was not removed, the president himself would be killed by it. I also told him that it was important that this cancer be removed immediately because it was growing more deadly every day." But from there, the actuality continues without interruption: "I then gave him what I told him would be a broad overview of the situation and I would come back and fill in details and answer any questions he might have about the matter. I proceeded to tell him how the matter had commenced in late-January, early February, but that I did not know how the plans had been finally approved." In all, that actuality on the NBC *Nightly News* ran for a total of *three minutes and forty-five seconds*, during which Dean recounts in detail names, dates, interactions, and presidential decisions. NBC's entire story on Dean's testimony that evening in 1973 lasted nearly nine minutes, seven and a half of which was Dean speaking.

On average, the Watergate actualities run surprisingly long—nearly thirty-six seconds apiece. Notably, those from members of the House and Senate—the lawmakers who would sit in judgment of Nixon—average nearly one and a half minutes, about the length of many entire stories on today's television news. Overall, federal lawmakers occupy a central position in the Watergate coverage, providing more than half of all actualities. Much of the coverage focuses on the public statements from and formal deliberations among those entrusted with the constitutional responsibility of deciding on impeachment. Here we can well see the agenda of high-modern news to serve as a conduit between state and citizen, to televise—that is, to represent across a distance—the political process to those who could not witness its unfolding in person.

Coverage of the House Judiciary Committee hearings on impeachment in the summer of 1974 provides further illustration. There, the vast majority of the coverage is comprised of lengthy actualities that convey the debate over Nixon's conduct and its constitutional implications. For example, an NBC story focused on a debate between Republican Representatives Charles Wiggins (California), who eventually would vote against all three articles of impeachment, and Robert McClory (Illinois), who would vote for two of the three. The uninterrupted give-and-take between the two men runs about as long as the Dean actuality discussed above: three minutes and forty-three seconds. Included in this is McClory's procedural request: "Mr. Chairman, I'd like to speak briefly in opposition," a snippet that today most certainly would wind up on the proverbial cutting-room floor. In a high-modern paradigm, though, such long-running and loosely edited actualities reveal the hope that watching the news could provide a functional substitute to witnessing the actual. The journalistic approach here is that of the stenographer, the textual insistence that the reporter is merely relaying the real. Thus NBC's

John Chancellor leads in to the Wiggins-McClory segment by simply suggesting: "Here is part of their exchange."

As the coverage of both Dean's testimony and the Judiciary Committee debates illustrates, the emphasis in the Watergate reports falls on the transmission of verbal information, argument, and exchange. The coverage is grounded in a typographic logic in which the linear assemblage of verbal language functions as the primary method of representing the real.[10] In this, the networks mimic traditions of print journalism or the radio news from which most of the networks' senior journalists had come. Indeed, the absence of visual imagery is remarkable—nearly 45 percent of the Watergate stories contain no filmed pictures or any full-screen visual elements other than the journalist's "talking head." Here the high-modern network news appears to be an effort to project a fundamentally verbal understanding of the world onto the television screen.

The treatment of the president himself is particularly revealing. Nixon rarely appears in the coverage of his own political downfall; only five of the more than a hundred stories examined here contain visual images of the president. In two of those, he appears in still photographs; only three contain moving pictures. Further, when Nixon does appear on camera, he is never framed in close-up, the networks still abiding by conventions that the president always be shown at the respectful distance of the medium or wide shot.[11] More often, Nixon is visually represented in the coverage by the official presidential seal or by an external shot of the White House.

In an age in which the technologies of moving-image acquisition and assemblage were costly and cumbersome, the visual aspect of television news was largely underdeveloped. In the Watergate coverage, the average prerecorded, reporter-voiced story—what the news business now tellingly calls the "package"—contained fewer than ten distinct visual images (and many of those were shots of the reporter), with each one remaining on the screen for nearly thirteen seconds. For the most part, those were pictures the network camera operators had shot that day—images of documents, government buildings, or people talking. If the actualities served a stenographic function, here the imagery functions as documentation, or visual evidence that confirms the reporters' verbal claims. If one borrows from Charles S. Pierce's typology of signs, the networks' approach to the visual can be considered indexical, with imagery used to provide evidentiary traces of the actual.[12]

In keeping, the imagery contains a minimum of camera movement or other production techniques that cinematographers well understand can add meaning to the visual field. Expressly forbidden, as Salant decreed, from using the "underscoring and the punctuations which entertainment and fiction may, and do, properly use,"[13] the high-modern news of Watergate strove to create the sense that its viewers were simply seeing the real, and not seeing through a technology or strategy of representation. In turn, the credibility of the network news was predicated on the authority of the indexical, the assumption that seeing is believing and the camera never lies.

For journalism, this faith in the possibility of representing truth led, as Walter Lippmann once put it, to the "habit of disinterested realism."[14] As a mode of representation, realism requires distance—between the camera and its object, between the observer and the observed. The credibility of the realist representation depends on the erasure of subjectivity, the elimination of any hint that what is being seen is being seen through someone's eyes. The endorsement of realism in news speaks to the "institutionalization of observers observing," the celebration of mediation without manipulation.[15] In the Watergate coverage, the network journalists presented themselves in this role of institutional observer. Although television may be inherently a personal medium, they strove to downplay their individual identities, functioning instead as institutional agents, representatives of the network news organization. A few standout reporters, including Dan Rather, Tom Brokaw, and Sam Donaldson, rose to fame amid the Watergate coverage, but they are the exception rather than the rule. As many as 40 percent of the reporters who appear in the stories examined here appear only once, and several of them are never even seen on camera.

None of the network reporters is referred to by his first name (and they are almost all men—a point we will consider more in the next chapter). Instead they are always introduced by their full name, along with their institutional position: "Sam Donaldson, ABC News." Even Walter Cronkite himself appears more as the embodiment of the institutional observer than he does the star personality. Never referred to as "Walter," his name is only mentioned during the show's introduction, when an unseen voice announces, "The CBS *Evening News* with Walter Cronkite." Similarly, the Watergate coverage is notable for the lack of interpersonal interaction between journalists. Reporters and anchors never talk to each other leading into or out of the reporter's story. They share no conversational pleasantries, nor engage in the now-standard question-and-answer sessions. Neither do two journalists ever appear on camera together.

Here the Watergate coverage illustrates the high-modern paradigm's endorsement of technocratic expertise, its use of representational techniques drawn from print journalism in which reporters are understood to be authoritative yet anonymous experts, disembodied professionals who disseminate democratically valuable information to the mass audience. In turn, the audience is assumed to be engaged in the rational process of seeking information. This distinctly modernist approach to journalism, Hallin argues, arose hand in hand with the ascendancy of science as the privileged mode of inquiry into the real.[16] Motivated by the logic of science, professional journalists were assumed to be value-free experts, not authors, scavengers, or editorialists.[17] Indeed, written guidelines at CBS codified this notion of professionalism, instructing journalists always to appear "in a restrained and disciplined manner." Tellingly, in the early 1970s Richard Salant refused a request from Tom Snyder's *Tomorrow Show* for an interview with Walter Cronkite and Dan Rather, explaining that he saw Snyder's late-night program as nothing more than a "straight old-fashioned New York graphic tabloid designed to titillate, not inform." As such, he rejected it as a "suitable framework" for the "excellent professional journalists" of CBS News.[18]

This high-modern assumption that the journalist was an informational expert is further illustrated by the nightly commentary, an element common to the newscast then but virtually nonexistent today. Regularly, the nightly news during Watergate would close with a commentary in which the networks' senior journalists—Eric Sevareid at CBS, David Brinkley at NBC, and Howard K. Smith at ABC—examined current events. Displaying no interest in the bells and whistles of TV, the commentaries run as long as three minutes and contain no images other than the grey-haired senior statesmen's talking head. As a rule, the commentaries are monologues: the commentator appears alone and speaks without interruption, always looking directly into the camera. An exception, perhaps, to high-modernism's aversion to subjectivity, the commentaries are presented as the work of the individual journalist. Brinkley's segments on NBC, for example, are labeled "Brinkley's Notebook" and begin with what appears to be his signature superimposed on the screen. Like the newspaper editorials they somewhat resemble, though, the commentaries are bracketed from the rest of the news and thus reaffirm the objectivity of the rest of the program. Subjectivity, they suggest, is contained in the commentary and does not impugn the objective work of reporting evident in the rest of the newscast.

The commentaries also make strong claims to informational authority and professional expertise. They cover weighty topics, including the nature of democracy, public opinion, and the role of the press (issues that we will consider in greater depth in the next chapter). Serious and erudite, the commentaries make references, at times esoteric, to world history, political theory, and even Greek mythology. They simultaneously presuppose the audience's literacy and celebrate the commentators' scope of knowledge and expert perspective. As such they reflect William Paley's suggestion that network commentators could apply the "special knowledge possessed by them or made available to them by this organization through its news sources" to "elucidate and illuminate the news."[19] The organizing logic here is the progressivist ideal of professionalized public service, itself the central concept articulated in the mid-twentieth century by the Hutchins Commission and its call for a socially responsible press. The Commission argued that the journalist should not only provide a "truthful, comprehensive, and intelligent account of the day's events," but also place them "in a context which gives them meaning."[20] In that vein, Paley explained that the function of the commentary was to help the audience "to understand, to weigh, and to judge."[21]

Postmodern News

The function of high-modern journalism was assumed to be providing the citizen with factual information and reasoned interpretation of the political process. In this labor, journalists conceptualized themselves as knowledge professionals whose technocratic expertise—their carefully cultivated and culturally credentialed ability to disseminate and interpret objective fact—was harnessed in the name of social progress. Seeking to minimize the particularly televisual aspects of their trade, they strove to use the techniques of television in an indexical fashion, providing the audience traces of the actual for their rational consideration. By the time the Monica Lewinsky scandal broke in January 1998, however, the "real" news of the high-modern paradigm had evolved into an altogether different enterprise.

If, during the network age, CBS's Salant had hoped to keep the form of broadcast journalism clearly distinguishable from the style of television entertainment, in the multichannel era those distinctions between genres had become deeply obscured. The coverage of the Clinton Affair is as much aesthetic-expressive as it is political-normative; it maximizes the capabilities of the televisual to create stories intended to entertain audiences perhaps more than to inform citizens. In place of the verbally oriented informational reports offered during Watergate, nearly two-thirds of the stories about the

Clinton impeachment were packages: tightly structured, highly visual, and fast-paced mini-narratives. In the Watergate coverage, only about one-third of all stories were packages, and those, as discussed above, were often the assemblage of lengthy actualities, a chronicle of the day's developments. By the time the Lewinsky scandal broke, however, the actual had become the raw material for the news package, a resource to be used by the television reporter in the nightly attempt to "impose the unity of a clear story line" on the political process.[22]

In this efforts to package—that is, to narrativize—the real, the networks largely abandoned the typographic approach of an earlier era, instead celebrating the formal techniques Salant had once passionately decried. At the forefront of this is the turn to the visual as the primary method of representing the world. Journalism scholars have documented that the average number of visual images in network news increased nearly twofold in the 1970s and 1980s, findings that are affirmed here.[23] The average package during the Clinton Affair—which, interestingly enough, averaged the same overall length as the Watergate packages—contained some 70 percent more visual images than those during Watergate, while the duration of each image drastically shrunk, with each one remaining on the screen only about six seconds. One story from the Clinton coverage—a report on public opinion in rural New Jersey—contained thirty-five different images in less than two and a half minutes, an average of less than four seconds per picture.

To feed this appetite for the visual, the networks continuously used and added to an extensive archive of imagery. For example, within days of Monica Lewinsky's name entering the headlines, the networks had obtained still pictures of her from a variety of sources, as well as home video of her college graduation and of an appearance in a school play. They also acquired three different shots in which Clinton and Lewinsky are seen in proximity, including two of them hugging. Similarly, when Washington lawyer Vernon Jordan's friendship with the president came under scrutiny, the networks quickly procured several pieces of video in which the two appear in public together, as well as historical footage of Jordan. Most importantly, the Clinton coverage is awash in images of the president. In the coverage of Nixon's political downfall, the president had remained largely an abstraction, a disembodied concept to be grasped through verbal description but not visual depiction. In the Clinton packages, however, more than 20 percent of all individual shots contain images of the president. Here he becomes primarily a visual entity, an embodied person rendered more readily available to the eye than to the ear.

The Clinton coverage reveals not just a quantitative increase in the number of visuals but also a significant qualitative shift in the use of that imagery—in a postmodern paradigm the very logic of televisual representation had changed distinctly. The visual portrayal of Nixon, for example, was largely dispassionate, the camera always remaining at a distance, insulating the president from the prying eyes of the onlooker. Nearly a fifth of the images of Clinton, however, are close-ups or extreme-close-ups. Regularly, his face fills the frame, his shoulders barely visible. At times the camera pulls in even closer, leaving neither his hairline nor his neck visible. These visual representations are highly intimate, the frequent use of the zoom lens offering subtle clues as to Clinton's mood and psyche. Bela Balazs once argued that the facial close-up was the essence of the "cinema," able to lift an individual character out of a crowd and illuminate the subject's humanity.[24] For Sergei Eisenstein, the close-up moreover was a powerful semiotic technique. Unlike wide or medium shots, the primary function of the close-up, he said, was "not so much to show or to present as to signify, to give meaning, to designate."[25] Here the indexical realism of the photographic image is conflated with symbolic representation, the visual frame actively invested with narrative meaning.

The Clinton coverage uses the full gamut of production techniques to enhance its aesthetic appeal and to construct meaning. For example, the camera is regularly on the move, at times spinning 360 degrees before settling on the object of focus, tilting from the ceiling down to its subject or moving through a room to increase the sensation that the viewer actually is in the scene. In one telling example, a shot from an NBC story on how Clinton would try to defend himself against Starr's accusations begins with a close-up of a portrait of George Washington. The camera then pulls out and pans to reveal the president speaking at a podium in the White House. The movement itself offers interpretation, emphasizing the perceived disconnect between Clinton, whose "problem with the truth" was a common topic for the nightly news, and George Washington, who supposedly could not tell a lie.

The networks also use a variety of postproduction effects such as slow motion or the altering of color and tone to complicate the imagery, an approach virtually nonexistent in the Watergate coverage. The general absence of such "postproduction" effects during Watergate was due in part to the technological limitations of the time, but it also reflects the high-modern hope of transparently representing reality. By contrast, the networks in 1998 readily sought to manipulate visual images in the effort to construct symbolic meaning and enhance the narrative frame. This approach also extends to techniques of editing, the linking of individual shots. Nearly all of the edits between visual images in the Nixon stories are hard cuts, in which one image simply replaces another. The hard cut is largely unobtrusive, directing the viewer's attention to the subject matter and not its visual construction. In the Clinton stories, hard cuts are still common, but the use of the dissolve, in which one shot is gradually replaced by the next, increased dramatically. Nearly 40 percent of all individual edits are dissolves, a technique that heightens the sense of drama and interconnection between images.

If the imagery of the Clinton Affair is often more symbolic than indexical—the relationship between sign and referent anchored not by its connection to the real but by the context of the surrounding narrative that it in turn is used to support—at times referentiality itself is obscured. In both impeachment processes, many of the key moments occurred well out of view of the camera. In those instances during Watergate, the networks often settled for images of the reporter speaking before a closed door. During the Clinton Affair, however, the networks still attempted to provide visual illustration, relying on pictures that bore at best only iconic resemblance to the reporters' copy. The shots of Clinton and Lewinsky hugging were used repeatedly to illustrate the accusation that the two had engaged in lascivious behavior in private, the potentially innocent hugs loosely resembling illicit sexual conduct. Similarly, when charges surfaced that the president had bought Lewinsky gifts and then had them returned, the networks showed pictures of Clinton apparently holding gifts—a coffee mug and shirts. Here the networks recontextualized the visual image, severing it from its original referent and attaching it to a new meaning.[26]

A more problematic example is found in an NBC story recounting the Starr Report, and specifically its allegations that Lewinsky often visited the president at night. The corresponding video was a shot taken from outside the White House at night. The camera zooms in to a second-floor window, and the viewer can see Clinton inside, talking with a brown-haired person seated with his or her back to the window. There was no evidence the person was Lewinsky (or even necessarily a woman), but the voyeuristic image was used nonetheless to illustrate the alleged late-night encounters. It is impossible here for the casual viewer to distinguish between a picture whose referent is what the reporter's copy suggests it is and one in which the connection between visual referent and verbal claim is tenuous at best.

The use of recontextualized imagery illustrates the wider inclination in this postmodern paradigm of broadcast news not to represent the actual but to use traces of the real to construct engaging, reality-based stories. Indeed, the Clinton coverage offers few examples of what during Watergate would have been called an actuality. Instead, it provides a stream of ten-second sound bites, small verbal nuggets carefully mined from the ongoing flow of public speech. For example, where members of Congress spoke for an average of ninety seconds during Watergate, that had fallen to an average of twenty-three seconds in the Clinton coverage. In the Clinton packages in particular, the average sound bite from federal lawmakers runs just over nine seconds. If members of Congress were once given several minutes to develop their arguments for and against impeachment, many lawmaker sound bites during the Clinton coverage ran as short as two seconds, as did the following bites from three different lawmakers in an ABC story on the growing sentiment for impeachment:

- "The president did obstruct justice."
- "I believe the president did not tell the truth."
- "I will vote to impeach the president of the United States."

If the high-modern actuality offered lawmakers the opportunity to develop their arguments on the evening news, the postmodern sound bite reduces the complexity of political discourse to informationally vacuous but easily packageable morsels of speech that the journalist in turn can assemble to illustrate the wider narrative frame. Unlike the actuality, which disguises its own construction, such short sound bites highlight the process of selection through which they have been generated and shift focus from the reality they represent to the story they help construct. As such, they reveal a shift in formal logic of news, away from the ideal of the stenographer and toward a narrative device more complex, one that overtly parses elements of the actual from the whole and reassembles them within the news narrative.

Perhaps even more significant, however, is the networks' increasing formal disinterest in the legislative branch. In comparison to the Watergate coverage, lawmakers play a vastly diminished role. Then, members of Congress accounted for close to half of all the sources who appear on camera, and well over half of all actualities. In 1998, federal lawmakers accounted for fewer than one-third of all sound bites and fewer than 30 percent of on-camera sources. In place of quotes from participants in the political process, the networks instead turned to a new kind of speaker to craft the story of

Clinton's impeachment. Nearly one-third of all sources in the Clinton stories examined here are analysts, a kind of speaker that for all practical purposes did not exist in the Watergate coverage. These are academics, lawyers, former government insiders—people whose only connection to the events in question is their talk. Interestingly, in the Clinton packages the analyst sound bite averages eleven seconds, longer than those from lawmakers.

If high-modern news strove to represent the unfolding of the political process to the viewer, the postmodern Clinton stories are engaged in a fundamentally more interpretive labor. Regularly, analysts are used to provide subjective characterization of the issues and the political actors. Psychology professor Bella DePaulo, for example, accuses the president of being a pathological liar, while writer Sally Quinn suggests that Hillary Clinton is going through "what I think must be hell." In contrast to the lawmaker actuality, which transcribed public speech, the analyst sound bite shifts from representing the real to probing the possible. No longer a formal technique to disseminate the actual, the analyst sound bite is a narrative device that imbricates interpretation within description and emphasizes the *journalist's* voice.

This becomes even clearer when one recognizes the diminished role of all sound bites within the Clinton stories. Where actualities comprised almost 40 percent of the Watergate coverage, sound bites made up less than a quarter of the Clinton story time. Thus during the Clinton impeachment, the journalists' own words filled more than three-quarters of the airtime. This speaks to the wider shift in the logic of broadcast news recognized by scholars who have noted that the journalists themselves, and not the reality on which they report, have become the primary focus of the news narrative.[27] Where during Watergate the reporter presented himself largely as an impersonal agent, during the Clinton Affair the reporters celebrate themselves and their own labor of storytelling. In comparison to the Watergate coverage, a far smaller pool of reporters produced a larger percentage of the Clinton stories. Regularly appearing on TV, the Clinton reporters become recognizable personalities, familiar players in the drama of the nightly news. Indeed, at ABC, which was now owned by the Disney media conglomerate, reporters and anchors had come to be referred to as "cast members" and not necessarily journalists.[28] In turn, much of their reportage is packaged as interpersonal interaction, give-and-take between television friends. In contrast to the Watergate coverage, multiple journalists often appear on camera together and regularly refer to one another on a first-name basis. Where Watergate reporters never talked to each other, more than half of the Clinton stories contain some form of conversation between anchors and reporters, including the sharing of personal greetings and expressing appreciation for each other's work.

This represents the wider shift in broadcast news from the impersonal presentation of information to interpersonal discussion. Indeed, the commentaries common to that earlier era were largely absent in the Clinton coverage. Instead, the networks regularly featured discussion segments in which anchors, reporters, and a range of analysts appeared on camera together, not to report on, but to talk about the news. On ABC, Peter Jennings continually turned to legal analyst Jeffery Toobin, as well as to political experts Cokie Roberts, George Stephanopolous, and Bill Kristol. The latter three teamed up for ABC's *Impeachment Watch*. "Well, there's so much to *digest*, and the country will have a whole weekend to do it," Jennings suggested one day. "We're going to try a little bit of it now." On CBS, that role of professional "digester" was filled largely by *US News and World Report* reporter Gloria Borger. Said Dan Rather, introducing Borger on the day of Clinton's impeachment, "We want to give you there in your living room or den, or wherever you may be watching, some context and perspective on this historic day." On NBC, it was Tim Russert, the moderator of *Meet the Press*, who joined Tom Brokaw "to help you put all of this in perspective."

One hears in this a residual trace of the ideals of public service journalism that motivated the high-modern network news, the same understanding that the journalist was a knowledgeable professional whose expertise could help the viewer understand the political situation. But where the commentators of Watergate strove to offer "context and perspective" on the actually occurring, the discussants of the Clinton Affair were quick to speculate about what might be. In Brokaw's discussion with Tim Russert on the first day of the breaking scandal, the word "if" was used five times in one minute of talk. Russert concluded by suggesting—quite inaccurately, as history was to show—that "if" the president had an affair and lied about it, "he's gonna have to leave town in disgrace." This form of "if-then" speculation, nonexistent in the news of 1973–74, was commonplace in the Clinton stories. Similarly, on the scandal's first day, Sam Donaldson suggested in an unattributed statement that allegations of an affair and a cover-up could lead to an impeachment inquiry. The next day on NBC, reporter Pete Williams noted that "it's far too early for any serious talk of impeachment," and then proceeded to suggest that impeachment might be exactly where this was heading.

This focus on the "might be" and "maybe was" is emblematic of a postmodern paradigm of broadcast journalism in which the attempt to faithfully document the actual has been eclipsed by the effort to manufacture narratives out of the raw materials of reality. Such postmodern news undoubtedly is a kind of infotainment, the packaging of information in the entertainment forms to which high-modern news was averse. In this new paradigm, the visual-aesthetic replaces the typographic as the central means of representing the real. The indexical and stenographic approach of high-modern broadcast journalism gives way to the symbolic—the postmodern representation of the actual made meaningful not by its correspondence to the real, but by its surrounding narrative context. The infotainment form of the Clinton coverage further diminishes attention to, and ultimately the authority of, political actors in favor of the journalists themselves, who, thus enhanced, function less as information disseminators than as narrators and television stars.

The form of television news has always been marked by a set of tensions or balance points between journalism and show business, the aesthetic and the informational, the televisual and the rational-verbal. The high-modern news of Watergate attempted to shape the rational-verbal dimension of the political world into a televisual form, at best an uneasy fit. In the effort to produce an authoritative record of the day's events, the televisual transcript of the political real, it sacrificed aesthetic appeal in favor of indexical realism. In so doing, it reinforced modernity's distinctions between the political-normative and the aesthetic-expressive: between news and entertainment, and ultimately between politics and pleasure. It offered its viewers little incentive to tune in beyond its promise of serious information, its commitment to serving the needs of the citizen. As such, it depended on its appeal to the audience's sense of duty, the obligation of citizenship. In the face of burgeoning entertainment choices and a decreasing tendency among Americans to self-identify as citizens, such an approach to news would seem increasingly untenable.

On a deeper level, though, the high-modern approach to broadcast journalism is further complicated by the unquestionable fact that the actuality is never the same thing as the actual; realism is never isomorphic with the real. As a mode of representation, realism elides its own construction; it denies that it is the product of a perspective. But it is, as Bill Nichols has argued, "a style, a form of textual construction, and a means of achieving specific effects, one of which is the appearance of a nonproblematic relationship to representation itself."[29] The Watergate coverage would ask its viewers to accept that they simply are seeing the real unfold each night, that the camera is but a neutral window to the world. Walter Benjamin once suggested that the great illusion advanced by modern media was a view of the world void of traces of the tools of mediation: "Mechanical equipment has penetrated so deeply into reality that its pure aspect freed from the foreign substance of equipment is the result of a special procedure.... The equipment-free aspect of reality here has become the height of artifice; the sight of immediate reality has become an orchid in the land of technology."[30] The Watergate coverage indulges in this artifice, its formal techniques designed to suggest that the view of the world presented on the nightly news is the immediate real—"the way it is," Cronkite insisted, or as Salant may have put it, the "actual fact."

The form of the Clinton stories, though, and of postmodern media in general, shatters this myth of mimesis. Calling direct attention to the technologies and techniques of mediation, it rejects the belief in transparency. In its pursuit of the aesthetic and the entertaining, it celebrates the construction of story and in so doing dismisses the very ideal that the news story could somehow be nonmediated. As such, the infotainment logic of the Clinton stories gives expression to a wider cultural turn that recognizes the unavoidable situatedness of any attempt to mediate the real. It reflects a deep cultural skepticism toward claims of transparency, of high-modernism's "news from nowhere." At the same time, however, that postmodern news reminds us that the "real" news of an earlier era was at best realistic, it also sacrifices the indexical credibility that authorized high-modern journalism. Its packaging of the real claims not to offer what is, but what may be. It conflates Salant's "actual fact" with possible facts and in so doing undermines the authority of its version of reality. Here broadcast news faces the problem confronting all contemporary televisual forms that represent reality. As it celebrates its own agency and its own particularity, as it uses the full spectrum of televisual techniques to craft stories from the raw materials of the real, it loses its basic distinctiveness from other televisual forms. It becomes another kind of reality TV, and, with that, it abdicates the authority to which news historically has laid claim.

The changes in the form of television news between Watergate and the Clinton Affair thus illustrate the turn toward infotainment, the hybridization of genres of broadcast journalism and televisual entertainment. At the same time, these shifts in representational techniques and narrative conventions reveal a more profound transformation in the underlying logic of news. They offer insight into the changing nature of journalistic authority, the stance from which broadcast journalists engage with the political world, and, in turn, the very nature of the claims they make about it. The changes in form between the high-modern and postmodern moments of television news therefore contain significant epistemological implications. They speak to a deeper reconceptualization of public inquiry and social knowledge itself.

3

♦ ♦ ♦

PUBLICIZING POLITICS

The "Hot Light" of Publicity

In the midst of Watergate, CBS's Eric Sevareid appeared on the *Evening News* for one of his regular commentaries, those weighty moments in an older paradigm in which the senior statesmen of broadcast journalism would offer their reasoned interpretations of the most serious issues of the day. For Sevareid, the question at hand that night was the function of the press in a democracy, especially in one on the verge of impeaching its president. The press, he eloquently explained, is a light of public inquiry, one that is "like the beam of a searchlight which moves restlessly about, bringing one episode and then another out of darkness and into view." This searchlight, he maintained, was an agent of democracy, serving the "public welfare" by exposing those in positions of power who would violate the public trust.

Sevareid's words, although moving, weren't exactly original. He quoted here virtually word for word from Walter Lippmann and his timeless treatise on journalism, democracy, and the public good—the 1922 book *Public Opinion*, in which Lippmann asserts that the press indeed is a "searchlight," a powerful tool of public inquiry.[1] For both Sevareid and Lippmann a half-century earlier, this metaphor of the searchlight captured the modernist assumption that public information, or what has long been referred to as "publicity," lay at the heart of democracy. John Stuart Mill, for example, once called for the "utmost possible publicity" to guarantee that the "whole public" could participate in its own governance. He suggested that a government exposed to the "light of publicity" must act in accordance with the will of the governed.[2] Jeremy Bentham similarly suggested that publicity was a necessary precondition for the formation of an enlightened public judgment. Only the basic principle of "distrustful surveillance" and a condition of "general visibility," he argued, could keep the exercise of power in check.[3] In Immanuel Kant's formulation, publicity would stimulate citizen involvement in public discourse by laying bare for "the public's eye all that is contained in an object, all that is presupposed by that object, and all that is meant by that object."[4]

Jürgen Habermas rightly argues that in Western democratic history, the press was the primary agent of publicity. He grounds the inception of his "public sphere" within the rise of the free press and suggests that Bentham's surveillance—the keeping of a watchful eye on power and its potential abuse—was the primary responsibility of the press.[5] James Carey has argued that publicity remains the vital function of the news media, exposing the actions of the state to public view. News has long played this role of political watchdog, he says, serving as the "eyes and ears of a public that could not see and hear for itself" and keeping those in power honest by "turning on the hot light of scandal and publicity."[6]

Carey's "hot light" of publicity invokes the same metaphor as Lippmann's searchlight, one that equates publicity with light and knowledge with illumination (enlightenment, that is). The "hot light" may be a clever turn of phrase, an ornamental use of language, but the broader metaphor of publicity as light, which recurs continuously in democratic theory, speaks to a deeper conceptual system that underlies both how we speak of the world and the ways in which we understand it. "Metaphor," scholars of language instruct us, "is not just a matter of language, but of thought and reason." Providing the conceptual maps that guide us through the mazes of abstract thought and everyday life, metaphors focus our perceptions and "afford different ways of viewing the world."[7]

The concept of vision itself structures the metaphor of publicity as light. To light something is to make it visible, observable, and knowable; to light is to see, and to see is to know. As the metaphor suggests, the way we understand something depends on the manner in which it is lit. Yet light is never constant: it can shine from different angles, with different intensity and hue; it can be tightly directed or widely diffused. The same object cast in different light may appear to be a different object altogether. To put the point another way, different kinds of publicity illuminate their objects in different lights. If news is the hot light of publicity, then different kinds of news project different kinds of light, contrasting conceptual maps that make sense of politics and the public domain in different ways.

In this chapter I turn from the form of news during Watergate and the Clinton impeachment to an analysis of the language of news—to the different metaphors of publicity that underlie network news coverage in the two contrasting eras and in turn express quite different assumptions about the nature of the political system and the role of journalism in a democracy.

The High-Modern Searchlight

The metaphor of the searchlight that Sevareid used to describe his vision of broadcast journalism provides a compelling place to begin. A searchlight is a directional beam of light: an intense and narrowly focused exposure that illuminates its subject yet leaves all else in shadows. It is a disciplinary tool, a device used to facilitate surveillance and supervision. Throughout the Watergate coverage, network news is conceptualized as a disciplinary agent. It is, says Sevareid, a "terrible spotlight" from which the Nixon administration cannot hide. When John Dean begins his incriminating testimony, White House Press Secretary Ron Ziegler is said to have agreed to answer questions only "under strong urging from newsmen." The next day, after Dean had accused, among others, White House Chief of Staff H. R. Haldeman, the networks confront Haldeman at his home in California with Dean's accusations. CBS suggests Haldeman had moved to California to escape the "Watergate limelight." But not even Nixon, let alone Haldeman, could hope to avoid the light of public inquiry. Haldeman "was *found* with his family living in this house," reads NBC's copy that evening, suggesting the beam of the searchlight is inescapable.

The searchlight is a light of political accountability, arrayed in battle against the forces of darkness, secrecy, and misinformation. The Watergate coverage often describes a White House cloaked in metaphorical darkness, posing an inherent threat to democracy. Following Dean's formal accusations of criminal wrongdoing, ABC suggests the White House is hiding behind "a wall of silence." There is a measure of metaphorical coherence here: the "wall" erected by the Nixon administration is designed to block out the searchlight and protect those behind it from public exposure. CBS calls this a "policy of studied non-involvement," while NBC suggests the Nixon administration will not be able to avoid a dialogue forever.

In the eyes of the searchlight, Nixon's silence, his refusal to step into that public light, appears guilty prima facie. A greater offense, though, is the Nixon administration's attempts to impede publicity—not simply to evade the searchlight, but to undermine its abilities to perform its democratic function. The networks pay considerable attention to Dean's accusations that Nixon ordered his staff to "keep a good list of the press people" who covered his administration unfavorably, suggested "wiretapping newsmen," and singled out CBS's Daniel Schorr for potential harassment. So too do they focus on Dean's revelations that he and the president purposefully fed Ziegler inaccurate information, so that he would in turn relay that misinformation to the press. CBS also calls attention to the unwillingness of the U.S. Information Agency to cooperate with foreign journalists in their effort to cover Watergate. In the eyes of the networks, Nixon's attempts to impede press coverage are among his most serious misdeeds.

Democratic Amplification

The networks unanimously celebrate their televisual exposure of Watergate as a welcome amplification of the public light. With live broadcasts during the day and detailed summaries on the nightly news, television was playing an unprecedented role in illuminating the political process and helping, they suggest, the public sort through what one woman in an ABC story on public opinion characterizes as "absolute confusion." Because of her confusion, she says, "I'm glad that it's out in the open." Here "out in the open" means to be "on television." "I think the American people are entitled to watch it on television and to hear as much as possible," she continues. "It's been a long time since a lot of things like this have been out in the open, and I think it's good." That story on the public's confusion ends with a "man-on-the-street" quote that well captures the idealism of the searchlight: "The Watergate makes me more cynical," he says, "but when there is a public investigation, it makes me more hopeful."

There is a certain ambiguity in the man's statement. It is not clear whether he refers to the public investigation being conducted in the halls of Congress or to the one unfolding on the nightly news. Regardless of his original intent, this quote, the story, and indeed the body of Watergate coverage agree that television news was extending the democratic potential of the searchlight. Sevareid proclaims that the "red eye of the television camera trained on the impeachment process brought millions of [people] into the meeting. It is something approaching direct democracy," he insists, "and it does seem manageable." Likewise, NBC's David Brinkley suggests that the presence of television cameras "opened those impeachment proceedings to the public," revealing that "this great national process is moving in a responsible way." Anticipating C-SPAN, ABC's Howard K. Smith likewise suggests that Congress should permanently open its doors and "let television bring in the nation to watch." When that happens, he says, "the public will know a lot more about how it is governed, and with the cameras watching, the way we are governed may improve."

Institutional Politics

In the high-modern news of Watergate, the central concern lies with the rational functioning of the institutions and processes of American government. Says Howard K. Smith during Dean's testimony, the fundamental issue is the public's trust in government. Smith here makes no mention of public feeling toward Nixon the person. He speaks of the "administration," "the government," "the president," and even "the man at the top," but remarkably, he never says the name "Richard Nixon." This illustrates the fundamentally institutional frame the Watergate coverage uses to understand politics. Nixon is conceptualized as an institution and an office, but rarely an individual. When Dean first accuses Nixon of complicity with the Watergate cover-up, Daniel Schorr concludes simply that "the *issue of the presidency* is deep in the hearings." So too does Dean, in his oft-repeated quote, insist that the "cancer" is "on the presidency," and not *in the man*.

The searchlight respects the "mystique of the president," even as "the presidency" comes under fire.[8] Neither Nixon's face nor his voice are recurring elements in the coverage. As noted in the previous chapter, when Nixon does appear, he is never framed closer than the traditional head-and-shoulders shot, a formal technique that emphasizes his official, institutional identity, not his humanity.[9] Throughout the coverage, the White House, not Nixon, is positioned as the central actor in the story. NBC expresses surprise at the White House's "deep involvement" in the cover-up and at Dean's revelation of just "how much trouble the White House was in." ABC speculates that prosecutor Archibald Cox was fired for being on the White House's trail, and later as the House Judiciary Committee's impeachment vote draws nearer, it is the White House, not the individual who resides there, that is said to be trying to maintain "an outward appearance of optimism."

This institutional light is extended to the other political actors as well. Congress is discussed as an institution—"the closest organ of government to the people"—and never a collection of individual partisans. The networks do not highlight any particular members of Congress, either as Nixon's defenders or as his foes. While Judge Sirica is positioned as Nixon's greatest enemy—says NBC following the Saturday Night Massacre, "the president was able to rid himself of Archibald Cox, but he cannot fire Chief Judge John Sirica"—none of the networks discusses Sirica's personality or life history, an approach that, as we shall see, becomes commonplace in a postmodern paradigm of news. The contemporary fondness for personal details calls into relief this textual silence of the Watergate coverage.

Finally, network news itself is understood as a disembodied institution, committed to the objective pursuit of truth. As discussed in the previous chapter, the network journalists downplay their own individuality, presenting themselves instead as professional agents, representatives of the institution of network news. The Watergate coverage is marked by the absence of first names or personal address, the avoidance of any indication of interpersonal interaction. This appears as a deliberate attempt to elide the subjectivity of the journalist. Reporters do not speak of themselves on air, their stories generally devoid of the words "I" and "me." Speaking in the third person and past tense, they obscure their own identity. Says NBC reporter Bob Jamieson, wondering if the Nixon administration's self-defense will "play" in Peoria, "the visitor to Peoria doesn't see much evidence of traditional Nixon support. He hears anger and sees confusion." Here Jamieson cloaks himself in the impersonal persona of "the visitor," the anybody. He claims a universalized subject position, insisting that his impressions would be anybody's and that his voice speaks for everybody.

Reasoned Argument

With its aversion to personality and its vision of politics as the domain of rational institutions, the searchlight gives expression to a long-standing tradition in Western philosophy that distrusts human nature left unchecked by the civilizing constraints of reasoned institutions.[10] Network news itself is thought to be one of those reasoned institutions, a bourgeois public sphere of the air that functions as a resource for information and evidence and as a forum for rational discussion and debate. One sees this in the coverage of John Dean's testimony before the Ervin Committee, which is structured largely as the presentation of evidence. Dean's opening statement, says NBC's John Chancellor, was "crammed with quotes, dates, memoranda, and detailed recollections." NBC's newscast that night, he assures his audience, will "cover that in detail." As noted earlier, actualities from Dean run strikingly long by contemporary standards, some lasting more than three minutes, as he presents detailed chronologies of his meetings with the president. Similarly, the networks replay extended segments of questions and answers between Dean and various senators on the Ervin Committee. Coverage of the House Judiciary Committee debates follows a similar pattern. The focus falls on the unfolding of specific arguments between representatives for and against impeachment. The networks highlight the process, as Sam Donaldson describes it, of "seeking evidence, measuring facts, struggling with conscience."

Ultimately, the emphasis of the searchlight falls on the rational conclusions that can be drawn from the available evidence. One hears this well expressed in a sound bite from Republican Lawrence Hogan (Maryland), broadcast on both CBS and ABC. Calling for approval of articles of impeachment, Hogan offers his colleagues a litmus test to help determine the proper course of action. He asks them to consider what "the reasonable and prudent man" would conclude from the mounting evidence against the president. The suggestion here is that the process of political decision making should be guided by the conclusions of "the reasonable and prudent man."

In this, one hears both the ideals and the limitations of the high-modern searchlight. It embraces a Kantian framework that understands publicity as critical exposure and rational scrutiny.[11] Kantian publicity, however, like Habermas's formulation of the public sphere that followed, depends upon the universality of the rational subject and the artificial bracketing of the particularities of one's inevitably situated identity, personality, and emotionality.[12] For the searchlight, "the reasonable and prudent man" is the assumed subject position—the ideal contributor to the public sphere is expected to be both rational and male, while those who differ from these norms are afforded few opportunities to participate.

These cultural biases pervade the Watergate coverage. Even as the newsworkers claim to be the unembodied representatives of the institution of network news, they are by their own description news*men*. Reporter Bob Jamieson's "visitor" to Peoria is by default a "he," and indeed, of the thirty-seven reporters and anchors who appear on air in the stories examined here, thirty-six are men. Likewise, while history might remember the speech Barbara Jordan gave to open the Judiciary Committee debates, *not one* of the networks include a sound bite from her in that evening's coverage. Although all three offer several lengthy sound bites from committee members, every one is from a white, male member. The committee itself contained thirty-eight members, thirty-six of whom were white, thirty-six of whom were men. Yet Eric Sevareid still concludes that the committee (95 percent white, 95 percent male) made up a "fair cross section" of the House, and "maybe of the country." The absurdity of this assumption (could Sevareid honestly have thought the population of the United States was 5 percent female and 5 percent nonwhite?) calls into relief the range of cultural identities denied representation in a discourse that claimed to speak for and in the public interest.

So too is the searchlight's celebration of the "reasonable and prudent" not without its problems. Critical scholar Nancy Fraser has argued that the historical insistence on the disembodied, rational voice restricts access to the political conversation to those who conform to dominant cultural identities and discursive voice. Discursive assimilation, she suggests, is a base condition for democratic participation.[13] Similarly, Alison Jaggar has argued that the "myth of dispassionate objectivity" both reaffirms and renders opaque the privileging of an epistemological system that is, at its root, patriarchal.[14] One must realize, then, that for all of its democratic intentions, the searchlight of Watergate assumed, and thus imposed, what Mikhail Bakhtin would have called a unitary language, one that naturalized the particularity of its patriarchal, dispassionate methods of inquiry, and implicitly marginalized alternative public identities and more affective forms of political reasoning.

A Postmodern Floodlight

Watergate, however, is a time of transition, as Sevareid suggests somewhat begrudgingly: "the press—or the media—as it, or they, are now called . . . " Sevareid here perceptively notes that the press—an *it*, that singular institution dedicated in his vision to serving American democracy—was transforming into the media—a *they*, a multinodal organization charged with serving multiple and often contradictory agendas. If Sevareid was witnessing the beginnings of this shift, his successors at the networks twenty-five years later had indeed become just one source of information in a continuously expanding multichannel environment. When Bill Clinton faced impeachment in 1998, the increased intensity of exposure was remarkable. ABC's Peter Jennings, for example, assures his viewers that "*Prime Time Live* will take this whole subject up again, as will *Nightline*." On CBS, Dan Rather proclaims, "More on all this tonight on *48 Hours*," and the next day promises continued coverage through the weekend, especially on Sunday's *Face the Nation*. NBC plugs *Meet the*

Press, as well as MSNBC's *The News with Brian Williams* on twenty-four-hour cable news. All three networks also urge their viewers to turn to an emerging medium—their websites—for expanded and continuous coverage.

The networks also reflect and refract lights shone by a wide variety of other news outlets. All three begin their coverage of the breaking scandal by replaying segments from President Clinton's interview with PBS's Jim Lehrer, a conversation that CBS tells its viewers can be seen in its entirety on that evening's *NewsHour*. ABC also replays parts of National Public Radio's interview with Clinton from the same day and follows with a live discussion with NPR's Mara Liasson about that interview. *Newsweek* reporter Michael Isikoff appears on NBC discussing his impressions of the Lewinsky-Tripp phone conversations, a sound bite that was first aired that morning on *Today*. ABC regularly turns to the *Weekly Standard*'s Bill Kristol for political insight; on CBS, *US News and World Report*'s Gloria Borger plays a similar role. Reporters from the *Washington Post*, *Chicago Tribune*, and even the *Louisville Courier-Journal* provide analysis.

This multifaceted illumination also extends well beyond the boundaries of the traditional news media. As Michael Delli Carpini and Bruce Williams have discussed, the Lewinsky scandal demonstrated the collapsing borders between "news and nonnews genres" characteristic of a multichannel media landscape.[15] Video of and references to numerous nonnews media outlets are interspersed throughout the networks' coverage. In stories on public opinion, talk radio is a favorite. Local talk radio hosts are interviewed more than once for their take on public opinion, while snippets from listener calls are used as examples of the public mood. The networks borrow video from cable's *Court TV*, *Entertainment Tonight*, and the *Rosie O'Donnell Show*. An NBC story on Hillary Clinton includes sound bites from the editor of *Vogue*, who explains why her magazine featured Mrs. Clinton on its cover. Finally, in perhaps the most bizarre example of this multiplicitous exposure, Larry Flynt, the publisher of the pornographic magazine *Hustler*, appears in two stories discussing his exposé that led to the resignation of House Speaker–elect Bob Livingston (a Republican from Louisiana).

In the multichannel era, network news came to function as a node in a complex web of illumination. To be sure, the metaphor of publicity-as-light continued to structure the Clinton coverage. ABC's Jackie Judd, says Peter Jennings, first "brought this story to light," while NBC suggests the scandal "has come to light" because Ken Starr was "looking in[to]" Whitewater. ABC says the scandal has forced presidential confidant Vernon Jordan into the "full glare of public scrutiny," a glare that is visually illustrated throughout the coverage by pictures of the television lights themselves. Indeed, if the camera were the televisual technology credited with revealing Watergate, in the Clinton coverage the lights themselves are emphasized as the primary tool of exposure.

Clearly, though, the light of publicity during the Clinton Affair was not what it was during Watergate. Says an ABC reporter in a telling metaphor, Judiciary Committee Chairman Henry Hyde is "ready for the spotlight." That verbal assertion is complemented by pictures of Hyde appearing in a parade, waving to the crowd as the marching band plays and American flags flutter in the background. A sense of theatrical pageantry pervades the scene, and one suspects that the disciplinary searchlight of Watergate has been replaced by a theatrical spotlight. Even that metaphor, though, seems inaccurate. A spotlight casts a narrow beam, illuminating a specific element of the story, while leaving much else in shadow. What we see instead is a much wider light, a diffused beam that illuminates far more than did an earlier paradigm of news. Reflecting and refracting countless other media lights, network news had instead become a floodlight, a dramaturgical exposure that bathes the political domain in light and, in so doing, fundamentally redefines the boundaries of that domain.

Politics as Dramaturgy

The metaphorical frame underlying the Clinton coverage is one of theater: a dramaturgical illumination that understands politics to be drama, publicity to provide the stage, and political actors to be just that—actors who star in the theater of politics. NBC suggests the Clinton love triangle is a "drama worthy of Shakespeare," while the impeachment debate is a "political life-and-death drama" unfolding on the nightly news. So too does ABC wonder how many people were watching the "impeachment drama" play out on television. Bill Clinton is the "central player in this drama," his emotional apology speech of September 11, 1998, a "performance" that casts him in the "role of confessed sinner." Hillary Clinton, meanwhile, is engaged in what "could be the performance of her life," all being played out "on this giant public stage." Mrs. Clinton, says reporter Pete Williams, is one of "many of the players in this drama" who "learned all about impeachment" during Watergate, an assertion illustrated by a visual flashback to a young Hillary Rodham attending the Ervin Committee hearings.

The networks do pay some attention to the legal and institutional dimensions of the impeachment process, but it is the narrative of sex and denial that occupies the floodlight's primary field of illumination. Early on, Peter Jennings admits that "reporters have been focusing on allegations of illicit sex." More than sex, though, the networks focus on the story. For CBS it is "the strange tale of Monica and Linda," which "could be the tale that brings down a president." The Starr Report, Watergate veteran Bob Schieffer explains, recounts "a tawdry tale told by a young woman who had become emotionally involved with an older, married man.... It is the story of a dreamy-eyed young woman. She called him handsome; he called her sweetie."

A truism of screenwriting holds that good dramas are built around compelling characters whose life histories, personal relationships, and innermost emotional states are revealed for the audience.[16] The floodlight characterizes all the major actors along these lines. The president is a "cool character," a "former law professor" who "had hundreds of affairs" in the early part of his marriage but had "tried to slow down" after he turned forty. Regularly framing him in extra-close-up and focusing attention on the personal, emotional dimensions of his character, the networks strip away any remaining vestiges of the presidential mystique. The "world has been watching the president seemingly bare his soul," says ABC, while all three networks report the details of his sexual preferences and perversions.

The floodlight exposes even the president's spiritual and mental well-being. In a story titled, by an on-screen banner, "Crisis of Faith," ABC interviews Clinton's personal pastor to gain insight into his spiritual health. The reporter asks the pastor, "What would you want people to know about him that only you might know?" The pastor answers, "I believe there's a real tension in his life related to faith. He wants to do some things and does not do them; he doesn't want to do some things, and does them. He's at a real crossroads in his life in a lot of different ways." Here the president's most private confidences are exposed in the glare of the floodlight. Continuing along these lines, ABC later notes that the president "is not under any psychiatric care" but will be meeting regularly with a "small group of trusted confidantes ... comparable to what is done in groups such as Alcoholics Anonymous."

The postmodern floodlight expresses a radically different understanding of the president than did the high-modern searchlight. In the Clinton coverage, the president is not an office but an individual whose emotionality receives continual inspection. He is "somber" and "deeply emotional." "He knows he's caused a lot of people pain," says Democratic Congressman David Bonior (Michigan), "and he's just devastated by it." As impeachment draws closer, however, reporters are surprised to find the president "smiling and upbeat," an emotional state another Watergate veteran, Sam Donaldson, attributes to the president having received "seven hours of sleep" the night before.

Lewinsky, however, is "an emotional wreck" and "virtually at the precipice." Her life, says NBC, further obscuring the tenuous boundary between news and narrative, had been "like an episode of *Beverly Hills 90210,* but now it's more like the *X-Files.*" She grew up "a child of privilege," notes ABC, but also was the "product of a bitter divorce" and had a "troubled adolescence." She may have been well-groomed for her role in floodlight, suggests NBC, noting that in high school she was voted "most likely to have her name in lights." That claim is illustrated by video of a young Lewinsky performing in a school musical. "She was in our chorus," says her theater coach. "She had a nice singing voice." Now she is illuminated on the giant public stage, and CBS reporter Scott Pelley wonders if he could "characterize her as a friend of the president."

So too do all three networks ask repeatedly whether Hillary Clinton will "stand by her man" one more time. Despite enduring "what must be the toughest days of her life," she remarkably shows "no sign of pain, embarrassment, or anger." Says one analyst, "She must have some kind of emotional armor to go through what I think is hell." Later, reporter Andrea Mitchell concludes that "an iciness" had come between the Clintons, "a distancing, perhaps even noticeable in public. *Barely visible to cameras,* she brushes away his arm," Mitchell says, directing the viewer's interpretation of her questionable visual evidence. Regardless, on the day of impeachment, Mrs. Clinton "assured Democrats of her love for the president" and emerged from the White House "arm in arm" with her husband.

Certainly the nature of the president's transgressions may have demanded some measure of journalistic inquiry into the mental states and emotional lives of the three central characters. In the floodlight, however, this dramaturgical frame is extended to all of the significant political actors. Presidential confidante Vernon Jordan is "a key player" in the story, the "first friend" whose life trajectory followed a remarkable course from the housing projects in Atlanta to a position of great power in Washington. He is "the other man in this," says ABC, noting that he "wears shirts handmade in London and drives a red Cadillac." Linda Tripp is an intriguing character as well, perhaps an "undercover operator trying to bring down the president, or a soccer mom shocked by wild behavior."

Prominent members of Congress also are characterized in the drama of impeachment, their "backstories" and emotional states revealed. House Judiciary Chairman Henry Hyde (a Republican from Illinois) is "a veteran of the navy, the father of four children." He was "born in Chicago, educated in Catholic schools." "Hank Hyde," the reporter says, was once a star basketball player with a strong hook shot. Majority Whip Tom Delay (a Republican from Texas) was "born in Laredo, Texas, fifty-one years ago." The "son of an oil rigger" had come to be known by Congressional insiders as "the 'hammer' . . . tough, shrewd, some say ruthless." Representative Jay Dickey (a Republican from Arkansas) is "having a miserable fifty-ninth birthday" as he tries to make up his mind on impeachment, while Dennis Hastert (a Republican from Illinois), the eventual successor as Speaker of the House, is described as having a certain "rumpled charm." The floodlight also focuses on the lawmakers' interpersonal affiliations. Delay "cannot stand Bill Clinton—never could." New York Democratic Senator Daniel Patrick Moynihan "is not a friend of this president," but Louisiana Democrat John Breaux is both "a close friend of the president" and Mississippi Republican "Trent Lott's best personal friend in the Senate."

Even Peter Rodino, the chairman of the 1974 House Judiciary Committee, is characterized in this light. In an interview with Tom Brokaw, Rodino admits that he suffered great "personal anguish" during Watergate. Following the approval of articles of impeachment against Nixon, Rodino says, "I then went into my cubbyhole in the back. I called up my wife, and I cried. I broke down and cried." During Watergate, Rodino was illuminated by the searchlight only as long as he stood in what could be called, to borrow from media scholar Joshua Meyrowitz, the frontstage of the political arena.[17] The floodlight, however, retrospectively shines into the "cubbyhole in the back," the backstage, where he is less a political statesman and more an emotional man, a husband who in private cries to his wife. In the glare of the floodlight, the traditional backstage of the political arena is no longer off stage and out of view. Rather, it becomes a central location for the construction of the public political narrative. In contrast to the rational-institutional frame through which the searchlight understands the political, the floodlight suggests instead that the political process is to a large extent a backstage drama driven by emotion and conducted through interpersonal channels.

Situated Journalism

In the Clinton coverage, the network journalists had abandoned the role of institutional observers, and instead become characters in their own stories, their individual identities celebrated rather than disguised. On air, they are presented with the informality of the first-name address. No longer "Tom Brokaw, NBC News," they are "Tom," "Dan," or "Peter," familiar personalities who regularly employ the first person, referring to themselves as "I" and "me." Interpersonal interaction between anchor and reporter similarly is a staple of postmodern news. Reporters and anchors appear live each night in conversation with their anchors. "David, what do you have for us?" Brokaw asks. "Well, Tom . . ." Bloom replies. "Bob?" says Rather, tossing to Bob Schieffer. "Dan" is his response. "Hi Tom," says Gwen Ifill, introducing her report on the congressional response to the Starr Report. At the end of their stories, they toss back to the anchors with a "Dan?" or a "Peter?" To that, the anchor invariably responds with something like "Thank you, Jackie—Jackie Judd reporting," or perhaps "Interesting point you make, Sam."

In the floodlight of contemporary publicity, the journalists' own engagement with the subject matter is presented as newsworthy copy. The networks highlight the act of reporting, illuminating what during Watergate was obscured by the use of third person and passive voice. "Bob Schieffer has been digging and working his sources all day," says Rather, while Jennings assures us that "Chris Wallace has been covering [Vernon Jordan] for years." Reporters are active doers in the news narratives, and they are also active thinkers, regularly reporting what they think and what they know. "Sam, can you lay out what you know?" asks Jennings. "It seems to me . . . ," says Brokaw, describing what he sees as long odds against the president. Speculating on the potential reaction to the Starr Report, Jennings turns to political analyst Cokie Roberts and says, "In a phrase—I hate to put too much emphasis on *intuition*—where do *you* think it's going?" This question reveals a profound shift both in network news' relationship to the political domain and its methods of inquiry. Roberts is asked to share neither her professional observations nor what her sources have confirmed to be fact, but rather her own thoughts and indeed her intuitions about that which has yet to occur.

In a postmodern paradigm, Roberts's intuitions and feelings have become legitimate journalistic avenues through which to examine the phenomenal world. The impeachment process, she says, is "sad; it's really sad." Similarly, when discussing the moment the House clerk formally read the impeachment charge, Roberts says, "I felt sick to my stomach." On the day of Clinton's impeachment, reporter Jackie Judd is asked by anchor Charlie Gibson if she ever expected this moment. "Oh my gosh, Charlie, no!" she exclaims. "Sitting here was still a shock; it was just a shock." The day before,

Sam Donaldson insists that President Clinton's apparent good mood was "really strange." Cokie was sick to her stomach, Jackie was shocked, and Sam found the whole thing strange. For postmodern network news, the nature of journalistic inquiry—its subject position and underlying epistemology—is situated and embodied, the sharing not just of methodologically verified knowledge, but of subjective thoughts, intuitions, and emotions.

Affective Discourse

In contrast to the searchlight's rational-institutional understanding of political discourse, the postmodern floodlight articulates a personal-emotional frame for political discussion. While it does not entirely reject the high-modern ideals of the reasonable and prudent assessment of available evidence, it endorses an affective, subjective model of political evaluation based on personal considerations and grounded in emotional reasoning. Says reporter Andrea Mitchell, quoting Clinton cabinet member Donna Shalala, "leaders are judged by good behavior, not just good policy." David Bonior, one of Clinton's strongest supporters, pleads the president's case, noting that he is "a father, a husband, the leader of our country who is very contrite and very sorry." Where Nixon was the office of the presidency, here Clinton is first a father, second a husband, and only third that institution of the presidency—"the leader of our country." One woman proclaims that she "felt sorry for him, because he made a fool of himself." On the day of impeachment, a man on the street says, "I wish Chelsea, and Hillary, and Mr. Clinton the best of times."

These examples illustrate the floodlight's move away from a high-modern paradigm of disembodied and dispassionate observation and toward a standpoint epistemology that considers situated knowledge, affective reasoning, and narrative logic to be legitimate methods of inquiry and decision making.[18] This underlying epistemological shift is well-illustrated in a final example from the Clinton coverage. Following the passage of impeachment in the House, CBS travels to the president's hometown of Hope, Arkansas, and offers this quote from an older woman: "I've known Bill since he was this high, and that may not be an excuse, but I just believe he is a good president." Here the woman is apologetic ("that may not be an *excuse*") for her conviction that Clinton is a good president because it is based more on her familiarity with him ("I've known *Bill* since he was this high") and her emotional instinct ("I just believe") than it is on reasoned argument. She understands that her methods of reasoning are nontraditional, historically excluded from the domain of legitimate political discourse. A postmodern paradigm of news, however, affirms her situated understanding of the political and the affective model of engagement upon which it is based.

Lost and Found

During both Watergate and the Clinton Affair, the networks agreed that publicity was light—an illumination that brings its objects into public view, rendering them knowable in the first instance. The two paradigms of news, however, vary substantially in their understanding of the nature of the public light. In the high-modern age, publicity is said to be a searchlight, a disciplinary tool of surveillance used to ensure political accountability. It offers an institutional frame through which to understand politics, understands journalism to be disembodied observation and objective inquiry, and assumes that political discourse is, or should be, the rational evaluation of argument and evidence. In more postmodern times, however, publicity is implicitly conceptualized as a floodlight, a voluminous light of theatrical exposure. In the glare of the floodlight, politics becomes emotional theater; journalism a kind of situated, subjective engagement; and political discourse an affective, embodied conversation.

For many, there is a sense that we have lost something profound in the turn from searchlight to floodlight, from the high-modern to the postmodern. Indeed, high-modern news explicitly envisioned itself as a democratic service, a resource for the formation of a critically informed public opinion. By contrast, the kind of postmodern news that is dominant today is largely the business of constructing dramatic narratives—televisual spectacles crafted for public consumption. In the name of storytelling, postmodern news has abandoned the goal of rational-critical exposure that underlies modernist ideals of publicity. Creating products for market, rather than pursuing critical inquiry, the floodlight has contributed to the wider depoliticization of the public sphere and the trivialization of publicity. It suggests that politics is aesthetic performance, that the citizen is but a passive spectator, and, perhaps most importantly, that "truthiness" is an adequate substitute for truth.

At the same time, however, the turn from the searchlight to the floodlight calls on us to think beyond the modernist divide between the discursive domains of the political-normative and the aesthetic-expressive. The familiar critique assumes that the arena of public affairs, governance, and the social good is necessarily distinguishable from the arena of private pleasure and affective play. The communication scholar John Durham Peters, though, has noted that in its Greek and Latin origins, the very term "publicity" contains *both* political-participatory *and* visual-aesthetic connotations.[19] The floodlight crisscrosses those boundaries, offering a discourse that is simultaneously news and entertainment, politics and dramaturgy. Illustrating the turn toward discursive integration enabled in the multichannel era, it erases a number of other conceptual distinctions that characterized modernity, including the arbitrary divides between the public and the private, the institutional and the personal, and the rational and the affective.

At least in one way, then, the floodlight provides a better fit for contemporary times. The searchlight was, to use the political theorist James Bohman's terms, a kind of "thin" publicity. It imposed a unitary language that narrowed what could count as legitimate public discourse to the abstract and the disembodied—to the "reasonable and prudent man." In this frame, the situated, emotional, and narrativistic were labeled as particular, illegitimate methods of political reasoning. Bohman argues that such forms of thin publicity limit access to the political arena to those culturally equipped to reason "correctly" and ultimately are inadequate in facing the challenges of a pluralistic society. To maintain an inclusive democracy, he suggests, citizens "must enter the public sphere with all their identities and roles intact," and public discourse must create spaces for a variety of cultural perspectives, epistemic resources, and social positions.[20] Thus at the same time that the floodlight represents the postmodern loss of the rational-critical impetus that motivated high-modern news, it also pushes at the boundaries of political discourse, laying the groundwork for the development of hybrid forms of public affairs media that can engage with politics in more imaginative and accessible ways.

4

♦ ♦ ♦

THE SLOW DEATH OF CBS NEWS

As the dust settled in the aftermath of the 2004 presidential election, the PBS journalist Bill Moyers posed a question to *New Yorker* writer Ken Auletta. "What's happened to the house that Murrow built?" he asked, referring, of course, to CBS News and its legendary hero Edward R. Murrow. Moyers, a former reporter for that erstwhile pinnacle of broadcast journalism, once one of the most trusted sources of news in the country, lamented that the mighty House of Murrow had crumbled, becoming merely a "shack on the side of the road."[1] Indeed, the 2004 campaign between George Bush and the Democrat John Kerry was a bellwether for CBS News. A noticeably aging Dan Rather still clung to the network's traditional "voice-of-god" posture—that centralized, hierarchical logic of news so characteristic of the high-modern paradigm—but that approach had come to resonate with fewer and fewer people. Rather's audience was older and smaller than it had ever been, leaving the CBS *Evening News* a perennial third out of three in the competition for ratings and earnings. The year 2004 also marked the final act of Rather's anchoring career: he was forced to resign just months later in the wake of the infamous Bush–National Guard story, whose strong accusations against the president rested upon transgressions of professional practice and in turn fueled the decades-old campaign by the conservative right to discredit Rather and the institution of CBS News.

The problems at CBS certainly were greater than those facing NBC and ABC, but network television news itself was in a state of crisis. As we have seen, the networks' high-modern democratic labor, pioneered by Murrow and polished by Walter Cronkite, had developed into a distinctly postmodern effort—a corporate product pitching drama, story, and character and no longer willing, or perhaps unable, to meet the responsibilities of the Fourth Estate. This became evident to many with the fiasco of election night 2000, when the networks called and recalled the winner far too many times, exposing an eventually self-admitted lack of professionalism and further undermining what little credibility the nightly news still retained. The next year, 2001, would see almost the complete collapse of the critical press. Like most sources of news in the dark months following the terrorist attacks of September 11, the networks were co-opted by aggressive Bush administration efforts to manage public information, becoming cheerleaders for the administration and its multiple wars in Afghanistan, on "terror," and in Iraq.[2] The climate of the times was epitomized by the president's 2003 "mission accomplished" moment, his beautifully backlit landing on the deck of the USS *Abraham Lincoln*, and his astoundingly premature proclamation of victory in Iraq. A carefully orchestrated exercise in propaganda, the spectacle would eventually backfire, but in the short run it was repeatedly circulated and celebrated by a remarkably acquiescent news media. Even though they were well aware that every detail of the spectacle had been arranged for effect, that awareness did little to dampen journalists' enthusiasm for it or spark any serious effort to question the president's basic claim.[3]

For many observers, the 2004 presidential campaign would also signify network news' further slide toward irrelevance. Late in the multichannel era, voters continued to turn to a remarkably broad array of media forms to make sense of the presidential campaign. From partisan talk to "docutainment" films, from afternoon self-help programs to sports and fishing shows, from late-night comedy to animated Internet videos, network news found itself competing against more sources offering qualitatively different kinds of news and information.[4] In turn, the number of people who reported learning something about the candidates or their campaigns from the nightly network news was down to 35 percent, a decline of 10 percent from the previous election cycle.[5] Perhaps even more problematic for the networks was the number of people who reported *believing* what they heard on the nightly news. According to one survey, only 16 percent of Republicans said they believed all or most of what the Big Three reported. While that may have been due in large part to the right's persistent accusations of liberal bias among network television, more than two-thirds of the Democrats surveyed said they didn't believe the networks either.[6]

Despite these bleak numbers, network television and its news divisions remained the central force in a multichannel media environment.[7] The three nightly newscasts combined to reach well over twenty million people each day, far eclipsing the audience for twenty-four-hour cable and making them still the most attended-to source of national news in the country. Network reporters continued to command front-row access at presidential press briefings, campaign appearances, and other governmental functions. Two of three presidential debates that year were moderated by journalists from the Big Three networks, including CBS's longtime political reporter Bob Schieffer, whose work at the network dated back to 1967 and Cronkite's *Evening News*. (Schieffer would also moderate one of the debates between Barack Obama and John McCain four year later, as would NBC's Tom Brokaw.)

Together the three network newsrooms continued to play a disproportionate role in shaping the national news agenda. Although no longer synonymous with "the news," the nightly network newscasts still had three of the loudest voices in the mass-mediated public sphere, or what many more commonly had come to refer to as the "mainstream media." Political communication scholar Lance Bennett and his colleagues have described a constellation of high-visibility news outlets—local and national, broadcast and print—that produce a largely homogenous take on the news each day. Relying on the same "widely shared news construction norms," the mainstream media turn to the same kinds of sources to report on the same issues and events. The result, Bennett and his coauthors argue, is the "default reality option"—the dominant interpretation of current events circulated through the mass media each day. Taken as both "official" and "authoritative," the default reality option establishes the baseline for public conversation and at the same time works to exclude alternative discourses from serious consideration.[8]

The underlying authority that still privileges the mainstream media and their default reality option is a legacy of the networks' high-modern heritage, that previous paradigm in which the self-proclaimed "excellent professional journalists" of network television sought to explain the "way it is" for the benefit of the citizenry. Late in the multichannel era, broadcast news and the wider paradigm of centralized, authoritative journalism were still propped up by this same, albeit increasingly tenuous, scaffolding. Network newscasters still claimed to be professional journalists engaged (although they wouldn't put it this way) in a high-modern enterprise, but as we've seen, they were now involved in a rather different endeavor. Examining the CBS *Evening News* coverage of the 2004 presidential campaign, this chapter extends the analysis. I consider what happened to the "house that Murrow built" and offer a snapshot of a house in disarray—a communicative form in decay. By 2004, the concept of the nightly news itself had become problematic and marked by incongruity—between its historical ideals and its postmodern practice, between its claim to speak truth to power and its ideological co-option, and ultimately between a network newscast and the eve of the post-network age.

Default Reality Option

According to the normative standards that once motivated the practice of network journalism, the nightly newscast ideally should function as a reliable source of politically viable information and argument, a discursive resource for the rational citizen's formation of reasoned opinion. For two decades, however, scholars have been documenting the ways in which it falls short of that democratic promise. Assessing network coverage of presidential elections over thirty years, Thomas Patterson rightly suggested something had become "out of order" with network news.[9] Stephen Farnsworth and Robert Lichter likewise argued that network coverage of elections from 1988 to 2000 amounted to a "nightmare"—a "devastating failure" to serve a useful democratic function.[10] Despite the networks' continual pledge to do better, the coverage of Campaign 2004 was remarkable for just how little had changed.

As during the Clinton impeachment six years earlier, the logic of infotainment and its metaphor of theater remained primary organizing devices. The candidates, said CBS, were fighting for command of "center stage," trying to outmaneuver each other for control of the "spotlight." According to White House Correspondent John Roberts, the parties' nominating conventions, once a critical moment of political argument and decision making, had become an "infomercial," a "narrative," or a "novel"—a ritual, explains one analyst, that has "all the trappings of theater." In turn, if the conventions once clarified party platforms, Roberts instead tells us the platform had become the "plot line," its advocates "performers" or "cast members," playing out the "script." Indeed, the party conventions are now entirely scripted, but CBS also insists that the debates are also "stage shows"—"televised showdowns" built upon an elaborate "behind-the-scenes production." Previewing the first presidential debate, reporter Richard Schlesinger says it will be "as carefully staged managed as a Broadway show, except minus the drama." Similarly, reporter Jim Axelrod argues that "vice-presidential debates historically have had all the interest of a paint-drying contest." Despite that, he holds out hope that in the midst of this particularly dramatic presidential campaign, the debate between the incumbent Dick Cheney and the Democratic challenger John Edwards "will be different."

Although the debates remain critical moments in the public decision-making process (some 62.5 million people watched the first presidential debate that year[11]), CBS suggests that ultimately they are bad theater, lacking the drama that would otherwise make them worth attending to. In this dramaturgical frame, CBS's primary concern lies not with the arguments the candidates will make—the content of their public speech—but rather with the quality of the televisual spectacle. No longer high-modern information disseminators or critical questioners, the CBS reporters function here as theater critics, their nightly role to dissect the campaign's political stagecraft. In his study of presidential election coverage, Thomas Patterson noted this increasing tendency among journalists to critique politicians' public performance rather than report on the substance of their speech. For Patterson, the journalist-as-theater-critic was symptomatic of a wider transformation in political journalism away from conceptualizing elections as critical moments in the process of governance and toward framing them as a kind of game—the candidates now understood as contestants in the ritualized competition of electoral politics.[12]

So it is with CBS, which both proclaimed the day before the election to be the "final act" in the theater of Campaign '04 and in the same story suggested that Bush and Kerry were in the "final sprint" in the race for the White House. As we have seen, metaphors speak to the underlying conceptual systems that organize knowledge of and practice within a given human domain. Thus it is revealing that after then political newcomer Barack Obama delivered the keynote address at the Democratic Convention, the speech that set him on the path to the presidency, reporter John Roberts would explain that he "hit what could *only* be called a home run into center field." For Roberts, sports provides the "only" discursive frame to make sense of Obama's successful speech and perhaps the entire political process. Elsewhere at the Democratic convention, Roberts sounds more like a sports commentator than a presidential reporter, explaining that "Democrats say that in the year 2000 they didn't want it badly enough, that Republicans wanted it more." Paying less attention to the party's platform than its will to win, he concludes that this year, "Democrats are saying they want it as bad if not more than the Republicans." So too does Roberts note prior to the second debate that "the president needs to bring his A *game*" if he hopes to get a much needed victory, and thus has been "working with aides, reviewing tapes"—his "strategy to make his opponent look defenseless." A few days later, Roberts concludes that indeed, "President Bush brought his A game," potentially saving his candidacy.

Patterson's research reveals that in what I've called the high-modern paradigm, news coverage of presidential elections was overwhelmingly descriptive in nature and largely interested in matters of policy. He notes that during the 1960 election, stories that explicitly assessed strategy were labeled "analysis" and thus demarcated from the factual reporting on policy issues that comprised the bulk of campaign news. By contrast, in a postmodern paradigm, the vast majority of stories had become interpretive, focusing primarily on questions of strategy and effect. Interestingly, Patterson notes that by 1992, issue-oriented stories were the ones explicitly labeled analysis, while the "game frame" had taken on the mantle of fact.[13] Extending the research to 2000, Farnsworth and Lichter found that 71 percent of network news stories that year focused on strategy, while according to the Project for Excellence in Journalism, only 13 percent of stories during the final weeks of the 2004 campaign discussed policy, compared to the 55 percent focused on strategic concerns.[14]

The CBS *Evening News* coverage of the election affirms the argument. In the newscasts examined here, CBS does produce stories exploring the candidates' stances on a number of issues, including tax cuts, stem-cell research, the nomination of Supreme Court justices, the use of the U.S. military, medical malpractice, and global warming. But most of those stories are packaged as special segments and appear later in the newscast, *after* stories whose overarching interest lies with the players' strategy. A story's location in a newscast largely is a sign of value—the earlier it runs, the greater its implied importance. Here the privileging of strategy over governance is clear. Despite the predominance of the game frame in mainstream media, however, Patterson argues that most voters still rightly conceptualize politics as the process of decision making and problem solving.[15] For a brief moment, CBS makes a similar point. Reporter Byron Pitts, who covers the Kerry campaign, notes on the day of Kerry's address at the party convention that "in Virginia, voters want substance" and "in New Jersey, issues matter." Despite that, Pitts's story that day fails to address any substantive issues; rather it simply notes that voters hope Kerry will talk about them.

Abdicating responsibility to carefully explore the candidates' policy stances, CBS instead examines their "playbooks." Before the first presidential debate, Pitts evaluates Kerry's playbook, his reporter copy complemented by a full-screen graphic that looks like it was drawn by the network sports department, depicting a notepad with Kerry's "strategy" laid out in tidy bullet points. These include facile admonitions to "lose the Senate speak," "talk like a regular guy," and convince voters that "he's not a flip-flopper" but a "sophisticated thinker." So too does Jim Axelrod discuss "the candidates' playbook" for the final debate, while the very next day Dan Rather tells us that John Roberts "has the candidate's playbooks for the run-up to election day." On the eve of election, the playbook becomes the candidates' "closing arguments," again illustrated graphically by brief lists of bullet points. Kerry's closing argument, Pitts reports, is that he would "make America safer at home and abroad, set a new course in Iraq, create and keep jobs in the U.S. by ending tax breaks for companies who ship jobs overseas, raise the minimum wage, expand health care coverage, and cut costs by rolling back tax cuts for the wealthiest of Americans." Here, Pitts does offer an explication, however brief, of Kerry's policy preferences, but quickly he transitions back into the familiar strategic frame. "It's a wish list the Bush campaign argues America can't afford," he continues, "but for John Kerry, it provides what he hopes will be a winning formula in a tight race."

For the CBS *Evening News*, this approach of reducing issues to strategy points reveals the network's own uncertainty about the place of the thirty-minute nightly newscast in a twenty-four-hour multichannel environment. The guiding assumption in the production of the nightly news became that the audience was already familiar with the day's headlines and could turn to a variety of on-demand sources for more extensive information. Quite intentionally, then, the evening news ceased to function as the news-of-record. Its producers continued to diminish its factual content—indeed, according to the Project for Excellence in Journalism, only 14 percent of stories in the final weeks of the campaign disseminated new information.[16] Instead, the evening news offered the inside story, the interpretive, behind-the-scenes assessment of character, strategy, and effect.

One sees this on display after the final presidential debate in a recurrent segment aptly titled *Inside Story*. "We have the latest info tonight from a high-tech CBS poll of uncommitted voters who watched last night's Bush-Kerry face-off," says Dan Rather. "Anthony Mason has the facts and figures and gives you the *Inside Story*." Mason's story then examines the results of

CBS's efforts to track debate viewers' moment-by-moment reactions along a sliding scale ranging from +5 (strongly approve) to—5 (strongly disapprove). His "high-tech facts and figures" reveal that Kerry "scored well when he talked about economic issues. Watch women respond when he talks about raising the minimum wage and women's pay," he instructs the audience, as a graphic shows the meter measuring women's responses bump up to +3.5. "The president," Mason continues, "scored some of *his* highest marks when he talked about his faith." Here the meters show the men's reactions at slightly over +2 and women's at about +2.5 as the president says, "I never want to impose my religion on anybody else, but when I make decisions, I stand on principle."

Translating the complexities of social issues and political argument to +/- 5 points, subdivided by gender, Mason's story imposes an instrumental rationality, or what the theorist Herbert Marcuse once called a "technological rationality," on the political process.[17] Transforming the autonomous, reasoning citizen into test subject, the poll reads the immediate, short-term, and necessarily unreflective effects of the candidates' use of words. The implicit assumption underlying both the poll and Mason's story is that the purpose of public speech is less to advance a reasoned argument or engage in dialogue in the name of understanding than to generate a strategic effect, to move the meter in pursuit of the pragmatic goal of technical control. In this instrumental frame, ideas and issues are no longer the substance of politics, but merely means to an end—a "winning formula in a tight race." Reporter Jim Axelrod expresses this political logic well, arguing that the lesson of the first Bush/Kerry debate—what John Roberts elsewhere referred to as "the takeaway"—is that "who wins and who loses can turn on moments that have nothing to do with policy at all."

Spectacle and Spin

CBS's suggestion that politics often has nothing to do with policy is both constituent and constitutive of the wider rationalization of public communication that has come to define the political landscape. Bennett and his colleagues describe a mutually dependent system of press and public office that each day manufactures a coherent and highly reductive interpretation of political reality. Engineered largely by a "dominant class of communication professionals who manage most high-level political situations," much political journalism has become largely the reporting of the scripts prepared by "pollsters, image shapers, marketers, handlers, and spin doctors," whose formulas now shape "nearly all aspects of our political communication."[18] In particular, running for president is now in no small part the systematic work of co-opting television news, of harnessing its ephemeral flow of rapid-fire imagery and sound bites to transform it into an instrument of "public opinion management" rather than an institution of public information and accountability.

As Republican campaigners Nicolle Devenish and Tucker Eskew have explained, "message development" is now "central to everything that happens in a campaign."[19] The two communication strategists describe a process of aggressively trying to "make news" within each day's news cycle in ways designed—visually, verbally, and conceptually—to construct what they revealingly refer to as "the narrative."[20] For the campaign engineer, political communication has become the highly rationalized production of a master narrative, one built, like the serialized fiction of an earlier era, through daily installments. To borrow from the scholar Murray Edelman, this daily stream of messages generates political spectacle, a "partly illusory parade of threats and reassurances" that "does not promote accurate expectation or understanding, but rather evokes a drama that objectifies hopes and fears."[21]

In 2004, Devenish, Eskew, and the rest of the Bush team were especially effective in using the nightly news to circulate their narrative and its corresponding conceptual frame. One sees this on the day before the election, when veteran reporter Bill Plante summarizes Bush's "closing arguments." The president, Plante reports, insists he "can be trusted to keep the nation's families safe, to win the war on terror, and to lead the nation to a better future in an uncertain time." Political spectacle, Edelman argues, is at its most potent when it is emotionally compelling but factually ambiguous.[22] Here Plante amplifies the Bush campaign's ambiguously emotive narrative of national security, one that paints Bush as the decisive and unwavering leader who could protect "the nation's families" from terror and uncertainty themselves.

Throughout the campaign, CBS actively co-constructs this narrative. For example, as the Democratic convention draws to a close, John Roberts explains that "the commander in chief reported for campaign duty today," the characterization of "Commander Bush" enhanced by imagery of the president proudly shaking hands with military personnel. A month later, at the start of the Republican convention, Roberts explains that the primary strategy will be to define Bush as the leader in the "war on terror" through heavy reference to the terrorist attacks of September 11. To illustrate this claim, Roberts's story replays the now-iconic clip of Bush standing amid the wreckage of the World Trade Center wearing a hard hat and proclaiming through the megaphone that "whoever did this will hear all of us soon." Notably, CBS here willfully interweaves spectacle into its campaign coverage, replaying for its audience the years-old clip highlighting the moment many consider to be the pinnacle of the Bush presidency.

Elsewhere, Roberts suggests that the Kerry campaign is in "a tough contest against a wartime White House that freely uses aircraft carriers and Iraq war veterans as a backdrop for speeches. Kerry can only challenge on a promise of performance and a proven record of military service." Although one can detect a note of criticism in Roberts's tone, he nonetheless contributes to the privileging of spectacle over the proven, or provable record, replaying and thus recirculating carefully staged pictures of Vice President Cheney speaking in front of a sea of uniformed personnel and Bush in his military flight suit on the deck of the USS *Abraham Lincoln*. Despite his between-the-lines critique of Bush's image-generating strategy, Roberts actively amplifies it. His reporting on strategy becomes the very tool through which the strategy is enacted.

In the face of the ubiquity of the Bush narrative, the Kerry campaign also tried to construct its own version of the national security narrative. Byron Pitts, for example, covers Kerry's "homecoming" to Boston for the Democratic convention—what Dan Rather refers to in dramatic, if not exactly factual, fashion as "the final mile of Senator Kerry's journey." Pitts's story opens with images of the senator sailing into Boston Harbor alongside fellow platoon members from the Vietnam War, as loudspeakers play Bruce Springsteen's song "No Surrender." A sound bite from Kerry immediately follows: "Bruce Springsteen had it right," he proclaims: "No retreat, no surrender!" Pitts then borrows from pop culture and World War II mythology to explain the Kerry narrative. "Kerry has used this 'Band of Brothers' as a metaphor for America: sons of poverty and privilege, side-by-side, one boat, with Senator Kerry at the helm." Pitts here clearly recognizes that Kerry's "homecoming" is a performance conducted for the television news cameras—he labels it a "picture-perfect photo op"—but conventions of campaign journalism demand that CBS cover it. It is, of course, what the candidate *did* that day. But rather than trying to determine the substance behind the spectacle, Pitts instead contrasts it with the Bush campaign's countermove, its release of a hostile web-based video intended to undermine Kerry's narrative.

Pitts demonstrates a postmodern understanding of objectivity—no longer the practice of neutral observation nor the correlation of claim to fact, but rather the comparing and contrasting of the two sides' machinery of spectacle generation. He does the same thing the day before Kerry's "homecoming," in a story about the "week in which every image matters." Pitts reports that Kerry was seeking to "one-up President Bush on national security" by visiting a military base and surrounding himself with "the sounds and symbols of the U.S. military." The Bush campaign, though, was quick to respond, "poking fun at pictures of Kerry in a protective suit as he toured the Kennedy Space Center." As the video shows a series of images of Kerry wrapped head-to-toe in a laboratory protective suit, including one of him foolishly prostrate on hands and knees, Pitts explains that the Bush camp was comparing those pictures to a "photo op of another presidential candidate, Michael Dukakis, riding in a tank in 1988." Here the video replays the archival image of Dukakis in the tank—an image, Pitts says, "that crippled his campaign." In the name of reporting on the day's events, CBS becomes an active conduit through which the campaigns' efforts to control imagery and manipulate perception is realized. Pitt's story sutures together images and explanation, constructing what Bennett elsewhere has called a "news reality frame," a carefully engineered simulacrum that substitutes itself for the reality it purports to represent.[23] Even as he implicitly challenges Kerry's national security claims and perhaps his masculinity, Pitts preserves his objectivity by noting that Democrats "were just as quick to point to a picture of Bush in goggles, with a Dukakis-like grin" and showing the audience one of the sillier photos of Bush from his top-gun landing on the *Abraham Lincoln*. "It's all politics at its pettiest," Pitts concludes, admitting the problematic nature of the contemporary campaign. "*But*," he continues, justifying his own complicity in the game, "this is a week when everything matters."

Amplifying the campaigns' image management, CBS likewise provides a highly visible venue for what reporter John Roberts calls the "battle to win the spin" or Jim Axelrod the "war of messages and messengers." After the second debate, for example, Dan Rather leads not by recapping what the candidates said, but by noting that the "spin doctors, political hit men, personal pollsters, and staffers" spent the day "trying to affect public perception of the outcome" of the debate. In the following story and throughout the campaign, CBS allows these "spin doctors and political hit men" to shape the discursive substance of the nightly news. After the election, Bush strategist Tucker Eskew credited the Republican victory in part to their successful "surrogate operation," the coordinated use of political insiders to speak each day on behalf of the candidates and advance the campaign's narrative frame.[24]

Thus as John Kerry prepared to speak at the Democratic convention, Rudy Giuliani, the former Republican mayor of New York City and Bush surrogate, tells John Roberts that Kerry is "asking to be the president of the United States at a time in which we're at war against terrorists, and his Senate career has been one that's been marked by indecision and inconsistency with regard to terrorists." Notably, Roberts here provides no examination of Kerry's record in the Senate and instead lets Giuliani's quote stand uninterrogated. Likewise, Roberts later gives airtime to Zell Miller—the Democratic senator from Georgia who had become an aggressive supporter of the president—and his declaration that Bush is "the kind of man we need as commander in chief during this time of war." Again Roberts makes no attempt to determine the factual basis for Miller's claim. Elsewhere, a sound bite from presidential adviser Karen Hughes prior to the first debate impugns Kerry's credibility before he even has the chance to speak. "You have to take whatever he says with a grain of salt tonight," she instructs the CBS audience, "because it's subject to change with no notice." So too does Republican strategist Mary Matalin offer claim without evidence, arguing before the vice-presidential debate that Dick Cheney is "a serious, wise man."

The reliance on surrogates is symptomatic of the professionalization, or rationalization, of contemporary campaigning. The candidates themselves are largely inaccessible to reporters, rarely leaving the confines of controlled settings nor deviating from carefully prepared scripts. The surrogates, by contrast, are seen as a welcome source of fresh material. As one print reporter who covered the Kerry campaign explains, when reporters interview the surrogates, they admittedly "get a certain amount of spin. But sometimes it's useful," he says, "just to get your questions answered, just to get something new for your story."[25] In practice, however, that "new" material functions to co-opt the news, to turn it into an echo chamber for campaign spin.

One sees a powerful example of this in CBS's coverage of the Republican convention, when Bob Schieffer, himself a remnant of the high-modern age, files a two-minute interview with Bush's primary strategist, Karl Rove. There, Rove "explains" that despite concerns about the war in Iraq and the sputtering economy (issues that favored Kerry), "There are going to be questions about values, questions about vision, questions about leadership, personal characteristics. People are going to want to know that they can relate to the president; the president's got values that don't change with the rising of the sun." The Rove interview may facilitate CBS's search for the "inside story," but at the same time it allows Rove and his well-coordinated apparatus to prioritize the issues and characterize the candidates in self-serving ways. Schieffer lets Rove set the terms of the debate, functioning as what the theorist Stuart Hall has called a "primary definer" for the discourse of news, dictating what it is that "people are going to want to know."[26]

As CBS becomes a tool for Rove's systematic effort to control the content of public knowledge, it illustrates the profound shift in political communication toward a strategic or instrumental rationality. It is emblematic of the breakdown of the high-modernist assumptions that the broadcast interview would, or could, function as a forum for rational-critical publicity. As Bennett and his coauthors argue, the journalistic convention of interviewing those in positions of power still rests on the "idealized belief in the open flow of public information and a shared commitment by elected officials to democratic values."[27] In a postcampaign debriefing, Democratic strategist Joe Lockhart made the same point. He suggested that there used to be a "shared sense of responsibility to the system, where both sides felt there was great value in these campaigns and in government." By contrast, he characterized the process of contemporary campaign communication as a group of "pretty skilled manipulators manipulating people who are very well aware of being manipulated."[28]

The Wellspring of Cynicism

Cognizant of their own manipulation, the CBS reporters struggle to regain some measure of professional autonomy—not by confronting strategic communication with critical challenge, but instead by seeking to exploit the uncontrollable and throw the candidates "off message." Late in the campaign, when news surfaces that a large stash of U.S. weapons has gone missing in Iraq, John Roberts reports that the news "had [the president's] campaign way off message today, losing in the headlines and in danger of losing momentum at the worst possible time." As the missing weapons remained in the headlines for two more days, Jim Axelrod reports that "the usually sure-footed Bush seemed a little off stride." Earlier, Roberts had the same take on Bush's unusually honest remark to the *Today* show's Matt Lauer during the Republican convention that he didn't think "you can win the war on terror." The "political firestorm" over Bush's statement, Roberts reports, had "yanked the carefully scripted convention badly off message." During the Democratic convention, it was a comment from John Kerry's wife—Teresa Heinz Kerry's exclamation to a conservative reporter to "shove it"—that was "a real distraction for the Kerry campaign." Says Byron Pitts, "it knocks them off message, if only temporarily." As did many mainstream media outlets, CBS returned to the "shove it" incident several times over the next two evenings, with a discussion of the comment serving as the crux of Dan Rather's interview with Heinz Kerry herself.

Indulging in such "gotcha journalism," CBS and the mainstream media's coverage of presidential politics delves into the trivial, ironic, and often absurd. As a result, it produces a fundamentally cynical discourse, one that provides an arena for the daily twists and turns of campaign strategy while suggesting that the whole endeavor is meaningless. Here, Jim Axelrod's report on the vice-presidential debate provides a powerful example. Recall that Axelrod had previewed the debate by hoping it would be more interesting than a "paint-drying contest." The day after, he argues that it proved to be a kind of boxing match: "more than ninety minutes of bare-knuckles politics" that "truth be told ... often crossed the line of civility." Avoiding any explanation of its substance, Axelrod instead reconstructs his version of the debate, a back-and-forth series of sound bites in which Cheney and Edwards snip at and talk over each other. "Edwards," Axelrod reports, "demonstrated why he won millions in the courtroom." Says Edwards in one sound bite, "I don't think this country can take four more years of this kind of experience." Cheney, Axelrod then explains, was "forcefully tough. He gave as good as he got—sometimes better." Says Cheney, "The senator's got his facts wrong." Without explaining what facts Cheney was referring to, Axelrod then proclaims: "Actually, both had a little *trouble* with the facts." Cheney, he notes, had insisted that he had never met Edwards before that evening. "*Reaaallly?*" Axelrod sneers, replaying a clip showing the two sitting side by side at a dinner in 2001. To preserve his objectivity, Axelrod then accuses Edwards of overstating the cost of the Iraq war, for citing the projected cost rather than the cost-to-date. Framing the debate entirely as a series of hostile attacks and misrepresentations, Axelrod finally reaches his conclusion. "So who won?" he asks. "There doesn't seem to be a clear-cut winner," he declares. "*And besides*, by the time the polls crystallize into some consensus about who won *this* debate, it will be time for the next one."

Notably, Axelrod's story provides the only coverage of the vice-presidential debate on the *Evening News* that night. Focusing entirely on form and effect, and offering no substantive information about the two candidates or their policy stances, Axelrod ultimately concludes that the debate is irrelevant. His disdain for the whole business is barely disguised, his tone marked by a dismissive smugness that is representative of the mainstream media's postmodern approach to politics, its deep distrust of public speech. Axelrod is fundamentally cynical; he assumes he is being deceived and celebrates his ability to see through the deception. The political rhetorician Roderick Hart argues that this kind of postmodern cleverness has "become the language of television," and in turn "the language of politics." Postmodern television, Hart suggests, dismisses politics as a "dastardly business," an exercise in linguistic manipulation absent of any inclination toward community building or problem solving.[29] As such, Axelrod, and CBS's coverage as a whole, contributes to a fundamentally ironic view of the political process, one that emphasizes the disjuncture between words and meanings and suggests not simply that candidates for high office inevitably will have "a little trouble with the facts," but that public language itself has become irreparably divorced from the real and the meaningful. Axelrod's brand of postmodern irony, the historian Hayden White once argued, "points to the potential foolishness of all linguistic characterizations of reality" and as a result "tends to dissolve all belief in the possibility of positive political actions."[30]

Authoritative Collapse

If Axelrod and CBS's ironic discourse undermines faith in the positive possibilities of politics, it ironically functions to undermine the nightly news as well. News is, after all, the characterizing of the real in language, a labor the postmodern cynic who dismisses the representational capacities of language necessarily must reject. With its endless attention to the play of surfaces—to the war of messages and messengers—deeper questions of truth, fact, and accountability become obscured. Reporting each evening not on the way it is, but the way those in positions of power say it is, the nightly news privileges the semiotic over the material, the narrative over the real. Becoming one more location in which the struggle to shape perception is waged, broadcast journalism abdicates its high-modern responsibility to determine the factual record; instead it articulates an epistemological position that rejects the very notion of a factual record and affirms the deeper distrust of anyone—itself included—who would try to make authoritative claims of what is.

For Bennett and his coauthors, contemporary news's disinterest in fact and its fixation with spin are correlated with the public's loss of confidence in the news media and a government that indulges in spin. "When the press becomes an echo chamber for well-managed but misleading information," they argue, "the result is only likely to deepen the spiral of cynicism and distrust among the public."[31] This point is not entirely lost on CBS, which, like most postmodern news, promotes itself throughout its election coverage, promising to provide "facts without spin." That claim is curiously similar to pundit Bill O'Reilly's insistence that his spin-laden *O'Reilly Factor* on Fox News is somehow a "No Spin Zone." In both instances, one sees the postmodern disconnect between words and reality. O'Reilly certainly cannot actually mean that his rabidly polemical program is spin-free, and neither does CBS's claim of "facts without spin" serve as an accurate characterization of its nightly amplification of spectacle and spin.

Presiding over the collapse of his own authority, there is a measure of despair in Rather's plea to his viewers to stay tuned to CBS during the Republican convention. "CBS News coverage," he says, "steady, reliable, independent. Coverage of the national convention will continue throughout the week." Here Rather invokes the increasingly obsolete value set of high-modern journalism—factual reliability and journalistic independence—but his last-ditch grasp at epistemic privilege quickly devolves into a marketing ploy posing as a mission statement. The irony of Rather's claim to authority that night was called into stark relief less than two weeks later when CBS would broadcast the story insisting that it had obtained documented proof that George Bush had been given preferential treatment during his days in the Texas Air National Guard.

Almost instantly, the story unleashed a fury—first among right-wing bloggers (including the pointedly titled RatherBiased.com), then quickly moving to the conservative talk radio and cable news apparatuses, and finally to the mainstream media themselves.[32] At issue was the authenticity of the incriminating documents, an authenticity that was immediately questioned, and that CBS finally was to conclude could not be verified. After two weeks of denial, Rather was forced to offer a formal on-air apology and, two months later, announce his resignation. When the panel CBS commissioned to investigate the matter released its 224-page report the following spring, it concluded that although there was no evidence that partisanship fueled the story, CBS News did violate the basic journalistic principle of verification in its rush to beat its competitors in the game of gotcha journalism. For many, so-called Memogate was a profound blow to the last vestiges of

CBS's journalistic authority. Driven by the desire to break the story, CBS had failed to determine the reliability of its source and the authenticity of its evidence, illustrating the increasingly tenuous basis of the "real" news' claim on the real.

This disconnect between story and actuality, however, was not just a problem at CBS. In its review of the affair, the *Columbia Journalism Review* argued that a lack of interest in fact characterized much of the mainstream media's handling of the incident. In a microcosm of the breakdown of high-modern journalism, reporters and pundits alike were quick to offer speculation without evidence and failed to adequately examine the complexity of the situation. "Rumors shaped the news and conventions of sourcing and skepticism fell by the wayside," wrote *CJR*. "Dan Rather is not alone on this one; respected journalists made mistakes all around."[33]

As the culmination of CBS's performance during the 2004 election, Memogate thus offers a window onto a powerful pivot point in the evolution of broadcast news. It demonstrates the increasingly interwoven nature of postmodern publicity late in the multichannel era and the decreasing role network news had come to—and indeed could—play as primary storytellers and arbiters of truth. Even more significantly, though, it reveals the extent to which the ostensibly real news had become, in actuality, *fake*: another version of reality TV more committed to story and spectacle than fact and evidence. Network news still postured as the same high-modern endeavor in which Cronkite was once engaged, but that high-modern veneer had grown brittle and unconvincing. Shortly after the election, with Rather's resignation, ABC's Peter Jennings's passing from cancer, and Tom Brokaw's celebrated retirement from the NBC *Nightly News*, the networks' last tenuous link to the high-modern paradigm would be broken. The Democratic strategist Joe Lockhart, therefore, is not alone in his conclusion that the 2004 campaign marked "the last gasp of the network news dominance and prominence."[34] Given the networks' increasingly negative contribution to the wider political culture, however, that is not necessarily a bad thing.

5

♦ ♦ ♦

NEWS FROM SOMEWHERE

HYBRID BLENDS IN THE MULTICHANNEL ERA

"I know, I know," admitted Walter Cronkite. "I'm the last person you'd expect to see on MTV." Cronkite certainly was right; old "Uncle Walter"—the "dean of TV journalism," the young MTV reporter called him—seemed more than a bit out of place on the youth-oriented channel, whose primary business is manufacturing teen culture. Here, though, the broadcast news legend was lending his gravitas to CBS's corporate partner MTV and its efforts to cover the 2004 presidential election. Such was the nature of broadcast news late in the multichannel era, a moment of unlikely combinations and hybrid blends.

By this time the paradigm of "real news" epitomized in our cultural imagination by Cronkite and his once-authoritative network newscast had been fractured. The nightly news had become a more postmodern form of reality TV, itself increasingly besieged by a growing number of alternative sources of news and information. In the wake of Memogate and Dan Rather's resignation, conservative columnist Peggy Noonan would claim that "the yeomen of the blogosphere and AM radio and the Internet" had "taken down" CBS News.[1] That might be debatable, but what is clear is that the networks and the rest of the mainstream news media were now in serious competition with a multitude of channels and outlets—not just for fragmented audiences, but for the very right to define the parameters of paradigm, for the profound epistemological privilege of claiming, as Cronkite often did, "the way it is."

In this shifting, tumultuous environment, news producers of all varieties were moving away from the one-size-fits-all approach of the mass media, instead targeting programs toward more narrowly defined audience clusters. The viewership of the nightly news may have been declining, but the networks were also striving to reinvent themselves in multiple forms and across delivery platforms. Spinning out from center, they were developing opportunities to extend their news "brands" and "repurpose" their content. Some of this was already commonplace *within* networks, where the news divisions had for years produced the weekly news magazines, the Sunday public affairs shows, and that other daily program—the morning news. Increasingly, though, the networks were seeking synergies across conglomerate structures. NBC, for example, had developed its partnership with Microsoft to repurpose the *Nightly News* on both cable and, to a smaller extent, the Internet. At CBS, which had never developed a twenty-four-hour cable news operation and whose web presence was minimal, news executives instead pursued strategies of integration with corporate parent Viacom's cable division, what Viacom calls the MTV Networks.

During the 2004 election, the Viacom/CBS partnership produced a variety of news aimed at a range of audiences. On CBS itself, these included the *Early Show,* the network's version of "breakfast TV," that daily mix of information and entertainment designed primarily for women. On cable, CBS extended its presence onto the Viacom-owned Black Entertainment Television channel (BET), where its news division coproduced the BET *Nightly News,* a national newscast explicitly targeting African-Americans. And on MTV, the CBS brand was interwoven with that channel's *Choose or Lose* project, a series of news reports and informational programs intended to educate teens about the presidential election and motivate their engagement.

In this chapter, I take up these three related efforts to recraft TV news in ways designed to reach culturally differentiated and historically marginalized audiences. In place of the network's increasingly uncompelling "news from nowhere," the CBS *Early Show,* the BET *Nightly News,* and MTV's *Choose or Lose* instead offered versions of news that were distinctly "from somewhere"; attempts to speak to and for audiences demarcated along axes of gender, ethnicity, and age. This effort was both necessitated by institutional transformations and enabled by the ongoing turn toward discursive integration—the blending of traditions, techniques, agendas, and voices. Experiments in hybridity, the three kinds of news I consider here generated multiple frames for understanding journalism, engaging with politics, and assessing the real, thus further accelerating uncertainty over the nature of credibility and journalistic authority itself.

The Early Show

The *Early Show* and the wider genre of breakfast TV are a more explicitly hybrid kind of TV than we usually have in mind when we think of "real" news. Seeking to translate the abstract and traditionally masculine world of national affairs into the everyday and traditionally feminine space of domestic life, it blends a number of journalistic traditions and television techniques. Shifting among serious information, feel-good human interest, celebrity chat, and home-and-beauty tips, breakfast television is set as a world "closer to home"; it strives to reproduce the rhythms and routines of daily life on the TV screen.[2]

The Early Show begins with a cheerful female voice singing about the joys of "taking in a brand new day," and from there the audience is introduced to the anchors—no longer the singular authority of the nightly news, but now four people, three of them women—who jocularly interact on a first-name basis. They are everyday people, they assure us: Hannah, Harry, Julie, and René, TV friends who join the audience each morning and mimic its "moods, schedules, and activities."[3] On the October morning following both a presidential debate and a Yankees–Red Sox playoff game, for example, the show begins with this exchange:

> HANNAH STORM: *(enthusiastically)* Good morning everybody, welcome to the *Early Show*!
>
> JULIE CHEN: Between the debate and the baseball playoffs, I'm wondering, did anybody get any sleep last night?
>
> HANNAH: It's easier to lose sleep when your team wins, right?
>
> HARRY SMITH: *(grumbling light-heartedly)* Sleep is overrated anyway.

Here the anchors situate themselves as ordinary people, suggesting they too are tired for having gotten up this early.

From there, however, the program abruptly shifts gears. "We want to get right to our top story," says Harry, transitioning from his musings on lack of sleep, "the final debate between President George Bush and Senator John Kerry." He tosses to veteran CBS reporter Bill Plante, who then offers a quite conventional television news story. Much of the show's content is familiar mainstream journalism: field pieces, newsmaker interviews, and insider punditry that cover the same topics and give voice to the same people that appear in other forms of broadcast news. At times, the show is surprisingly more substantive than the *Evening News*—the events of the previous evening are considered current enough to cover in some measure of detail—but the journalistic effort is still largely guided by the same norms of news construction as the rest of the mainstream media.

Reproducing the "default reality option,"[4] *Early* all too readily indulges in the "game frame" that fills the *Evening News*. It rebroadcasts all of reporter Anthony Mason's *Evening News* stories, for example, that celebrate CBS's "high-tech" techniques for measuring the short-term effects of the debates on undecided voters (see chapter 4). So too does it give considerable airtime to pundit Craig Crawford, who regularly giggles at the absurdity of it all. Voicing the same postmodern cleverness that characterizes so much mainstream news, *Early* re-creates the masculinist, expert-driven, and ultimately cynical discourse that feminist critics argue severs politics from the lifeworld, restricting it to an "alien sphere" divorced from the "everyday culture of its citizens."[5]

Empathetic Engagement

At other times, though, the show constructs a markedly different manner of journalistic engagement. In contrast to the nightly news, whose persona is grounded in institutional privilege and hierarchical access, the morning anchors position themselves as representative of the audience. They are our TV friends, but more importantly the conduits through which we can experience public affairs. Thus on the morning that Barack Obama, at that point a little-known Illinois politician, would address the Democratic convention, Hannah Storm appears sitting by his side on the Fleet Center floor. Grinning broadly, she exclaims, "Great to meet you!" suggesting that through her the audience also can "meet" Obama. Rejecting the traditional dictate that the news interviewer must pose as an impersonal agent of the newsgathering institution,[6] Hannah instead frames the interview as interpersonal exchange.

Beginning on a clearly personal note, she references Obama's rapid rise to political notoriety, asking, "What has this whirlwind been like for you?" Here the interview functions less to teach the audience about Obama the politician than to help them become familiar with Obama the person. From there, however, Hannah segues into a serious discussion of race, the Democratic party, and African-American representation in the federal government—more the stuff of traditional public affairs interviewing. Finally at the end, she returns to the personal frame, suggesting, "You've got the speech of your life tonight; you seem really calm and cool. Good luck!"

In this interview, and throughout its election coverage, *Early* views politics through the lens of empathy. Its connection with the political process is developed not as abstract knowledge but as an emotive and personal exploration of the individuals who occupy the political sphere. Thus Hannah asks Democratic vice-presidential candidate John Edwards to describe his relationship with his running mate. "We trust each other," he says. "We are very very close." She then concludes the interview asking if he's going to "dress up" for Halloween and take his kids trick-or-treating. Earlier, she interviews Edwards's wife and daughter in a discussion that traverses from the personal to the political and back again. "Mrs. Edwards," Hannah asks, "how are you juggling traveling with two young children and all of the demands of the campaign?" At the Democratic convention, she talks with Teresa Heinz Kerry in the wake of the "shove it" debacle. Here, however, the emphasis is not on the comment's political impact—the story line that dominated the *Evening News*—but on Heinz Kerry's feelings about it. "Everything you say and do is going to be scrutinized," Hannah asks. "Is that hard?" She continues, "Do you get hurt? Do you have a pretty thick skin?" Later in the week, *Early* returns to the Heinz Kerry interview and focuses entirely on her "maternal side," which, Hannah suggests, "really came out when I sat down with her earlier."

In this feminized model of public affairs television, the emphasis falls on the personal emotions and familial relations of the central figures. At the Republican convention, Harry Smith asks Cindy McCain, who sits alongside her husband, if she would like John to run for president in 2008. Mrs. McCain answers, "I want him to be happy and do what he wants to do. If that means going home to Sedona, that's great too." So too does Harry sit down with Lynne Cheney and daughter Liz, primarily to discuss the controversy over Mary Cheney's sexuality. "I have a very personal question," Harry asks the vice president's wife. "How is [Mary] doing?" "Oh," Mrs. Cheney answers, "she's just terrific." "The important thing to know about this family," Liz suggests, "is how hard we're working together as a family." It is the First Family, of course, that gets the most attention. In his interview with Laura Bush, Harry focuses on her relationship with the president. "We have the same values," she explains. "We both grew up in Texas." The next day, Hannah narrates an extensive profile of the Bush daughters. From it we learn that Barbara is "very similar to my mom and her temperament. She's very level headed and I think I am too." Jenna explains that their mother has a "wicked sense of humor" and a "really cute personality," although she is "bizarrely clean." The parents, they note, "have a really unconditional love" for each other. Even the president's father is examined in this affective light. "Is there an emotional factor for you," Harry asks George H. W. Bush, "when you're sitting there watching him in these times of testing? Talk about it as a father." The former president answers, "It *is* emotional for me, and it hurts when some of this unfair criticism is leveled against him.... You asked what's it like as a father? It hurts a lot to see your son constantly pummeled."

Perhaps the most curious example of this affective approach comes following the appearance of Ronald Reagan's son Ron at the Democratic convention to speak in favor of federal support for stem-cell research. In response, Hannah interviews Ron Reagan's half-brother, Michael, in a conversation that winds its way through the topics of stem-cell research, political partisanship, and family drama. Michael offers a rebuttal to his half-brother's arguments but more importantly uses his appearance to attack Ron and his sister Patty for allegedly turning their backs on the Reagan family. "If we're gonna use our father's name," he laments, "then we need to sometimes honor our father and show up to be with *their mother* Nancy."

In these moments, *Early* seems to be as much soap opera as newscast, using the emotional and relational focus that defines the genre as a "frame of reference" for talking about and making sense of politics. The media scholar Liesbet van Zoonen has celebrated the soap opera as an alternative conceptual frame, an explicitly feminized model of political understanding that draws on the "themes and values associated with the private sphere" to engage with public life. She rightly contrasts that with the standard fare on most news programs, which construct politics through consistently "masculine metaphors and symbols."[7] A hybrid form of public affairs, *Early* offers both the traditionally masculinist discourse of politics and power common to the nightly news and a feminized conversation of empathy and emotional understanding.

Incoherence

Both of those discourses in turn are interwoven within the program's wider soft-news fare of celebrity gossip, human interest, and home-and-beauty tips.

Every morning, the anchors interrupt their coverage of politics for stories on pressing topics such as actress Kirstie Alley's weight gain, a "remarkable father-daughter reunion," and grilled nectarines—that "sweet summer treat you don't want to miss." This underlying incoherence, the effort to interject politics into the most unlikely of spaces, is on display elsewhere, such as when the show's resident "stylist to the stars" treats "drab blonde" Cheri Hottinger, a Republican convention delegate, to a makeover. He dyes her hair a "really pretty walnut-pecanny color" and dresses her in a tailored brown business suit, because "browns are really hot for the fall." To that, Cheri proclaims that her state senator husband and their fellow Republicans will "love" her new look, "as long as I'm still Republican." Similarly, on the day of the election, the show's Euro-chic "party planner" offers tips for throwing a last-minute election-night soiree, complete with American flags in the cocktails. He suggests the audience could print their own election ballots so they could "have a mock election and have fun with that" and then throws in the air a handful of "cute little confetti"—red-white-and-blue chips printed with the faces of the candidates, their wives, and other political personalities.

In the midst of a rabidly partisan campaign, there is no small measure of disconnect here. These segments flirt with the surreal, offering a mix of incompatible discourses, a jumble of "distant and unrelated signifiers" that, to borrow from the theorist Fredric Jameson, has become one of the primary markers of postmodernity.[8] For van Zoonen, the soap opera frame such as one finds on breakfast TV may have the potential to open alternative avenues of political engagement. At the same time, however, the *Early Show* illustrates the pitfalls of hybridity, producing a kind of fragmented discursive environment that Jameson argues resists the effort to cognitively map one's surroundings, to know exactly where it is that one stands. If news is a form of social orientation, the effect here becomes one of disorientation—a sort of postmodern confusion that makes it difficult to know of and take action within the political world. It may be unsurprising, then, that researchers consistently find that despite breakfast TV's efforts to link politics to the audience's lifeworld, the morning news audience knows less about politics than do the viewers of almost every other kind of news or public affairs program on television.[9]

BET Nightly News

The BET *Nightly News* likewise blends a range of voices. Relying on CBS's journalistic and technical staff, *Nightly* hoped to meld an explicit ethnic approach—its promise to cover "Our World, Our Issues, Our Culture"—with CBS's traditional posture of universality, its default white, affluent, and male perspective. Occupying this tenuous discursive space, the program also sat at the intersection of mainstream news and "black entertainment"—BET's larger business of profiting through circulating what the scholar Beretta Smith-Shomade has described as "beat, bling, and bodies."[10]

For *Nightly*, these tensions are embodied in anchor Jacque Reed—who, like her network counterparts, appears alone on camera and speaks with confidence of what is. Here, though, the authoritative persona comes in the form of a striking African-American woman, whose self-presentation falls between the night club and the corporate boardroom. Speaking about the "issues that affect you," Reed directly addresses her audience. "I wish you guys could be here," she says from the Democratic Convention. "The energy is amazing!" Speaking in the vernacular, she says the Democrats are hoping black voters will "*be down* with the Kerry-Edwards team."

Positioned as both institutional authority and representative of "you guys," the African-American audience, Reed orchestrates a newscast that crisscrosses a range of conceptual frames. On one end, *Nightly* uses material drawn directly from the CBS *Evening News*. The light-skinned African-American Byron Pitts, who covered the Kerry campaign for CBS, appears multiple times in the BET coverage, his stories on the Kerry campaign little changed from their original version, save the out-cue: "Byron Pitts, CBS News, *for the BET Nightly News*." Crafted originally for the *Evening News* audience, Pitts's stories often seem misplaced on BET. He covers a Kerry appearance in Iowa, for example, showing the senator surrounded by a group of white children—an effort, he suggests, to appeal to their parents. Offering short sound bites from rural white men for and against, Pitts tritely concludes that night that "Kerry's argument amounts to: he can chew gum and walk at the same time."

In these instances, the BET news hardly resembles the ethnic alternative it promised to be. Elsewhere, however, it provides something remarkably different: "A convention party," says Jacque Reed from Boston, "and we've got the soundtrack!" The "soundtrack" that night was a hip-hop remix of the day's political events, a bit Reed says is from "BET's own DJ Co-Co Butter, giving us some flavor." Throughout the conventions, Co-Co Butter offers daily digests that present the day's events in rap-video form, or as Reed puts it, that "wrap it up for us, BET style." Consider, then, the "BET-style" take on Bill Clinton's speech at the Democratic convention:

Unh, the Democratic convention
Had me paying attention.
Al Gore put it down,
So did Hillary Clinton.
But when Billy came up, I was like "No he didn't!"
He went straight for the jugular vein.
Talked about everything from the government plan
To where we would be if the country was ran
By the Democrats instead of the Republicans, ehh?

Referring to the former president as "Billy," Co-Co Butter establishes an alternative discursive frame for understanding politics. He uses the language of hip-hop ("Bill Clinton got me crunk," he says—"crunk" being slang for energized) as a means of accessing the abstract and distant domain of politics. Perhaps because of that, Reed closes the newscast suggesting that "Co-Co Butter takes us home"—implying, maybe, that for the BET audience, the end of the newscast returns us to a more familiar place, or that hip-hop itself functions to translate politics into something closer to home.

Advocacy Journalism

At the Democratic convention, Co-Co Butter finishes on an intriguing note. "One rhyme, one vote," he says, "Got me concerned about how it's gonna go. We the people got the power in 2004." Traversing the divides between news and hip-hop, politics and entertainment, white speech and black idiom, Co-Co Butter concludes with a clear call for "people power." With that he hints at the wider agenda that underlies the BET News. Each night exhorting its audience to "Speak about it; Be about it; Vote," *Nightly* fashions itself as the televisual equivalent of the black press, mimicking its historical agenda to "serve, speak, and fight for the black minority."[11]

In part, this meant far less attention paid to the spectacle and spin that dominates the mainstream media and much more to issues of significance for what BET calls "the black community." *Nightly* downplays the strategic construction of campaign narratives: John Kerry's "picture-perfect photo op" sailing into Boston Harbor, which led the CBS *Evening News*, does not warrant even a mention. The next day, Andre Showell reports instead on Kerry's promises to "invest in technologies to create jobs, cut taxes for the middle class, and make health care more affordable." Similarly, during the Republican convention, stories focus less on the theatrical show and more on Bush's promises to help "people buy homes, start businesses, improve job skills, and open tax-free retirement and health care accounts—issues black delegates say should resonate with African-Americans."

BET also explores issues ignored by the mainstream media. Following a brief mention of AIDS during the vice-presidential debate, *Nightly* reports on the two party's stances on "the AIDS crisis in black communities." The next week it examines the president's cold relationship with the Congressional Black Caucus, a response to Bush's claim during the second debate that he had an open-door friendship with African-American representatives. Later it explains the president's role in nominating Supreme Court justices, referencing the court's landmark civil rights cases, including *Plessy v. Ferguson* and *Brown v. Board of Education*. Says Jesse Jackson in a sound bite, "We run a great risk this time." He explains: "*This* court would not have passed *Brown v. Board of Education* 9–0."

Rejecting objectivity in favor of advocacy, *Nightly* pays particular attention to members of the Democratic establishment seen to be friendly to the black agenda. It offers lengthy interviews with Bill Clinton and John Edwards, and it celebrates Barack Obama. It extensively covers his role in the 2004 Democratic convention, speaks with him multiple times, and then follows his successful campaign for the U.S. Senate. The emphasis falls both on his rising political star and on his promise to pursue "an agenda of rebirth and growth in our communities." Says Co-Co Butter, "Give that boy a clap."

Throughout its coverage, *Nightly* represents black engagement with the political process, reporting on "people of color who are making their presence felt." At the party conventions, it highlights the black politicians and speakers who remain all but invisible in the mainstream news, as well as the black convention delegates, the ordinary people who carry out the real work of the convention. Focusing less on the stage and more on the floor, BET frames the conventions not as theaters of power but as processes of political engagement. If CBS presents politics as a top-down phenomenon—a democracy, as Robert Entman has written, without citizens[12]—BET instead creates a space for the visualization of citizenship: a celebration of political engagement.

BET also leaves the convention hall to seek out African-American perspectives. At the Democratic convention, Kevin Powell interviews delegates, but then, to the song "Everyday People," he heads out "to the street." There, Powell offers a series of sound bites from African-Americans who speak of continued anger at the 2000 election, as well as a lively exchange with a black woman who expresses her fondness for John Edwards, whom she refers to as "my boy Ed." At the Republican convention, Powell constructs a debate of sorts, intercutting between an African-American delegate—a woman who wears a star-spangled shirt and a white cowboy hat—and a young dreadlocked man outside on the New York street. As she makes claims about Bush's record on education and employment, he counters with statistics about African-American school drop-out and unemployment rates. When she praises the administration's waging of war, he insists: "They pimped 9/11."

Unlike the *Evening News*, which amplified the Bush 9/11 narrative, BET instead creates a space for oppositional voice, the kind that falls outside the consensual sphere crafted by the mainstream media. Scholars suggest that the black press historically provided "the foundation from which to launch challenges at the white public sphere."[13] BET News likewise functions as an alternative public sphere. At the Democratic convention, Manuel Gallegus files a story on the so-called free speech zone outside the Fleet Center. Reporting from within the cage of chain-link fence and razor wire to which protestors were confined, Gallegus illuminates what for the *Evening News* was a blind spot, a site of public demonstration that ran counter to the seamless narrative being constructed on the convention stage. "This is our public space," a woman proclaims to a Boston police officer keeping a close eye on the demonstrators. Says a convention delegate, "We don't even hear the demonstrators except as echoing sounds in the distance, and I think that's a shame." Gallegus concludes that "while the delegates celebrate inside the Fleet Center fortress, outside, democracy often falls on deaf ears in the birthplace of the revolution." As did the mainstream media, BET also covers the massive protests at the Republican convention. But here, BET rejects the dominant frame that sees the demonstrators as a threat to public safety. Instead, the emphasis of the coverage is on the performance of protest, on "action and civil disobedience" as the spirit of democratic practice. "Where the barricades end," says reporter Jennifer Donelan, "democracy begins."

As election day draws closer, BET explicitly takes on the role of advocate, both reporting on efforts to fight potential voter suppression and instructing the audience on their rights as voters. Jacque Reed tells her viewers to visit the BET website and "print out our voter-rights guide" if they have questions about their voting rights. Two days before the election, a sound bite from a representative of the ACLU warns that polling stations could be crowded but encourages black voters to "stay the course, remain in line." On election day, Andre Showell asks the question "What should you do if your vote is challenged?" A spokeswoman from the Racial Justice Legal Organization urges voters to call the hotline so that the "civil rights community can respond if needed."

Envisioning itself as an extension of that "civil rights community," *Nightly* also tries to get more African-Americans, and especially young ones, to vote. "We have a lot of young people who watch our network, our news," Reed says to Obama. "How can we energize them?" In a segment entitled the "BET Bookbag," Showell offers "tips on how the hip-hop generation can become more politically active." BET consistently publicizes efforts by representatives of the hip-hop industry, and particularly business mogul Russell Simmons and the superstar P Diddy, to increase youth engagement. "They're making it cool to be good citizens," says Bill Clinton in his interview with Showell. "They're showing people that politics matters." Likewise, John Edwards celebrates the two: "those great leaders from a different part of our world," he calls them, implicitly recognizing the multiple sites of power in a discursively integrated age.

BET News itself was an exercise in discursive integration. It melded, although not always smoothly, mainstream news and advocacy journalism, white speech and black representation, hip-hop celebrity and political power. This discursive amalgam is well-captured in the channel's motto—"black star power"—which itself encapsulates the tensions that mark BET News. Beretta Smith-Shomade suggests the concept of "black star power" seeks an uneasy balance between "black power"—the ethno-political demand for "self-determination, self-respect, and self-defense" grounded in a sense of solidarity and community—and "star power"—the commodification of the black entertainer and the individualistic ideals of capitalism upon which BET's wider business of "selling blackness" depends.[14] That tension would ultimately make the BET *Nightly News* untenable. The *Nightly News* failed to attract a large enough audience to appease its corporate overseers, and the experiment in journalism would be short-lived. Less than a year after the election—and well before Barack Obama's historic campaign for the presidency—BET canceled its *Nightly News* and, with it, its efforts at daily newscasting.[15]

MTV News

MTV's 2004 *Choose or Lose* series also seemed an unlikely blend, an explicit public-service campaign from the often vacuous, hypercommercialized MTV.

A number of informational reports, newsmagazine-style programs, and documentary films that explored issues ranging from presidential campaigning to the politics of sex, drugs, and the economy, to youth engagement with the political, the series was both surprisingly insightful and highly viewed. Audiences for individual programs reached as large as five million people.[16] It also was experimental, integrating MTV's standard fare of pop culture and teen style with serious issue coverage and social advocacy, and in turn constructing a number of models of journalism that complemented and complicated mainstream news.

Gideon Yago: Neo-Anchor

Gideon Yago, then twenty-six, was the front man for *Choose or Lose*. He anchors several topical half-hour programs, and much of his labor is to build credibility for the tenuous journalistic institution of MTV News. He does this in part by grounding his identity in a familiar high-modern paradigm. Positioning himself as an expert member of a hierarchically privileged agency that seeks knowledge and commands the resources to do so, he assures us that MTV is *real* news. One sees this effort clearly in the program "Work It," which focused on questions of economy and jobs. At one point Yago does an on-camera "standup" in what appears to be a newsroom, despite the fact that it is unlikely MTV maintains a "newsroom" in any traditional sense of the word. The newsroom can be understood as a privileged site in the circuit of knowledge production, a locus of institutional authority closed to most members of the public. The program also features a segment in which Yago travels to India to report on outsourcing. "I went halfway around the globe," he says, to learn why American jobs were migrating out of the country. That report is quality journalism—a revealing exploration of the economic attractiveness of India—and it also authorizes him as a member of an elite news-gathering team, one that can send its people "halfway around the globe" to uncover the story.

It is also in "Work It" that Walter Cronkite makes his unlikely appearance on MTV. Explaining that Cronkite is the "dean of TV journalism," Yago introduces him to an audience too young to remember him. Despite the fact that Cronkite may be the epitome of the residual news anchor who has become "anathema" to young people,[17] his appearance functions to authorize Yago. It endorses his claim to what Mikhail Bakhtin has called "authoritative discourse"—a mode of speech akin to "the word of a father, of adults and of teachers." Existing in a "distanced zone, organically connected with a past that is felt to be hierarchically higher," authoritative discourse claims the unchallengeable right to speak of what is.[18] As the show cuts directly from Yago to Cronkite (the dean) and back again, Yago is positioned as heir to Cronkite's authoritative legacy. In keeping with this theme, Yago's reportorial mode is dispassionate observation and objective inquiry. He conducts impartial interviews with advocates on both sides of the issues and offers equal airtime to representatives from both campaigns. Quoting statistics and marshaling verbal and visual evidence to support his claims about what is, he offers a discourse of fact and epistemological certainty. Like Cronkite, he is expert, not author—his vantage point universal, not local.

Even as he positions himself as professional expert, however, Yago complicates his identity, equally situating himself as representative of young America. "This is it," he says at the start of his program on John Kerry, "*our* chance to get to know the man who would be president." Here he shifts from an authority claim based on institutional privilege to one that seeks credibility for its personal familiarity.[19] He tells his audience that he got to "tag along" with the Kerry campaign, a point illustrated by video of him walking on to the press plane. Wearing a leather jacket, sunglasses, and a backpack slung over his shoulder, he looks at the camera and flashes the "rock on" hand sign. Here covering the campaign more resembles a college road trip than a professional journalistic assignment.

Yago constructs his identity as youth representative both in image and in language. Rarely wearing a jacket or tie, he instead appears slightly unshaven, in shirts untucked and open-necked. He wears jewelry and has tattoos on both forearms. He also speaks in a "youth" vernacular. He tells the audience that he gets "to *hang* with the candidate's daughter," notes that the president always travels with a "gi-normous security apparatus," and says the Bush campaign "dropped bank" on a "humungo" banner. Then, as Kerry's campaign plane lands, he exclaims, "Look at that thing! Pimp my ride, indeed."

The last phrase alludes to MTV's program *Pimp My Ride,* in which a young person gets a surprise makeover for his or her car. Yago draws linkages to a target audience he presumes will appreciate the reference. He assumes his audience will recognize the use of "pimp" as a verb, but more importantly, he uses popular culture as a reference point to help his audience make sense of the political sphere. Most producers of youth-oriented news take it as a truism that popular culture is the "leading force" in young people's lives and the foundational ground from which their appreciation of the political sphere begins.[20] For Yago, his fluency in pop culture allows him to blend the authority of institutional hierarchy with the persuasiveness of cultural familiarity and bridge the spheres of news, politics, and entertainment.

Sway: Cultural Differentiation

MTV constructs a second journalistic model in the African-American reporter known by the one-word moniker "Sway," who, like Yago, moves fluidly between MTV's journalism and entertainment programming. During the 2004 campaign, he files reports from the party conventions and anchors the program *Drug Laws*. Sway resembles Yago, assuming the position of institutional authority, speaking in the voice of objective fact and explanation. So too does he position himself as youth representative, explaining that drug laws are "our issue, a young person's issue."

If, however, Yago is an updated version of an old model—white and male, insisting upon the universality of his perspective—the African-American Sway is ethnically marked. His one-word name distinguishes him from the norm, connoting a "cool" persona marked by personal style. He is barrel-chested and deep-voiced and keeps his hair in thick dreadlocks. On one program, he appears wearing a Rastafarian cap over his hair, dark jeans, and a dark T-shirt featuring an image of the slain rapper Tupac Shakur, who has come to symbolize urban, ethnic counterculture. Similarly, he visits a maximum-security prison to interview a "young prisoner of the drug war." Wearing a dark cloth wrap around his hair and a plain blue sweatshirt, Sway greets the young man with an elaborate handshake. Through dress and gesture he subtly establishes his cultural affiliations. At the Democratic convention, he calls P Diddy " Bro'." So too does he urge "those *in the hood* who think their votes don't count" to register and vote.

Explicitly raced, Sway is authorized to speak both to and for young African-Americans. Thus he leads a pseudopolitical rally (complete with picket signs reading "Choose or Lose") that works its way up the street and into MTV's studio. Dressed in his rasta cap with a bullhorn in hand, Sway leads the "demonstrators" (the studio audience) in chanting "CHOOSE ... OR LOSE!" As he passes the camera, he shouts, "We're coming!" Although obviously staged, the scene connotes political activism, perhaps reminiscent of the civil rights movement. Further blurring the line between journalism and advocacy, Sway's purpose is not just to inform but, like the BET News, to give voice to a group that traditionally has had little expression in the spheres of news or politics.

Christina Aguilera: Celebrated Expertise

A third model of journalist comes in the unlikely form of pop singer Christina Aguilera, who hosts a program exploring the politics of sexual issues. In many ways, her performance is familiar. Her narration is written in the language of objective fact and unbiased explanation, while her claims about what is are supported by statistics, sound bites, and standard news footage. She conducts neutral interviews with a range of people, at times asking challenging questions, but never revealing her own stand on the issues. Given the fact that most network news stories are crafted by a team of unseen producers, Aguilera's work looks like much contemporary television journalism. Of course the point remains, though, that she's a pop singer and only playing a journalist on television.

In place of journalistic credentials, Aguilera is authorized by her celebrity. Despite resistance from mainstream journalists, the lines between celebrity and journalism have grown deeply blurred. Able to command the credibility of parasocial familiarity, celebrity itself has become a fluid asset, no longer limited to the domain of entertainment but translatable to the spheres of journalism and politics. "The categorical distinction of forms of power is dissolving," cultural scholars suggest, "in favor of a unified system of celebrity status."[21] MTV, however, offers a different explanation. "Christina Aguilera," says reporter John Norris, previewing her program, "you would have to agree knows a little something about sex, right? So *it only makes sense* that Christina would host our next *Choose or Lose* special." For MTV, it is Aguilera's highly sexualized public persona that authorizes her to report on sexual politics. Scholars suggest that the privileging of celebrity represents "a leveling of the epistemological hierarchy."[22] Because she "knows a little something" about sex, that is, Aguilera becomes a new kind of expert, one for whom self-identity and lived experience translate into journalistic expertise.

Aguilera's performance in turn is framed by her own emotions and personal life. The program is based in her hometown of Pittsburgh; she "returns home" to meet people and learn more about the issues. When the program turns to the topic of domestic abuse, she asserts her credibility in starkly personal terms: "I know domestic violence can happen in any family," she says, "because it happened in mine." That is illustrated by a clip from her own music video dramatizing her experiences with domestic violence. She then interviews a young woman who left an abusive relationship, explaining that hers is a struggle "which I know about coming from my own domestic abusive past, so I know how that whole process goes." Finally, she concludes the program noting, "after my trip home I understand more than ever just how much the government touches the most intimate aspects of my personal life." Authorized by her celebrity expertise, Aguilera offers a journalistic discourse of equal parts fact and affect, of objective information grounded in subjective engagement.

Drew Barrymore: Sympathetic Credibility

Drew Barrymore provides a strikingly different model of the journalist-celebrity in her film *The Best Place to Start*. Produced four years before Barack Obama's run for the presidency would revitalize many young people's interest in presidential politics, Barrymore's film explored why so many young Americans were disengaged from politics. Making no claim to expertise, Barrymore instead presents herself as the embodiment of the politically disaffected youth. On the day her film airs, she tells the audience she is "honored" her film will be shown on MTV because "we watch this"—"we as young people," that is, "our generation." She then urges the audience to vote, because if they do, they can force politicians to "talk to you on your level—a level that I certainly want to be spoken to."

Barrymore is authorized to appear on MTV, make her film, and speak for a generation because of her celebrity status. The film, however, tries to elide her celebrity persona, instead crafting her as the "everygirl." Early in the film she appears in a harshly lit and slightly out-of-focus scene shot with a home-video camera—a clear distinction from Hollywood film and television news. With her hair slightly messy, wearing little makeup and no jewelry, she steps into the frame, awkwardly adjusts the camera, and introduces herself: "Hi, um, my name is Drew. And I am a repressed voter. I want to learn about the voting system; I want to be a voter." This is neither the Hollywood star nor the broadcast journalist reading scripted lines, but rather a supposedly raw look at the authentic "Drew." In turn, the film repeatedly takes the viewer "backstage," showing her riding in the car, sleeping on the train, studying politics in the library. There she confesses, "I never got my diploma. That's another thing I'd like to do."

Presenting her as vulnerable, subject to the same weaknesses that others suffer, the film asks the audience to sympathize with Barrymore, to see her as enacting the daily struggles that they routinely face.[23] Indeed, Barrymore's struggle to overcome her own ignorance and fear of the political process provides the story's crisis point. Again shot with a home-video camera, the pivotal scene shows Drew at home, calling her producer to discuss her lack of progress. She breaks into tears and sobs, "I don't know what I'm doing." The authenticity of the scene is further established as she loudly blows her nose—the kind of backstage behavior one rarely sees from a film star. The producer encourages her: "The good news," she says, "is you don't have to pretend you know what you're doing." Her credibility is grounded in her *lack* of expertise, the perceived authenticity of the fact that she *doesn't know what she's doing.*

Barrymore's sympathetic identity serves not just to authorize her to speak, but it functions as the mode of reporting. Rather than soliciting information for the audience, she takes them along with her on a personal journey of self-education. The contrast between modes of reporting—between disinterested information-gathering and personal exploration—is drawn explicitly as Barrymore, along with the national press, attempts to "cover" the Democratic primary in New Hampshire. She gets press credentials for a campaign appearance by General Wesley Clark, where we see her moving awkwardly through a crowd of reporters. At one point Clark walks past her without giving a second look, to which she shrugs and smiles meekly. The culmination of the scene comes on Clark's campaign bus, when she gets the chance to ask the candidate a question about youth disengagement from politics. Clearly nervous, she speaks too softly, and other reporters yell for her to speak louder. Clark then gives her a trite answer, condescendingly pats her on the shoulder, and tells her he has to take other, presumably more legitimate, questions.

Clark's refusal to take Barrymore seriously is echoed in the next scene, which shows her reading the local paper the following morning. The camera zooms in to reveal an article with a photograph of her questioning Clark under the headline "Get Off the Bus, Angel." An attempt at paradigm repair, the New Hampshire paper suggests her efforts at political reporting are illegitimate. Denigrating her for her celebrity identity (she was a costar in the two *Charlie's Angels* films), the headline uses the word "angel" to belittlingly suggest that this pretty girl does not belong, literally, with the boys on the bus. In an age when more and more people—and especially the younger ones—are tuning out the mainstream media, however, Barrymore's film asks us to think carefully about who does belong "on the bus"—what it means to be a journalist and how one can understand the political.

P Diddy: Admiring Authority

Finally, the hip-hop star P Diddy offers a third version of the celebrity/journalist. He serves as a reporter at the party conventions and hosts the program *Hip Hop Politics*, which tries to encourage members of the broadly defined hip-hop community to become active in the political sphere. Says the scholar and activist Cornell West in a sound bite, "The correct response is not apathy and indifference, but engagement and truth telling." Like all of MTV's reporters, Diddy positions himself as representative of his audience. At the Democratic convention, he tells Hillary Clinton, "I am here representing the young people of America." He continually speaks of "we"—"we're a lifestyle, a culture, a community," he says, referring specifically to hip-hop, but more symbolically to poor, young African-Americans. At the start of *Hip Hop Politics*, we see him driving in an open convertible through Harlem. As he yells greetings to people along the streets, he says to the camera, "You can't never escape where you're from—I'll always be a part of this community. That's what makes me me."

At the same time, Diddy stresses his sociocultural privilege, reminding his viewers of all "the cars, the money, the jewelry, the clothing sales, the record sales" he has amassed. When he decides he wants to know what politicians are willing to do for "our communities," he says, "you know how I do: I took my questions right to the top." That comment is immediately followed by shots of Diddy sharing a faux kiss with Hillary Clinton and talking with Al Sharpton and Jesse Jackson, and also actors Ben Affleck and John Cusack. As comfortable in the streets as he is alongside political power brokers and Hollywood stars, Diddy lays claim to a complex form of cultural authority, one that is grounded in his ability to represent ordinary people and authorized by his access to the halls of power and prestige. He encourages a form of "admiring identification"; he becomes the hero whose actions "serve as exemplary models for a particular community."[24] Indeed, he labels himself "America's dream … young, gifted, black, talented, powerful," an assertion visually reinforced by a shot of him wearing a T-shirt proclaiming, "I am the American dream." He concludes that "I was one of the lucky ones," and because of that, "I got a responsibility, whether it's to educate, whether it's to help, whether it's to empower, whether it's to hip my people to the hustle of what's really going on."

Music celebrities often function as "the public representation of change." In particular, minority celebrities give voice to "the various discourses of the excluded and marginal in the social world" and seek avenues to reintegrate them "into the social mainstream."[25] For Diddy, who led the organization "Citizen Change" and its campaign "Vote or Die," an agenda of change defines his journalistic persona. He embraces Barack Obama, literally and figuratively, sharing a warm handshake four years prior to

Obama's run for the presidency, and proclaiming enthusiastically, "You making sense to me, boy!" Elsewhere, he explains to the audience that "us gaining political power . . . it's gonna be a process." As the video shows images drawn from the civil rights movement, Diddy insists, "We gotta build on a process that's gotten us this far." He continues, "We got an agenda. . . . We ain't going nowhere." If Diddy's status as cultural hero authorizes him to "hip" his "people to the hustle of what's really going on"—which itself may be a discursively integrated definition of public-interest journalism—hipping people to the hustle inevitably is a means to an end. Diddy's model of authority reminds us that information always has an agenda and fact can never be isolated from social value.

Emerging Voices

In 2004, Diddy would optimistically insist, on both BET and MTV, that "the revolution will be televised." Of course he was wrong—at least that year. The change he was working to incite would take longer to come to fruition. Four years later, though, change had become the narrative of the times, not just from Republican to Democrat, but from homogeneity to heterogeneity and, as we will see in the following chapters, from the postmodern to something altogether new. It is difficult to draw a straight line from the various versions of "news from somewhere" discussed here to the political transformations that would occur shortly thereafter. Indeed, the *Early Show* would be reformatted, the BET *Nightly News* canceled, and most of MTV's 2008 *Choose or Lose* moved online. Nevertheless, the suspicion is that without these kinds of experiments in hybrid blends, these varied efforts to broaden the range of voices heard in the mediated public sphere, the status quo represented both by the Bush presidency and by the network nightly news would have proven far harder to dislodge.

For the political scientist Doris Graber, the "abominable quality" of most television news and the "deplorable nature of politics as painted by cynical journalists"—in short, what I've described as the postmodern paradigm—has been to blame for much of the population's disengagement from politics.[26] To hear James Carey tell it, the high-modern paradigm, with its conceptualization of the journalist as informational expert, may also have been at fault. He worries that a form of news that merely translated the "arcane language of experts into a publicly accessible language for the masses" also "confirmed the psychological incompetence" of the people to participate in their own governance. In the absence of a discourse focused on public engagement, he argues, citizens could become either "consumers of politics or escapists from it."[27] With only those two choices, escapism became a reasonable option.

Underlying both arguments is a concern for the quality and character of public voice. From such a perspective, mainstream journalism's efforts to provide a "language for the masses" may be the largest obstacle to widespread citizen engagement. Rejecting the very notion of "the masses," rhetorician Gerald Hauser instead describes a "montage of publics" that come to exist through local and shared languages—"vernacular rhetorics," he calls them—and are often elided in dominant forms of public discourse. Without a mediated political discourse reflective of such publics, he suggests, "it is small wonder that those who should be interested and active participants in the public sphere find themselves in full retreat, filled with bewilderment at the character of public conversation and cynicism at the unresponsiveness of their institutions to the concerns of their lives."[28] The multiple models of journalism we've seen in this chapter thus provided much-needed experiments with the possibilities of public discourse. Some worked better than others, but all of them offered intriguing alternatives to a nightly news that had lost its democratic vitality. As such, they accelerated the centrifugal forces of paradigmatic reinvention that are still at work, radically changing the nature of news and American political culture.

6

♦ ♦ ♦

THE DAILY SHOW AND THE REINVENTION OF POLITICAL JOURNALISM

In September 2008, the Republican vice-presidential nominee Sarah Palin had her grand unveiling at the GOP convention. With her folksy quips about hockey moms and pit bulls, the little-known Alaskan governor charmed the partisan crowd and, at least for a few days, the national media. Like most news outlets, *The Daily Show* covered Palin's speech, rebroadcasting her lipstick-on-a-pit-bull joke as well as her less charming attack on Barack Obama for having worked as a community organizer. "I guess a small-town mayor is sort of like a community organizer," she taunted, referring to her background as mayor of the little town of Wasilla, "except that you have *actual* responsibilities!" The crowd cheered, and many news analysts took it as a sign that Palin was tough enough for national politics. *The Daily Show,* however, was quick to point out the hypocrisy of Palin's barb—its mean-spirited contradiction of the compassionate conservative ideal of a "thousand points of light." "Yeah!" Jon Stewart responded in satiric outrage. "So to everyone out there trying to make difference in your communities . . . fuck you! You know what you are? A thousand points of bullshit!"

In some ways, *The Daily Show* looked like the real news that night, playing many of the same sound bites that filled the mainstream media's coverage. But in other ways, the so-called fake news seemed to come far closer to the ideal of critical publicity that theorists have long suggested democracy demands, holding up Palin's comments not for public consumption, but for public scrutiny. And unlike much of the real news, for whom yesterday fades quickly, *The Daily Show* would return to Palin's attack on community organizers through the rest of the campaign. Comedian Jason Jones, for example, examined the assertion that the "actual responsibilities" she had as mayor of Wasilla were good training for the vice presidency. Jones traveled to Alaska, where he interviewed Dianne Keller, then the current mayor of Wasilla. The two share a chuckle over Palin's jab, but when Keller insists that being mayor had prepared Palin for the office of vice president, Jones prods her, and she reveals that the Wasilla mayor does not oversee a fire department, the local schools, or any social services. "What *do* you do?" Jones asks quizzically. "Take me through the mayor of Wasilla's day." A straightforward question, but Keller struggles to answer. "Just different things on different days," she sputters. "Uh . . . well . . . Monday at ten o'clock we always have a staff meeting, and then . . . um . . . uh . . . every Thursday is check-signing day, so I sign all the checks for the city, pay the bills." With that hectic schedule in mind, Jones concludes that Palin is right: "The town's top job is anything but easy."

Comedian John Oliver also pretends to agree with Palin in his story on community organizers, whom he concurs are "absolutely hilarious." He interviews a community organizer in New York City who explains, to Oliver's amusement, that she fights for the rights of low-income residents. "Get this," he proclaims in mock disdain. "They help people find affordable health care, lobby for a living wage, and even make sure [people] have heat in their homes!" His story then cuts from New York to southeast Ohio, where he interviews a white woman, a self-described "conservative Christian" who usually votes Republican. When Oliver asks her what she most dislikes about community organizers, she scowls and tells him that *she* is a community organizer who fights hunger in her rural community. She then explains that she was so offended by Palin's comments that she decided not just to vote for Obama but to *organize* for him.

Through satire and parody, *The Daily Show* offers a pointed rebuke to Palin's sound bite—information that places her comment in context and interrogation that challenges its sensibility. During the 2008 campaign, it was that mixture of information and interrogation, always expressed through laughter and play, that the program's domestic audience of two million people had come to expect and an increasingly international audience had come to enjoy. Four years earlier, it was that unfamiliar approach to public affairs television that led the New York newspaper *Newsday* to name Jon Stewart the most important newscaster in the country. It also was one of the reasons Bill Moyers insisted the year before that "you simply can't understand American politics in the new millennium without *The Daily Show*."[1]

Moyers and *Newsday* were early adopters, aware of the transformations that were reshaping the landscape of public affairs and political media. Although they didn't put it this way, *The Daily Show* was a leading indicator of the end of the multichannel period and the emergence of the post-network age. The network structure that had long dominated the television business and had continued to shape the industry through the multichannel era was being displaced by radical innovation in the technologies of video production, distribution, and consumption.[2] The continued expansion of cable and satellite broadcasting, broadband Internet connections, and a wide variety of portable screens was deeply fragmenting the audience and multiplying the sources and styles of news. In turn, the cultural logic that organized the network approach to television was also being dislodged. If CBS's Richard Salant could once insist that his "field is journalism, not show business," the very concept of the "field"—that bounded domain of identities, practices, and concepts—had become subject to slippage, with once-definable fields now flexible and fluid, overlapping and intermingling in unprecedented ways.[3]

That point was on display during Jon Stewart's much discussed appearance on the CNN debate show *Crossfire*, a moment that perhaps more than any other established *The Daily Show*'s prominence in the serious world of American politics. Much to the dismay of *Crossfire*'s hosts, who were expecting lighthearted humor, Stewart instead was quite serious, accusing them of "hurting America," of failing "miserably" to live up to their "responsibility to the public discourse" when they substituted show business and spectacle for democratic debate. Claiming that his program was fake news, Stewart suggested that *Crossfire* also was fake news—a contrived bit of political theater that indulged in partisan spin while posing as a viable public affairs program. Stewart was right that *Crossfire* was infotainment, a largely vacuous and cynical form of TV entertainment. But he was guilty of a deception of his own. His continued insistence that *The Daily Show* was fake news masked the real significance of his program. Parodying the "real" news that has become so often fake, *The Daily Show* illustrates the flip side of infotainment: the emergence of innovative approaches to political television enabled by the fusion of "field logics" and the multiplication of media forms.

This chapter examines *The Daily Show*, another variety of informational program produced under the Viacom corporate umbrella. Unlike the other Viacom-owned experiments in journalism we've considered thus far, *The Daily Show* more thoroughly effaces the boundaries between information and entertainment, drawing equally from traditions of network news and late-night talk to produce a powerful, discursively integrated kind of public affairs programming—a comedy show that has become one of the best sources of news and most critical voices on contemporary television. In seeking to make sense of this unlikely turn of events, I pay particular attention in this chapter to the role the program played for several years as a critical counterweight to the Bush administration and its aggressive efforts to manipulate public information, as well as to a corporate news media that, following the terrorist attacks of September 11, had largely abandoned their democratic responsibility.

News or Entertainment?

In just the first few seconds of each night's program, *The Daily Show* links itself to the traditionally authoritative network news. "From Comedy Central's world news headquarters in New York," the unseen announcer proclaims as the screen shows a full-screen graphic with the date, an American flag, and the globe, "this is *The Daily Show with Jon Stewart.*" Set to a music track serious in tone, the show's opening invokes the power of the New York–based news media and their residual tradition of global, institutional prestige. Of course, the joke is that the comedy channel claims to have a "world news headquarters," and immediately the introduction cuts to a live camera shot that swings though the studio, a technique of fast motion more common to late-night talk than to news. So too does the audio cut to an upbeat, rock-and-roll soundtrack, while the live studio audience—a clear marker that we're no longer in the domain of traditional news—cheers in the background.

From the start, then, the program interweaves at least two sets of discourses, collapsing two formerly distinct fields. Although the opening may suggest that entertainment supersedes news, the two are placed not in binary opposition but in complementary arrangements. Demanding that we move beyond the either-or—news or comedy, entertainment or information—the show instead pushes us to recognize the both-and, the fundamentally hybrid nature of public affairs media in a discursively integrated age. Reworking multiple generic approaches, it functions as both entertainment and news, simultaneously informative and comedic, serious and silly.

Stewart begins each night in the posture of late-night entertainment host. Engaging with and energizing the audience with whom he interacts throughout the show, he cracks a few silly jokes, assuring us, "We've got a great show for you!" Just like his counterparts on the other late-night chat shows, Stewart enthusiastically previews the guest that will join him "later in the program." And like his counterparts, he then launches into his introductory monologue, a version of the familiar late-night format common since the 1950s and still apparent on programs such as *The Tonight Show* and CBS's *Late Night*. In its traditional form, the host uses politics as comedic fodder. Current events provide the setup for snappy one-liners that dig at the personal foibles and character flaws of the people who headline the news.[4] Attacking people but rarely policy, the usual late-night jokes amount to a kind of "benign" humor—more personal than political, containing little relevance to the serious arena of policy and debate.[5]

The Daily Show's approach can also be traced to the more complex style of political humor on *Saturday Night Live*'s "Weekend Update," a feature on that program since its inception in the mid-1970s. There, cast members play the role of news anchors, seated at what looks like a standard television news set. The segment complicates the late-night monologue with the addition of visual elements—usually suggestive photographs or newspaper headlines placed in an over-the-shoulder graphic. The "anchors" offer a brief explanation of the image and then the punch line. Again, like the late-night joke, "Weekend Update" rarely focuses on substantive political issues (with the notable exception of Tina Fey's powerful parody of Sarah Palin) and often turns to the surreal to find its humor.

The Daily Show, however, while borrowing from both of these traditions, more deeply melds them with the content and concerns of news. Although it does at times focus on the trivial aspects of the political domain, more often it tackles issues of national and global significance. Despite its label of "late-night comedy," nearly half the show's content deals with foreign affairs, federal governance, and electoral politics.[6] During the Bush presidency, topics regularly included the conduct of the administration and its political allies, the invasion and occupation of Iraq, and the Bush war on terrorism. Further unlike comedy and more like news, much of its content is built around sound bites from the primary political actors, an approach reminiscent of a high-modern journalistic paradigm and its emphasis on the actuality. The president and his top administration officials appear regularly, but the show also focuses on congressional hearings, speeches, and press conferences with various governmental figures. The show's writers and staff cull this material from CSPAN, twenty-four-hour cable news, and other readily available sources. They complement the visuals with information gained from major newspapers such as the *New York Times*, *USA Today*, and the *Wall Street Journal*.

The Daily Show is thus enabled by the sheer abundance of news and information in the post-network era. Stewart acknowledges the point after the resignation of Bush's director of the CIA, George Tenet, who secured his place in history by insisting that Iraq did indeed have weapons of mass destruction—describing his profoundly inaccurate information as a "slam dunk." "Huge breaking news story," Stewart begins. "We're gonna get right to it, because you know when news breaks . . . we may not be the first people on the scene, but we've got televisions; we know what's going on." Stewart's line appears to be self-deprecating humor, a reminder that the show refuses to take itself seriously. It also is significant commentary, however, on the volume of informational resources now publicly available and the decreasing role traditional news outlets play in filtering the flow of news. It is possible, *The Daily Show* suggests, to construct a newscast by mining the raw material provided by the average cable TV system.

Critical Inquiry

Drawing on live broadcast coverage of public statements and government proceedings, *The Daily Show* looks much more like the mainstream news media than it does its comedy counterparts. Empowered by the label of "fake news," however, *The Daily Show* routinely violates contemporary journalistic conventions in ways that allow it do things the "real" news cannot. For one, although it covers the same raw material, its choice of sound bites turns contemporary conventions on their head. The unwritten rules of journalism define a good quote as a coherent statement of policy or attitude, ideally containing emotion or character, and completed neatly in about eight to twelve seconds. Professional journalists are trained to ignore long, rambling verbal presentations, quotes with poor grammar or misstatements, and sound bites with long pauses or any significant absence of verbal content. In the effort to package eight seconds of speech, that which does not conform to conventional expectations is left on the cutting-room floor. *The Daily Show*, however, mines those outtakes for a wealth of informative content.

Consider the coverage of Bush's statement following Tenet's resignation. Bush, of course, refused to suggest Tenet had made any mistakes (and indeed, would bestow upon him the Presidential Medal of Freedor ABC's *World News Tonight*, viewers would see the following sound bi the president: "I told him I'm sorry he's leaving. He's done a superb behalf of the American people." On the CBS *Evening News*, the only sound bite from Bush showed him proclaiming, "He's strong, he's resolute, and I will miss him." *The Daily Show*, however, does something quite different. Here is part of Bush's statement that the show includes: "George Tenet is uh ... is ... a ... the kind of public service, uh, servant, you like to work with. He has been a, a, um ... a strong and able leader at the agency. He's been a, uh ... he's been a strong leader in the war on terror." In their coverage of Bush's statement, the networks hold to standard conventions and in so doing reduce Bush's sloppy, pause-saturated speech to a tightly constructed set of words that suggest a clarity of thought and purpose. *The Daily Show*, however, reveals a different aspect of Bush's statement, one that calls into question his focus and his sincerity. Both versions are "accurate" in the strict sense of the word, but each achieves a markedly different textual effect.

In rejecting the standard conventions of quote selection, *The Daily Show* achieves a critical distance that cannot be said of the networks. As we have seen, mainstream journalism's reliance on predictable conventions renders it susceptible to manipulation by the professional speech writers and media handlers who seed public information with prescripted sound bites and spin. As we have seen, especially in the years between September 11 and Hurricane Katrina, the Bush administration was remarkably adept at playing to journalistic conventions in ways that limited inquiry and encouraged the news media to amplify its rhetoric without critical challenge.[7] As "fake news," however, *The Daily Show* is not beholden to conventions that have outlived their usefulness. Its refusal to abide by standard practices offers a measure of resistance to manipulation, a counterbalance to the mutual embrace between press and politics.

A second convention *The Daily Show* freely rejects is the mainstream news media's insistence, at least in name, on a dispassionate observation that elides the journalist's subjectivity. If the insistence on objectivity too easily can become amplification, *The Daily Show* instead engages in subjective interrogation. Consider the treatment of the Bush statement quoted above. Here is how it appeared on air:

Bush: George Tenet is uh ... is ... a ...

Stewart: Um, a convenient fall guy ... um ... liability to our intelligence operation.

> BUSH: ... the kind of public service, uh, servant, you like to work with.
>
> STEWART: I was gonna say that, that was on the tip of my tongue.
>
> BUSH: He has been a, a, um ... a ...
>
> STEWART: Uh, uh, an albatross around the neck of your administration, an albatross.
>
> BUSH: ... a strong and able leader at the agency. He's been a, uh ... he's been a ...
>
> STEWART: He's been around too long. No, that's not it.
>
> BUSH: ... been a strong leader in the war on terror.
>
> STEWART: No, that's not it. It's right here—I don't know what it is ...

The humor lies in Stewart's interruptions, in his willingness to read Bush's statement against the grain and confront it with his own reactions and responses. Stewart's presentation is explicitly situated; he speaks with the voice, as media scholar Susan Douglas has noted, of the "outraged individual who, comparing official pronouncements with his own basic common sense, simply cannot believe what he—and all of us—are expected to swallow."[8] This kind of juxtaposition, between official pronouncements and Stewart's version of common sense, is *The Daily Show's* primary strategy. Juxtaposition is also the basic principle of political satire, which pits the "presumptions and pretensions of the politicians" against the "intuitions and instincts of the commonplace."[9] Like all satire, *The Daily Show* is dialogic in the Bakhtinian sense, the playing of multiple voices against each other in a discursive exchange that forces the original statement into revealing contexts.[10]

One can see the strategy of dialogic confrontation at work following the release of a Senate report documenting the breakdown in U.S. intelligence prior to the invasion of Iraq. To defend the ongoing occupation, Bush gave a thirty-two-minute speech in which, as Stewart notes, he "used a particular phrase eight times." This exchange then follows:

> BUSH: Because America and our coalition helped to end the violent regime of Saddam Hussein, and because we're helping to raise a peaceful democracy in its place, the American people are safer.
>
> STEWART: (*surprised and enthusiastic*) Oh! Oh good! We're, we're, we're safer! That's why we did this, because America is safer! *(changes tone)* Granted, some have said that Iraq now is a bigger breeding ground for anti-American groups, and even Tom Ridge [the secretary of Homeland Security]

has said that Al-Qaida plans on attacking us before the election, uh, so, some might think we're ... *less safe* ... but ...

BUSH: The American people are safer.

STEWART: Oh! So, uh, well, he said it again! That was his second time. So, you know, the thing is, even Bush's own State Department released a report that, once that report was *de-fucked* up, it said that there were more terrorist attacks last year than at almost any point since it's been tracked.

At this point, a clock is superimposed on the screen while Bush is talking and tracks the time from which his sound bites were drawn.

BUSH: [11:37 am] And the American people are safer.

STEWART: (*hanging head*) Oh, oh, ok. But let me ask you this, just for shnicks between the two of us ... what criteria are you using to prove that? I mean what evidence is there other than you saying it?

BUSH: [11:39] The American people are safer.

BUSH: [11:43] And the American people are safer.

BUSH: [11:45] The American people are safer.

BUSH: [11:47] And the American people ... are safer.

STEWART: (*after a moment of silence*) So basically, what it comes down to is this, the Bush administration's strategy to fight terrorism is ... *repetition*. (*pause*) You know what, give us one final "America is safer," and this time, give it a flourish that says "stop questioning me about any of this."

BUSH: [11:50, with his finger pointing] And America and the world are safer.

STEWART: Boom! Nicely done.

The treatment of Bush's speech functions on multiple levels. By emphasizing his rhetorical strategy of repetition, it lays bare Bush's clear attempt to plant the sound bite "the American people are safer" in that day's news. At the same time, Bush's one-sided, singular-voiced presentation is reworked into dialogue ("let me ask you this, just for shnicks between the two of us"), his certainty forced into critical exchange. Stewart speaks as interlocutor, confronting the president with counterargument and suggesting he lacks both the factual evidence and logical criteria to support his claim. Here Stewart engages in a kind of "undermining" humor, challenging not just the legitimacy of the president's statement but the wider authority on which it relies.[11] Finally, Stewart shifts to the voice of choreographer ("this time, give it a flourish") to make the point that Bush's speech is more theatrical spectacle than it is reasoned argument, designed ultimately to shut down avenues of inquiry ("stop questioning me") rather than inform the public.

Both Bush's rhetoric and the mainstream news are monologic, one-way speech directed at a distant, passive audience and claming to "possess a ready-made truth."[12] Satire instead represents a searching for truth through the process of dialogical interaction. Unlike traditional news, which claims epistemological certainty, satire is a discourse of inquiry, a rhetoric of challenge that seeks through the asking of unanswered questions to clarify the underlying morality of a situation. One sees this regularly on *The Daily Show* as it discusses the treatment of prisoners in the Bush war on terror, especially in the wake of the Abu Ghraib torture scandal. Says Stewart after the infamous photographs of prisoner abuse had become public, the revelation of torture is "difficult for all of us to wrap our heads around. Clearly this is a time for our defense secretary to speak clearly and honestly to the American people about these egregious instances of torture." A sound bite from then Secretary of Defense Donald Rumsfeld follows:

> RUMSFELD: Uh, I think that ... uh (*scratches his head*) ... I'm not a lawyer; my impression is that what has been charged thus far is abuse, which I believe, technically, is different from torture (*audience groans*), and therefore I'm not gonna address the torture word.
>
> STEWART: I'm also not a lawyer, so I don't know, technically, if you're *human*, but as a fake news person, I can tell you, what we've been reading about in the newspapers, the pictures we've been seeing ... it's fucking torture.

Stewart's response is distinctly subjective ("*I* can tell you"), an approach he suggests he is allowed to pursue because he is not a journalist but a "fake news person." Conventions of objectivity would disallow comment here: traditional journalists can reiterate Rumsfeld's troubling quote in hopes it will "speak for itself," but they cannot engage with it as Stewart does. Presenting this bit of news in front of a live audience, whose own subjective response adds a powerful layer of commentary, Stewart uses satire to challenge Rumsfeld with a statement of morality. He suggests, and the audience concurs, that both the incidences of torture and Rumsfeld's obfuscation—his refusal to speak "honestly and clearly"—are fundamental violations of human decency.

In an age of disconnect between words and actions, *The Daily Show* uses satire to hold the leadership accountable to both. One sees this clearly in the show's coverage of the Bush administration's rationale for war in Iraq, which shortly after the invasion had shifted from weapons of mass des tion to an alleged connection between Iraq and Al-Qaida. The follo year, however, the 9/11 Commission released its report flatly rejecting that argument. In response, *The Daily Show* plays a recent clip of a CNBC interview with Dick Cheney, who aggressively insists, much to the interviewer's surprise, that he "absolutely never said" that an alleged meeting between 9/11 hijacker Mohammed Atta and an agent of the Iraqi government had been "pretty well confirmed." From there we return to Stewart, who merely scratches his chin in puzzlement. A replay immediately follows of Cheney on NBC's *Meet the Press* in which he says, word for word, that the meeting had been "pretty well confirmed." Mining the video archive to expose Cheney's blatant lie, Stewart follows simply by saying, "Mr. Vice President, your pants are on fire."

The Daily Show's satirical take on the news can be understood as a discourse of inquiry that seeks to penetrate a political communication system Stewart himself suggests has become "purposefully obtuse."[13] In an age in which few power holders are willing to speak clearly and honestly, *The Daily Show* uses humor as license to confront political dissembling and misinformation and to demand a measure of accountability. In so doing, the program enacts a high-modern agenda, attempting to revive a spirit of critical inquiry, of the press as an agent of public interrogation that largely was abdicated by the news media post–September 11. In the frantic competition for ratings, in the fear of appearing "unpatriotic," and in the professional need to avoid alienation from the halls of power, the high-modern ideals of supervision and accountability had been replaced by a journalism of conformity and complicity. As the scholar Dustin Griffin argues, it is in such times that satire most readily appears:

> It is the limitation on free inquiry and dissent that provokes one to irony—and to satire. If open challenge to orthodoxy is freely permitted, then writers will take the most direct route and debate the ideas and characters of political leaders openly in newspapers, protected by guarantees of free speech. It is difficult, or unnecessary, to satirize our political leaders when the newspapers are filled with open attacks on their integrity and intelligence. But if open challenge is not permitted, writers will turn to irony, indirection, innuendo, allegory, fable—to the fictions of satire.[14]

In the days following September 11, when Bush's press secretary Ari Fleischer would suggest that "people need to watch what they say,"[15] *The Daily*

Show emerged, not as fake news but as a much-needed alternative kind of journalism, one that turned to satire to achieve that which apostmodern media had all but abandoned.

Critiquing News

The Daily Show also turns its critical lens onto that postmodern media, the "real" news that too often fails its democratic function. For example, Stewart replays a clip from a British press conference following Prime Minister Tony Blair's meeting with a representative of the Chinese government. In it, a reporter asks, "Who are we to talk to the Chinese about human rights, when we are an active member of a coalition which has detained, without trial, without access to lawyers, in often inhumane and, we now know, degrading conditions, both in Iraq and in other places in the world. What right do we, then, have to question the Chinese about human rights?" Before Blair answers, we cut back to Stewart, who says, "Dude, where can we get a reporter like that? Seriously, you know what I was wondering? England, I'm just throwing this out there—let me ask you this. We'll trade you one Aaron Brown, two Brit Humes, and a Van Susteren, and I'm not talking about the *old* Van Susteren—I'm talking about the *new* Van Susteren." Stewart refers to the anchors of CNN and Fox News, and to the lawyer-turned-TV-news-personality Greta Van Susteren, who dyed her hair and underwent plastic surgery on moving from CNN to Fox. Here Van Susteren becomes emblematic of much that is wrong with contemporary news.

If the news updates provide a venue for explicit criticism of the media, such criticism functions more implicitly in *The Daily Show*'s second primary element—its parody news reports. As we saw with John Oliver and Jason Jones earlier, the show's cast of comedians appear each night as news reporters. Often they are on set with Stewart or in a pretend "live" shot, standing in front of a chroma-key background (or blue screen) said to be the scene of the big story. In these segments they offer mock versions of the instant analysis common to contemporary news. They also appear in preproduced news packages, as Jones and Oliver did, traveling around the country and the world to cover real and sometimes substantive stories from the domain of public affairs. Thus Rob Riggle would spend a week with the troops in Iraq and later would cover the 2008 summer Olympics from Beijing, China. In 2004, *The Daily Show*'s Ed Helms was one of the few national reporters—real or fake—who ventured into the caged-in and heavily policed "free speech zone" established in Boston for the Democratic convention.

Always silly and at times ridiculous, their stories offer a measure of insight into significant topics. The greater purpose of *The Daily Show*'s parody reports, however, may be to mock the very genre of postmodern television news. "Parody" can be defined as a polemical imitation of a particular cultural practice, an aping that both reinvokes and challenges the styles and standards of a particular genre.[16] Parody is a moment of criticism, one that employs exaggeration, often to the point of ludicrousness, to invite its audience to examine, evaluate, and resituate the genre and its practices. The parody pieces on *The Daily Show* may generate a laugh, but their deeper thrust is subversion, an attack on the conventions and pretensions of contemporary television news.

The comedians delight in emphasizing that they are playing the role of reporter, suggesting that many of those who posture as "real" journalists likewise are playing a role. They claim a constantly changing list of praiseworthy titles, including "senior Baghdad bureau chief," "senior election/terrorism correspondent," "senior vice-presidential historian," and "senior black correspondent." Here they expose the tenuous claim to expertise the postmodern broadcast journalist so often makes. Their revolving credentials emphasize the collapse of the modernist paradigm of expertise, the point that like Van Susteren, one now becomes an expert by being on television, rather than the reverse. Armed with fake credentials, the reporters pretend to travel the globe to cover the big story. Often stretching the point to absurdity, they mock television news's overuse of the live shot, its insistence that the reporter's physical presence is isomorphic with good journalism. So too do they indulge in self-celebration. Focusing more on themselves than on the subject matter, they call into relief the trend in today's theatrical broadcast news to celebrate the reporter as the central actor in the story.

Suggesting that too many "journalists" are only playing the role on TV, the parody pieces further critique television news for the vacuousness of its content. Thus Rob Corddry, during his time as a *Daily Show* correspondent, asks a California election official to explain "in a nutshell" the problems facing the state's electoral system. After she gives a thoughtful and lengthy answer, Corddry responds, "Great. Now can you take that long-ass answer and put it in a nutshell, like I asked you?" Calling attention to television news' aversion to complex argument, the parody pieces likewise expose the media's reliance on stock narratives. Reporting the night before a presidential debate, Ed Helms reads the prewritten story he says he intends to file *after* the debate. Playing the straight man bewildered by Helms, Stewart interrupts and asks, "Ed, you've written your story already? In advance?" Helms replies, "Yeah, we all do. We write the narratives in advance based on conventional wisdom, and then whatever happens, we make it fit that story line." When Stewart asks why journalists do this, Helms shrugs his shoulders and suggests, "We're lazy?"

Ultimately, it is this disinterest in the real, the construction of televisual spectacle at the expense of accurate understanding, for which the parody pieces most criticize mainstream television news. John Oliver, for example, appears on the program the night of Hillary Clinton's speech at the 2008 Democratic National Convention. Although Stewart introduces him as *The Daily Show*'s senior political analyst, his on-screen title proclaims him to be the "Distilled Essence of Media." From that lofty perch, Oliver reports on whether Clinton was successful in "healing the Democrats" in the wake of the hard-fought party nomination process. For much of the news media, the dominant story line had been that Clinton supporters were going to refuse to vote for Obama, despite Clinton's endorsement of him (a media narrative that might have prodded the McCain camp to pick Sarah Palin as his running mate). As the "distilled essence of the media," Oliver couldn't agree more. Despite Stewart's questioning whether that particular narrative frame might have been a fiction created by "you and your type," Oliver insists that the rift between Clinton and Obama would certainly ruin Obama's chances to win the presidency. "I used to be like you, thinking this party could come together," he explains, "until I spent an entire evening trying to find a woman who would undercut that theory." His following report from the convention hall does indeed re-create the story line of irreparable party conflict—"tomorrow's press narrative" Oliver calls it. Says the woman he spent all night trying to find: "I don't think we can use a Band-Aid to cover this wound at this point."

Oliver admits to Stewart that night that he was engaging in "asinine analysis," largely because "it's fun and easy, and I've got time to kill." Four years earlier, though, Rob Corddry insisted he was doing good journalism in his reporting on the Bush-Kerry presidential race. When the ongoing story was speculation over whom Kerry would select as his running mate, Corddry literally holds his hands to his ears to avoid hearing the name. He then explains in a serious tone, "As a journalist, my job is to speculate wildly about these things. I can't let that responsibility be compromised by the facts." Elsewhere, when discussing the "Swift Boat" ads that attacked Kerry's military service, Corddry rejects Stewart's suggestion that he has an obligation to determine the factual basis of the allegations. In a highly sarcastic tone, he mocks Stewart's point: "Oh, this allegation is spurious, and upon investigation this clam lacks any basis in reality." Dismissing any responsibility to identify the truth, he explains, "I'm a journalist, Jon. My job is to spend half the time reporting what one side says and half the time reporting the other. A little thing called ob-jec-tivity. You might want to look it up some day."

The parody pieces thus ask us to consider just what a reporter's job *should* be. As such, they play a diagnostic function, identifying much that is wrong with news in its current form. If imitation is the highest form of flattery, *The Daily Show* reminds us we need broadcast journalism. At the same time, it illuminates several contemporary conventions that have rendered television news increasingly irrelevant and at times harmful to the democratic process. It asks us to be skeptical of much that passes for news today, but in an age when the conventions of journalism are open to reconsideration, it equally argues that there can, and should, be new alternatives.

Hybrid Conversations

The Daily Show's interview segment offers such an alternative model of public affairs programming. Running as long as ten minutes, the studio interview can constitute more than half the show's content. While it is modeled in the tradition of the late-night celebrity interview, the discussion segment differs from its predecessors in important ways. Although the guests at times are the familiar movie stars who frequent the late-night circuit to promote their latest films—and Stewart often seems most comfortable clowning around with male actors—only about a third of the guests are entertainers.[17] More often they are national politicians running for office or managing their public personas, an occasional former president or international leader, and authors of nonfiction books—journalists and scholars, government insiders and political pundits who address a wide range of issues.

Like the rest of the program, the interviews are hybrid affairs, melding the lighthearted sociability of entertainment chat with the serious topical concerns of more traditional public affairs programming. Stewart always approaches them as an interpersonal exchange—a conversation among friends, or at least respectful acquaintances. For example, he shares tea with then Pakistani leader Pervez Musharraf, suggests that he and U.S. Senator

Ben Nelson take a road trip to Nebraska so they could eat steak together, and tells Tom Brokaw, on the eve of his retirement from the *Nightly News*, that "I'm looking forward to seeing you when you've got a little more time on your hands. Maybe we can go out and have a sandwich." In contrast to most late-night shows, however, where this kind of informal chit-chat is the purpose of the interview, on *The Daily Show* such interpersonal warmth provides the frame for often-heady conversations about public affairs. On any given night, the guests discuss topics ranging from war and economy, to politics and policy, to history, science, and sociology. Often rich in analysis and argument, many interviews also explore background and context of current events, and some explain basic institutional processes—the kind of information essential to understanding public affairs but usually missing in most forms of news.

Despite the somber nature of many topics and the serious concerns of many guests, Stewart always interweaves the irreverent and silly into the conversations. He regularly throws in humorous asides that keep the interviews from becoming too serious, too dissimilar from the rest of the late-night landscape. In his interview with Barack Obama four days before the 2008 election, for example, Stewart raises the question of the so-called Bradley Effect, the idea that polls overestimate the popularity of black candidates because many white voters say they will vote for black candidates but ultimately do not. Noting Obama's multiracial heritage, Stewart asks, "Are you concerned ... that *you* may go into the voting booth, and your white half will suddenly decide, '*I can't do this*'?" Stewart's humor here interjects verbal style; it adds a playful burst of irrationality that gives the interviews a measure of unpredictability and momentarily breaks, but does not derail, the otherwise linear, logical flow of the discussion. For his part, Obama rolls with the joke, explaining tongue in cheek that "I've been going to therapy to make sure I can vote properly on the 4th." Thoroughly interweaving the serious and the silly, the interviews result in a more dynamic, layered form of political talk than one finds in either traditional public affairs interviews or late-night chat.

There is also a significant aspect of marketing in the segment. As with other forms of late-night entertainment, the guests appear on the show largely to promote themselves or their work—usually some form of political information or comment, be it a book, a documentary film, a television program, or the like. The trade publication *Advertising Age* has labeled the show "the Oprah Book Club of the political press," because of its ability to reach an educated audience that reads political nonfiction.[18] The interviews are in large part an economic undertaking, but at the same time they provide a portal into the wider exchange of political discourse. Show producers have suggested that part of the goal is to connect to a national conversation or, to put the point differently, to provide a point of intersection between entertainment TV and a political public sphere.

Dialogue and Democracy

The well-being of that public sphere is itself a central concern in the interviews, as it is in Stewart's conversation with conservative columnist Peggy Noonan a few weeks before the 2008 election. The two lament that the campaign had become, in many ways, a disappointment. When Stewart says he had hoped that Obama and McCain would have been able to "raise the level of discourse," Noonan agrees. "The campaign has not been big enough for the moment," she says. Stewart suggests that "the conversation in America has gotten so off base" that "for eight years," politicians "have spoken to us as children" and are more interested in manufacturing consent than in seriously engaging with issues. For her part, Noonan puts the blame on the professional political operatives who script public communication in the interests of manipulating the electorate.

Noonan echoes a recurring focus in the *Daily Show* interviews on the lack of honesty in political talk and the proclivity among public figures to adhere strictly to the talking points and partisan spin that turn public discourse into marketing. On this point, former Bush Press Secretary Ari Fleischer is both straightforward and unapologetic, simply answering "yes" to Stewart's question of whether the Bush White House had restricted the flow of information more than previous presidencies. Stewart seems unprepared for the honest answer and responds, "Oh my, Ari Fleischer was just candid with me! I don't know how to take this." He then asks why the administration was unwilling to engage in candid dialogue. "It's not candid or not-candid," Fleischer responds. "It's the power of TV. Who doesn't want to craft a beautiful image for somebody who is on the air?" Fleischer takes it as a given that the power of postmodern spectacle renders moot any responsibility to engage in reasoned discussion. Stewart then pushes the point. "It's very clear," he says, "that governments use marketing strategies, talking points, carpet bombing with phrases and such." Again, Fleischer responds with an almost-celebratory "you bet!" Despite Stewart's subtle prodding, Fleischer refuses to suggest that such practices might be problematic. Finally, Stewart concludes the interview by telling Fleischer, "I could talk about this for hours, and you could deflect me for hours." He laughs and then tears up his note cards, emphasizing the disjuncture between "talk" and "deflection"—the former being open dialogue, the latter verbal manipulation.

Fleischer's defense of communication-as-manipulation might be, in the words of philosopher Harry Frankfurt, only so much bullshit. Frankfurt appears on the program less than two weeks after Fleischer to discuss his essay titled "On Bullshit." Frankfurt's concern lies with the language of marketing, of political spin—with speech, he tells Stewart, that "undermines our commitment to the truth." Frankfurt contrasts "bullshit" with lying. The latter he argues is a willful misrepresentation of the truth and therefore an act that depends upon a conception of what exactly *is* the truth. By contrast, he explains that "the bullshitter really doesn't care if what he's saying is true or false." Because of that, Frankfurt suggests that "bullshit is a more insidious threat to society because it undermines respect for the truth and it manifests a lack of concern for the truth." Still in the shadow of the Fleischer interview, Stewart asks Frankfurt if political spin counts as BS. He agrees that it "is a form of bullshit, a subset of bullshit," because its practitioners "don't care about the truth." Instead, "they care about producing a particular impression in the mind of the people to whom they're addressing their speech. They're engaged in the enterprise of manipulating opinion, not in the enterprise of reporting the facts."

In his essay, Frankfurt relates "bullshit" to "hot air," suggesting that speech emptied of informational content is akin to "shit," which lacks "everything nutritive." Thus bullshit, he argues, "cannot serve the purpose of sustenance or of communication."[19] Frankfurt echoes the theorist Jürgen Habermas's argument about communicative ethics, which suggests that every statement makes a claim to validity—that it corresponds with an external reality—and to truthfulness—that it accurately reflects the speaker's true intentions. For Habermas, validity and truthfulness are required elements of communication, which he defines as speech oriented toward mutual understanding. Habermas contrasts communication with "strategic speech," which, like Frankfurt's bullshit, is intended only to generate an effect on its audience, not to move the participants toward consensus, agreement, or understanding.[20]

Articulating the same kind of faith in communication, *The Daily Show* ultimately advocates a deliberative theory of democracy—the notion that only civil and honest conversation can provide the legitimate foundation for governance. A theory of deliberative democracy can be distinguished from a market theory of politics, which begins from the assumption that the polity is comprised of instrumentally rational individuals who enter the debate with fully formed preferences, intent on maximizing their own self-interest. In such an economic theory of democracy, politics is seen as conflict between divergent interests, while political discourse becomes competition that at best can produce functional compromises.[21] It is this logic that appears to underlie political discussion programs such as *Crossfire* or *Hardball* and their "You're wrong; I'm not" model of political argument. Such shows reduce political discourse to a zero-sum game, an unreflexive contest in which only one side can win.

In contrast to a market or instrumental understanding of democracy, a theory of deliberative democracy as expressed on *The Daily Show* understands the political system ideally to be comprised of individuals engaged in reasoned discussion, a cooperative discourse that seeks to reach a consensual notion of the common good. It is a dialogical notion of democracy, one that "requires citizens to go beyond private self-interest of the 'market' and orient themselves to public interests of the 'forum.'"[22] The forum provides the central metaphor of deliberative democracy, which depends in the first instance on active deliberation among citizens. Dialogue here is the locus of democracy, the public process through which citizens determine their preferences and define the public will.

For advocates of a deliberative democracy, reasoned conversation is the defining feature of a democratic system, a feature clearly lacking in much of the reactionary, frenzied, and often unintelligible twenty-four-hour news media. It is this shortcoming of the mainstream news media and politicians alike that motivates *The Daily Show*'s interview segments, and much of the program's criticism of contemporary political communication practices. One sees this expressed in Stewart's interview with former Treasury Secretary Robert Reich, who pleads for a "return to reason" in political argument. "Irrationality rules the day," Reich insists, "but reason is in the wings." Before Stewart can respond, the audience bursts into applause, at which point Stewart leans toward Reich and says, "By the way, the people clamoring for reason? You hear that? You don't see that too often." *The Daily Show*, however, regularly offers a model of and resources for political dialogue and reasoned conversation.

"The Way of the Future"

Paul O'Neill, the former Bush treasury secretary, was one of the first Bush insiders to speak out against the administration, complaining, as he did on

The Daily Show that the president's inner circle refused to listen to criticism or "candid advice." In his interview with Stewart, he also argues that the news media are no longer interested in reasoned explanations of policy and that they "hammered me really hard for telling the truth." To that, Stewart proclaims, "This is why, and I hate to toot our own horn, . . . fake news is the way of the future." O'Neill responds tellingly. "I like what you're doing," he says. "Keep making fun." The suggestion here is intriguing—that by "making fun" *The Daily Show* is at the same time engaged in the serious exploration of political issues, an exploration that is vital to the conduct of democracy but all too often missing in the contemporary media. That point runs counter to the argument offered by some critics, who worry that the show is yet another offshoot of the same postmodern cynicism that encourages "false knowledge" and saps any sense of "political possibility." Such is the view articulated by the rhetorician Roderick Hart, whose concerns about television and its culture of postmodern cynicism we saw in chapter 4. More recently, Hart has argued that in the crass pursuit of profit, *The Daily Show* has made "cynicism atmospheric, a mist that hovers over us each day." He and his coauthor Johanna Hartelius dismiss Jon Stewart's brand of political humor as a kind of debilitating aesthetic spectacle: "a type of display more than a type of argument," one that suggests that "social organizations and continuing commitments—the very essence of politics—are passé."[23]

I suggest, however, that theirs is a misreading of *The Daily Show,* one entrenched in a modernist worldview that imagines that the aesthetic and the political could, or should, be distinct—that humor is incompatible with argument and that entertainment necessarily diverts and distracts one from the consideration of serious matters. Rather than dismiss *The Daily Show* as entertainment posturing as political news, we must recognize that entertainment is a doubly articulated concept. On one hand, "to entertain" means to amuse and to give one pleasure, but it also can mean to engage with and to consider. Stewart's humor does indeed give pleasure, but, more than that, it continuously calls on its viewers to consider. Lying just beneath—or perhaps imbricated within—the laughter is a quite serious critique of much that passes for public discourse in a postmodern age.

The Daily Show's blending of news and satire confronts a system of political communication that has honed the art of manipulation and misinformation, while its use of parody unmasks the artifice in contemporary news practices that all too often echo the scripts of power. So too is it grounded in a faith in fact, accountability, and dialogue; the interview segment endorses and enacts a deliberative model of democracy based on civility of exchange, complexity of argument, and the goal of mutual understanding. Advancing a kind of "serious comedy" that is entertaining in both senses of the word, *The Daily Show* ultimately is not really postmodern at all. In an age in which the real cynics may be the professional political communicators and the mainstream media who regularly substitute style for substance and the absurd for the sensible, *The Daily Show* is less cynical than it is skeptical, rightly distrustful of the postmodern comedy that too often pretends to be political conversation.

As in the world of Joseph Heller's *Catch-22*, where insanity is the norm and the sane appear crazy, it is now left up to the comedian to pierce the bubble of spectacle and spin. The scholar Robert Hariman has made a similar point, suggesting perhaps paradoxically that "only by admitting to absurdity and moving through the laughter can one become really serious today."[24] Despite the critics' insistence that it rejects "the very essence of politics," *The Daily Show* holds out the hope of reinvigorating political journalism and public discourse, celebrating the quite modernist hope that we might be able to reason our way out of the predicament in which we have been mired for too long.

7

♦ ♦ ♦

"NOTHING I'M SAYING MEANS ANYTHING"

STEPHEN COLBERT AND THE NEW LANGUAGE OF PUBLIC AFFAIRS

In the spring of 2006, the fake newsman and pundit Stephen Colbert took to the podium as the keynote speaker at the annual White House Correspondents' Association dinner. At first blush, the late-night comedian, who regularly lampoons current events from an ostensibly conservative point of view, appeared to be an ideal choice for that strange annual ritual in which politicians and journalists suspend their supposedly serious professional identities for a night of good-natured ribbing. Standing just a few seats away from the president, however, Colbert instead unleashed a powerful stream of satire—sarcasm, irony, and double-entendre that sounded like praise but in actuality was blistering criticism. "I stand by this man," Colbert proclaimed, "because he stands for things. Not only *for* things, he stands *on* things. Things like aircraft carriers, and rubble, and recently flooded city squares. And that sends a strong message that no matter what happens to America, she will always rebound . . . with the most powerfully staged photo ops in the world."[1]

Accusing the president, among many other things, of responding to national tragedy with spectacle instead of substance, with publicity in place of policy, Colbert's address was a watershed moment, one that spoke volumes about the contemporary nature of politics and public conversation. By all accounts, the president didn't care much for criticism, and those who disagreed with him rarely got a seat at the same table. Yet here, months before Bush would become a figure of broad public ridicule, was a serious challenge, a stinging critique clad in the guise of good humor. "The greatest thing about this man is he's steady, you know where he stands," Colbert blustered. "He believes the same thing on Wednesday that he believed on Monday, no matter what happened on Tuesday. Events may change, but this man never will." Bragging that both he and the president were little interested in reality, because it has a "well-known liberal bias," Colbert lauded Bush for rejecting fact in favor of wishful thinking and privileging emotion over intellect—in short, for substituting "truthiness" for truth: "Guys like us, we're not some brainiacs on the nerd patrol; we're not members of the 'factanista.' We go straight from the gut, right sir? That's where the truth lies, right down here in the gut."

Refusing to conform to expectations that he would be politely funny and avoid issues of significance, Colbert equally skewered the Washington press corps. As Jon Stewart had done on *Crossfire* two years earlier, Colbert seized the moment to criticize a hypercorporatized, post–September 11 news media that had been all too complicit in the Bush administration's manipulation of public information. Again, his critique came in the form of backhanded compliments. He praised Fox News for always reporting "both sides of the story—the president's and the vice president's," but he worried that the rest of the media might be awaking from their noncritical slumber. "Over the last five years, you people were so good. Over tax cuts, WMD intelligence, the effects of global warming—we Americans didn't want to know, and you had the courtesy not to try to find out. Those were good times ... as far as we knew." Colbert then reminded the reporters in the room of the unspoken "rules" of contemporary political journalism:

> The president makes decisions; he's the decider. The press secretary announces those decisions, and you people in the press type those decisions down. Make, announce, type. Just put 'em through a spell check, and go home. Get to know your family again. Make love to your wife. Write that novel you've got kicking around in your head. You know, the one about the intrepid Washington reporter with the courage to stand up to the administration. You know ... *fiction*!

Although few of the reporters in the audience laughed, Colbert's performance struck a nerve with millions of other people. Within just forty-eight hours of its original broadcast on CSPAN, nearly three million of them had downloaded the clip from YouTube.[2] A year later, the address remained among the top-five audiobooks on iTunes. That was despite the mainstream press's almost universal dismissal of the event. The network breakfast shows and CNN all refused to mention Colbert in their coverage the next morning, as did the *New York Times* for several days after. The *Washington Post* covered the performance but dismissed it as "so not funny."[3] The significance of Colbert's address, however, may lie precisely in that point. It wasn't exactly "funny"—at least not in the way Rich Little's banal imitations were the following year. It wasn't the kind of benign humor that leads to a chuckle and not much else.[4] Instead it was a form of serious comedy, a much-needed exploration of presidential leadership, political journalism, and truth in a postmodern world. The moment was made all the more remarkable by the fact that it was the comedian—not the professional journalists in the room—who was willing to do the heavy lifting of the Fourth Estate. For his part, Jon Stewart marveled at the performance but expressed astonishment over the media's reaction, noting that Colbert must have assumed that he had been hired to perform the act "he does on television *every night*."

The Colbert Report

Indeed, four nights a week on his self-celebratory *Colbert Report*, the improv comic takes on the role of the egregious right-wing pundit who is all too quick to insist on the bright line between right (i.e., him) and wrong (i.e., anyone who might disagree). *The Colbert Report* emerged from *The Daily Show*, where for seven years Stephen Colbert honed his character—the enigmatically foolish and deeply ironic television personality whose blatant disregard for accuracy and political correctness often results in piercing humor. Like *The Daily Show*, Colbert's character is an example of discursive border crossing, a blend of the serious and the silly, the real and the surreal, the sensible and the absurd. In differing combinations each night, he borrows from and reassembles a number of generic traditions, melding the content of news and public affairs, the form of cable television's partisan punditry, and the style of edgy nightclub comedy. Thus *The Colbert Report* is a discursively integrated form of television, offering a topical blend ranging from the significant to the ridiculous, from pointed examinations of war, foreign policy, and presidential politics, to lighthearted and sometimes inane commentary on entertainment celebrity and pop-culture headlines.

A multilayered assemblage, the *Report* is a complex performance, one that functions simultaneously as entertainment, spectacle, information, and critique. It is also a site of a wide-ranging public conversation—lively and at times subversive—that features a remarkable diversity of politicians, journalists, intellectuals, social activists, and public personalities. In this chapter I suggest that *The Colbert Report* represents a new brand of public affairs television, a significant innovation in the ways—in terms of both content and form—in which television can talk, and people can learn, about the political. On one hand, it is a kind of postmodern TV. Colbert seems to be an abstract, a spectacle created for the screen, while his program is marked by the sort of border-effacing slippage that postmodern theorists have suggested characterizes a distinct break from the social and discursive order of modernity.[5] On the other hand, like *The Daily Show*, Colbert enacts and endorses a *modernist* agenda, one that ultimately rejects the postmodern logic of spectacle and simulacrum and the now-commonplace assumption that truth is relative and fact a product of power. As such, *The Colbert Report* is a neo-modern form of public affairs television, a new way of pursuing the old goal of public information and democratic accountability.

Feeling the News

On his debut program in October 2005, Colbert lays claim to an intriguing agenda. "Anyone can *read the news to you*," he suggests, but "I promise to *feel the news at you*." That was the culmination of his pledge to pursue "truthiness"—the concept that he introduced that first night and that quickly worked its way into the popular vernacular (with help from Merriam-Webster, which named it "word of the year" for 2006). Like the president he insists he supports, Colbert explains that the *Report* will gleefully reject evidence in favor of emotion and celebrate opinion over reason. "Every night on my show," he later explains at the Correspondents Dinner, "I give people the truth, unfiltered by rational argument. I call it the *No Fact Zone*. . . . Fox News, I hold a copyright on that term." Specifically highlighting Fox, Colbert placed the critical focus on that problematic trend away from objective reporting and toward partisan bluster, the profit-driven attempt not to inform a democratic citizenry but to provide market segments with the kind of emotive reassurance they most want to hear.

The Colbert Report thus cannot be understood without considering Fox News and its remarkable insistence that a network owned by the avowed conservative Rupert Murdoch and run by the former Bush media operative Roger Ailes could somehow also embody that modernist ideal of being "fair and balanced." Most specifically, Colbert targets Fox's flagship commentator Bill O'Reilly, the archetypical right-wing pundit who rose from playing a reporter on the early tabloid program *Inside Edition* to become the star of another kind of infotainment TV—Fox News. The connection between Colbert and O'Reilly (and his hard-to-swallow suggestion that his *O'Reilly Factor* could possibly be a "No Spin Zone") was drawn as early as August 2004, when a series of spoof commercials on *The Daily Show* imagined an "exciting new *Daily Show* spin-off." Envisioning a program that would be hosted by an angry, know-it-all Colbert, the first of these fake promos featured a sequence of split screens in which Colbert appeared to be interviewing newsmakers—John Edwards, John McCain, and Donald Rumsfeld—and in each one ordering the imaginary production crew to "cut his mic"—a jab at O'Reilly, who can only tolerate disagreement to a certain point, before he orders his guests to "shut up" or turns off their microphones altogether. In the second of the fake promos, Colbert promised to "tear the news a new one," concluding that "right or wrong, I'm right, and you're wrong."

The founding premise of the *Report* is Colbert's parody of O'Reilly, whom he glowingly calls "Papa Bear." Colbert insists that he is crafted in O'Reilly's image, patterning his verbal performance and nonverbal mannerisms after him. Thus when Colbert appears as a guest on the *O'Reilly Factor*—the night Colbert celebrates as the "Pundit Exchange," when O'Reilly also visits the *Report*—he showers "Papa Bear" with praise, insisting that it is "an amazing honor" to be "at the foot of the master." Together the two delight in celebrating O'Reilly and attacking those, such as the *New York Times*, who would condemn him. "They're haters, Bill," Colbert proclaims of the same "liberal media" he lambasted at the Correspondents Dinner for not being critical *enough*. "They are," agrees O'Reilly. "They're scum." Colbert continues, "You know what I hate about people who criticize you? They criticize you for what you say, but they never give you credit for how loud you say it." Without a hint of reflexivity, O'Reilly agrees. "That's true," he says, "not many people are as loud as I am."

Largely substituting volume for thought, O'Reilly insists that he is a "culture warrior" in the fight against liberals and what he calls their "San Francisco values." Notably, his interview with Colbert on the *Factor* was part of his ongoing segment entitled "Culture War," which he explains later on the *Report* that night is a struggle "between secular progressives such as yourself . . . and traditionalists like me." The self-appointed title of "warrior" might be an overstatement, but O'Reilly does wield his words like a club. Journalism researcher Mike Conway and his colleagues have found that O'Reilly employs many of the traditional techniques of twentieth-century propaganda, constructing a fearful and simplistic world of heroes and villains fighting over some imagined American way of life. His most frequently recurrent villains—the evildoers—are, of course, terrorists and illegal immigrants, but the bad people in O'Reilly's world also include academics, non-Christians, and *both* left-leaning and politically neutral media. By contrast, he insists the virtuous are the right-leaning media, George Bush and the Republican party, Christians, and a vague notion of the American people.[6] As such, his "No Spin Zone" ironically functions as a key circuit in the generation of political spectacle—right-wing political artistry that imagines problems and invents enemies to sell a predetermined, but often undisclosed, political and economic agenda.[7]

Playing the role of the megalomaniacal and xenophobic demagogue, Colbert insists, like O'Reilly, that he is objective, but he regularly spouts proclamations such as: "We have a very simple system in America. Republicans believe in God, and Democrats believe in a welfare state where we tax the rich." Often sounding like O'Reilly, Colbert regularly invokes "Papa Bear," as he does in a segment with Michigan Congresswoman Carolyn Cheeks Kilpatrick. When Kilpatrick blasts the Bush administration for its failed response to Hurricane Katrina, Colbert recites verbatim an O'Reilly commentary blaming the victims of Katrina for their own victimhood. "The aftermath of Hurricane Katrina should be taught in every American school," he quotes. "If you don't get educated, if you don't develop a skill and force yourself to work hard, you'll most likely be poor, and sooner or later you'll be standing on a symbolic rooftop waiting for help." As he reads, O'Reilly's head is superimposed over Colbert's, and Colbert's voice fades into O'Reilly's. At least in this instance, Colbert is no longer playing an O'Reilly-like character but becomes O'Reilly, assuming his words, his head, and his voice.[8]

Thus O'Reilly explains to his audience the night of the Pundit Exchange that Colbert "owes everything to me," that he "tries to convince people that he *is* me." What O'Reilly fails to acknowledge, however, is that the imitation is parody, a critical examination that targets the absurdities of its referent and invites the audience to "examine, evaluate and re-situate the hypotextual material."[9] Indeed, Colbert rarely passes on the opportunity to expose O'Reilly at his most absurd. When a viral video briefly circulated on the Internet revealing a much younger O'Reilly throwing a temper tantrum on the set of *Inside Edition* because he didn't understand the words that had been scripted for him, Colbert pretends to rush to his defense. First, of course, he replays the entire clip of O'Reilly berating his crew, but then he plays what he insists is his own self-revealing video, a segment in which an allegedly younger, mustachioed Colbert appears to be anchoring a local television news program. When he's asked to correct a factual error made the day before, Colbert loses his cool: "OK, we got a problem! There's something wrong with the prompter. Those aren't the right words. Those aren't words. What does that mean: 'I'm sorry; I was wrong'? What is that!? I've never seen those words before in my life!" When an off-camera voice explains, "It's an apology," Colbert screams in O'Reilly-like fashion, "You mean like, I made a mistake? *I'm not research!*" Calling into relief O'Reilly's belligerence and, more importantly, his refusal to admit when he is wrong, the parody demonstrates that at least in this case, imitation is not always flattery.

Satiric Interrogation

Much of Colbert's act is the ridicule of O'Reilly and his ilk, but that parodic mocking is never simply fun, or to put the point differently, *simple* fun. Rather, the *Report* is a complex form of political engagement, commentary, and criticism. Like *The Daily Show,* its main technique is satire—the juxtaposition of contradictory voices and perspectives that force the singular presumptions of monologue into dialogic engagement. Like all good political satire from Swift to Stewart, the unspoken agenda is to puncture political orthodoxies and challenge conventional practices. This is well-illustrated on the *Report* the night in late 2006 when Colbert decides its time to "clean out the TiVo." Brandishing a remote control, Colbert pretends to browse through various programs he supposedly has stored on his DVR. He begins by replaying a recent bit from *The Daily Show,* in which Jon Stewart explains that the Iraq war had now lasted longer than the entirety of U.S. involvement in World War II. In response to that Colbert winces and quickly hits "delete." He then turns to a segment from ABC's *This Week,* in which host George Stephanopoulos asks Dick Cheney to respond to that point. Not surprisingly, the vice president answers with the kind of dissembling that has become all too conventional practice. "The analogy of World War II," he insists, "is just not a valid analogy. It's a totally different set of circumstances." Colbert celebrates that answer: "Thank you, Mr. President [*sic*]," he exclaims, and then says he'll save that clip on his TiVo "until forever."

But from there, Colbert takes an interesting turn. Saying, "OK, let's go back a ways," he plays an earlier clip from Fox's *Hannity and Colmes*, in which the right-winger Sean Hannity explains that "for the last number of days, the president, the vice president, Donald Rumsfeld, our secretary of defense . . . they've all made the case. . . . They're using the analogy of World War II and appeasement" (all this while presidential press secretary and former Fox News personality Tony Snow nods along in agreement). Colbert again quickly hits "delete," noting that he doesn't "need *that* anymore." Clips then follow from other high-ranking Republican officials previously asserting the similarities between Iraq and World War II. Says Ken Mehlman, then the chairman of the Republican Party, arguing against timetables for withdrawal from Iraq, "Could you imagine in World War II if we had said in 1943, here's when we're going to withdraw from the battlefield . . . ?" The juxtaposition of past and present administration rhetoric reveals the strategic machinations behind Cheney's dismissal of the "World War II analogy" and leaves a seemingly agitated Colbert no choice but to give up on his task of reviewing recent history.

In many ways, that segment is similar to what one sees on *The Daily Show*, but one can identify significant differences between the two approaches. At the least, Colbert is more theatrical. Where Jon Stewart summarizes headlines and introduces sound bites much the same as the nightly newscaster does, Colbert weaves his informational content into artfully staged scenarios—in the example just discussed, his juxtaposition of contradictory sound bites is framed as "cleaning out the TiVo," complete with appropriate props. *The Daily Show* draws tighter linkages to the traditional form of news and its generic conventions. Stewart generally reports the news—albeit in multiple voices of comedy, satire, and earnest despair—while Colbert enacts spectacle scripted for the stage. In that regard the names of the programs seem reversed—*The Jon Stewart Report* and *The Colbert Show* might be more appropriate descriptors for the different endeavors in which the two are engaged. As such, while Stewart appears as himself, articulating the same values and embodying the same ethos he offers in other public presentations, Colbert is fundamentally a character. His on-camera performance offers little trace of the real person behind the act; he appears as a mask or an invented fiction. In turn, Colbert is far less *literal* than Stewart, his performance continuously double-layered, his speech marked by the perpetual ironic juxtaposition between what he says and what he might actually mean.

"The Word"

Colbert's ironic duality is both a kind of aesthetic play and a powerful vehicle for argument and criticism, one whose edge always exists at a measure of interpretive distance. This is most evident in his segment "The Word," an explicit parody of O'Reilly's "Talking Points Memo." Mimicking the form of "Talking Points," Colbert appears in close-up on one side of the screen, his finger regularly wagging at the camera as he pontificates on topics such as foreign affairs, national policies, and presidential politics. On the other side of the screen, key words related to the monologue are presented in graphic form. But unlike O'Reilly's "Talking Points," in which the on-screen text simply repeats his argument, on Colbert's "Word," the written text provides an unspoken voice, a second level of meaning that complicates his spoken language.

During the 2008 campaign, for example, Colbert examines Sarah Palin's disinterest in the cause of global warming and John McCain's similar refusal to discuss the causes for the invasion of Iraq. In a "Word" segment entitled "Mavericks Without A Cause," Colbert suggests that "Every problem that has ever threatened our country can be traced back to a cause (*Or Blamed On Immigrants*). I say that makes causes our country's greatest enemy (*Sorry Gay Marriage*)." The Democrats, though, want to "understand causes," Colbert laments, and "attention is just what these causes want. I say we ignore them (*Worked With Afghanistan*)." In the spoken words, Colbert sounds much like O'Reilly, insisting the Democrats are empowering "our country's greatest enemy." But the on-screen text (expressed here in brackets and italics) turns monologue into dialogue, inviting its audience to critically deconstruct the sensibilities of the monologue's literal content. The written text thus functions as an ironic "corrective," a textual device through which an "assumed or asserted fact is shown not to be true, an idea or belief to be untenable, an expectation to be unwarranted or a confidence to be misplaced."[10]

Even the title "The Word" is multilayered, invoking the talking point and at the same time deconstructing the political use of language. In that vein, Colbert turns his critical focus onto then–presidential hopeful Rudy Giuliani, the former New York mayor who, Colbert notes, had "used the words 'Islamic terrorism' so many times" in his attempt to win the 2008 Republican presidential nomination that "the phrase 'September 11' is starting to get jealous." That was in response to Giuliani's charge that the Democratic presidential candidates were not using the phrase "Islamic terrorist" to describe "the enemy." In a "Word" segment entitled "Clarity," Colbert worries that in avoiding reductive labels, the Democrats were making it "sound like we're in the middle of a complex, nuanced struggle that requires deep understanding of the differences between politically and religiously diverse groups." That, he suggests, is

> worse than political correctness, it's actual correctness. And we all know too often correctness gets bogged down in detail (*Fails To See Bigger Caricature*). If we really want to win this war, we have to paint with broad strokes.... We need to return to the clarity of the good old days, before there was any difference between Sunnis and Shias, back when there were "freedom fries," and our justification for war was three simple letters, W-M-D (*L-I-E*).

As the letters *L-I-E* appear on the screen, the audience bursts into uproarious laughter. When that subsides, Colbert continues: "I propose Rudy Giuliani be appointed America's language czar. He could decide which words help America (*President Giuliani*), and which words weaken us (*"Habeas Corpus"?*).... If we don't use his simple, all-encompassing label for all of our enemies, he knows there's no way to win (*The Election*)." As this example illustrates, the "Word" segment often is an exercise in rhetorical criticism, an interrogation of public discourse. Here he critiques the pitfalls of reductive characterizations of complex situations and the use of language to mask dangerous governmental policies.

Colbert also uses "The Word" to probe topics that are largely ignored by the mainstream media. For example, when, in February 2007, the Pentagon's inspector-general released a report condemning former Defense Undersecretary Douglas Feith for fabricating prewar intelligence to facilitate the invasion of Iraq, Colbert devoted more than three minutes to the issue, which was largely glossed over by the mainstream press.[11] Colbert's "Word" that night was "Inappropriate," which he explained was "the word the inspector-general used to describe Feith's manipulation of intelligence." He then provides a kind of neo-journalistic explanation of the situation—a mixture of information, interpretation, and humor. "You see folks, back in 2002, Feith's job was to analyze the American intelligence community's conclusions about Iraq and Al-Qaida. He found a major flaw in the CIA's intelligence—namely that it didn't support the administration's desire to attack Iraq. And he wasn't afraid to be 'inappropriate' and say the CIA was wrong (*If By Wrong, You Mean Right*). And folks, that took courage." By 2007, of course, Feith was downplaying his attempts at misinformation, as he does in a quote Colbert both reads and displays on the screen: "In presenting it," Feith insists, "I was not endorsing its substance." To Feith's contorted logic that he was not responsible for his words because he personally didn't mean what he said, Colbert responds, "Don't be so modest, Doug. Putting Al-Qaida in Iraq back then may have taken some imagination, but thanks to inappropriateness, you made it a reality (*Feith-Based Initiative*)."

Finally, Colbert explores the implication of the Pentagon report's careful language, its conclusion that the manipulation of intelligence was "inappropriate" but not "illegal," which he suggests is "an important victory for the administration (*Misleading Accomplished*)." Using the word "illegal," he explains, "would just start a whole new round of investigations, and questions like 'how far up the chain of command does this illegality go?' Nobody wants that (*The Buck Stops Way Over There*). But calling Feith's actions inappropriate puts an end to the investigations. What happened happened. And the administration knows never to do this again, or they will suffer the same punishment as Feith (*None*)." This is a powerful moment of television, a kind of critical illumination reminiscent of the high-modern hope that broadcast journalism could be the hot light of public inquiry. Colbert suggests that Feith was taking the fall to protect those higher in the chain of command who were avoiding accountability for their actions. That point is made all the more compelling by the fact that it is not the press but the comedian, whose tools are the brazenness of satire and the subtleties of irony, who asks the critical questions and demands democratic accountability.

Conversation

If *The Colbert Report* provides an unlikely source of information and criticism—two of the requisite contributions public affairs media ideally should make within a democratic system—it likewise functions as a kind of neo-modern public sphere, a gathering place in which a wide variety of public figures discuss a vast range of issues. Much of the program is devoted to conversation. Like *The Daily Show*, the third block of the program always features an interview, at times with celebrity entertainers (although even they often want to talk about politics), but regularly with politicians, journalists, and authors drawn from across the political spectrum. Similarly, experts and activists often appear during the first block of the show for topical discussions interwoven with the satirical examination of contemporary issues. Colbert also has interviewed dozens of sitting members of the U.S. House of Representatives as part of his ongoing effort to profile every one of the 435 U.S. Congressional districts.

In the discursively integrated world that is *The Colbert Report,* these interviews don't always meet the standards of rational-critical discourse that Jürgen Habermas suggests a public sphere requires.[12] Colbert's congressional profiles (what he calls "Better Know a District"), for example, are highly illogical, much more theatrical spectacle than deliberative exchange. Similarly, when Democratic Congressman and presidential candidate Dennis Kucinich appears on the program, he doesn't discuss policies or politics, but instead performs in a surrealistic sketch in which he "emptied his pockets"—that a challenge from Colbert after news reports identified a number of small items (including a pocket Constitution, a baseball card, and a tea bag) that Kucinich always carries with him. Among the many things he pretends to pull from his pockets on the *Report* are a tea pot and cups, as well as a miniature Colbert, a digitally generated effect that stands on the desk and, to Colbert's horror, sings. Likewise, at the height of the 2008 primary season, Hillary Clinton appears on the program just long enough to "fix" the screen behind Colbert's desk, Barack Obama adds "petty distractions" to the "On Notice" board (Colbert's list of things he does not approve of), and John Edwards reads "The Word" segment ("Ed-Words" it was called that night). So too does Republican Mike Huckabee play air hockey with Colbert, using the state of Texas as the puck.

At the same time that these otherwise serious people engage in lighthearted fun, Colbert's guests regularly delve into level-headed discussions of significant public issues—issues that often go unexplored in other forms of public affairs media. For example, well before the Supreme Court was to rule that the detainees at Guantanamo Bay have the legal right to request a hearing, Ken Roth of the group Human Rights Watch appears to discuss the prison and the treatment of its prisoners. Congressional scholar Norm Ornstein talks about the need for and possibilities of reforming Congress, Government Accountability Office head David Walker offers a sobering overview of the federal budget deficit and the future of social entitlement programs, and Illinois Congresswoman Jan Schakowsky explains her efforts to understand the realities of living on food stamps, part of Colbert's coverage of Hunger Awareness Day.

In all of these interviews, Colbert remains in character, occupying the same ironic stance that characterizes his performance elsewhere—for example, accusing the Democrat Schakowsky of being "in the pocket of big poverty." He seems to be the belligerent and mindless conservative blowhard, but the voice always remains multilayered, with words and meanings never quite adding up. With his conservative guests, he postures as their unconditional ally, proclaiming, as he does to Jed Babbin, editor of the reactionary publication *Human Events,* that "you're a man after my own heart" and "I am with you, my friend." Likewise, when Georgia Republican Phil Gingrey, explains that his opposition to gay marriage is rooted in his faith in the inerrancy of the Bible, Colbert assures him that "it's so nice to be talking with someone I agree with." But from there, Colbert subtly challenges Gingrey's position. "Where do you come down on gays having *driver's* licenses?" he asks, and then argues with Gingrey when he uncomfortably admits "they have every right" to drive a car. "See, that's where you and I part ways, sir," Colbert responds. "I don't want my highways all 'gayed' up.... I don't want to be driving down the road and see a car's bumper sticker that says, 'My other car is having sex with a man.'"

When Gingrey awkwardly suggests that "that's a good point," Colbert refuses to let him off the hook. "Really?" he answers. "Thank you. Not many people say that." As he does elsewhere, Colbert provides the keys to his own translation. His surprise at Gingrey's affirmation of his absurd point emphasizes his own foolishness and, in so doing, reveals that he does not—that he *could not*—mean what he says.[13] While he poses as a friend in order to play the foil, Colbert's false praise masks a deeper antagonism that forces the exchange into a form of dialectical tension. He does the same thing with *Human Events*' Babbin, who suggests that Democrats "hate America" but reluctantly admits that their victory in the 2006 election was in part a statement of opposition to the Iraq war. Without batting an eye, Colbert asks him, "What *can* we do to shut the American people up?" So too does Colbert play the role of false friend in his interview with antitax advocate Grover Norquist, who explains his "leave us alone" philosophy—that the only legitimate role he sees for government is to maintain a police force to arrest criminals and a military "to make sure we don't get attacked by foreigners." "I applaud you," Colbert responds, "for resurrecting some of the rhetoric of the nineteenth-century South.... Aren't you really capturing the spirit of *E Pluribus Unum,* which literally in Latin means, 'out of many, just me'?"

Playing the role of the false friend with conservatives, cloaking critical questions in ironic praise, Colbert often inverts this dynamic in his interviews with liberals. With them, he is gratuitously bellicose and antagonistic on the surface, as he is with progressive journalist Amy Goodman. He begins by attacking her, accusing her of being a "communist—a liberal leftie outside agitator," and telling her sternly that she will "have to earn every inch of this interview, lady." But from there, he gives her space to talk about widespread opposition to the Iraq war and to criticize the corporate media for its distorted war coverage. Here Goodman, whose voice usually is relegated to the margins of corporate television, is given several minutes to advocate her concerns. Following the interview, Goodman explains that she was prepared by the show's producers to "imagine yourself speaking to a drunk in a bar" and that in turn, she appreciates "what he was doing," giving her the high-profile platform, even briefly, to stretch the boundaries of televisual discourse.[14]

One sees something similar in Colbert's 2008 interview with Susan Eisenhower, the granddaughter of President Dwight Eisenhower, who renounced her affiliation with the Republican party and spoke at the Democratic Convention in support of Obama. "Why won't you support the Republicans?" Colbert chides her. "They're the ones who made your grandfather's vision of an out-of-control military-industrial complex come true. Don't you owe them?" Similarly, he pesters Kim Gandy, president of the National Organization for Women, for backing Obama and not the McCain-Palin ticket. When Gandy explains that she is supporting Obama for his stand on the issues, Colbert asks, "Isn't focusing on 'issues' clouding your judgment? I think you are losing sight of the fact that [Palin] is a *woman*." As did Goodman, both Eisenhower and Gandy understand that Colbert's real strategy is playing the foil without actually being the foil. This ironic duality serves a narrative function, crafting verbal conflict that evokes the dramatic appeal of antagonism. As such, it creates an agora-like setting, a Socratic interrogation in which the guests are forced to articulate and defend their ideas.[15] But because he is only playing, as opposed to O'Reilly or Rush Limbaugh, whose game is anger and verbal attack, the guests often delight in the exchange. Laughter regularly punctuates the discussions, and they become moments of playful engagement. In turn, the guests grant Colbert greater latitude to throw more and more absurd verbal roadblocks in their way, until he leaves the domain of rationality altogether, and the guests no longer are obligated to respond seriously.

Colbert himself, in a moment out of character, has explained his strategy:

> I say to all my guests, "You know I'm playing a character; you know I'm an idiot. I'm willfully ignorant of the subjects I talk about—disabuse me of my ignorance. Don't try to play my game. Be real; be passionate; give me traction I can work against." It's the friction between the reality, or the truly held

> concerns of the person and the farcical concerns that I have, or my need to seem important as opposed to actually understanding what's true. . . . Where those two things meet is where the comedy happens.[16]

Such is the case in Colbert's raucous interview with author Susan Jacoby, who appears on the show to promote her book *The Age of American Unreason.* In a discussion filled with laughter and faux outrage, Jacoby bemoans the fact that an inordinately large number of Americans cannot find Iraq on a world map nor know what DNA is. Playing the false foil, Colbert yells back at her that he knows what DNA is—it's "a fraud perpetrated by science to make us not believe in God!" He continues, gleefully asking if she could date the onset of the "age of unreason" to the day the *Report* first went on air. Personally taking credit for the rise of unreason, Colbert explains that "I'm not a big fan of reason. There's *reason* and then there's *feelings.* I'll bet those kids who can't find Iraq on a map can tell you how they *feel* about Iraq!" Not to be undone, Jacoby draws linkages between what she calls "unreason" and contemporary politics, identifying the common rhetorical trope of attacking the opposition for being "elitist"—a "stupid word," she suggests, symptomatic of the age of unreason. "Of course you say that 'elitist' is a stupid word," Colbert counters, "because you *are* an elitist." Accusing her of being one of those people "who read books and know things," Colbert yells that "knowing things that other people don't know is the *definition* of elitist!" Finally, however, Colbert tips his hand, suggesting that Jacoby has actually stolen her entire argument *from* him. "You describe something you call 'junk thought,'" he explains, "where 'people only know what they want to know, while facts that challenge their beliefs are brushed aside.' I believe that's called 'truthiness,' and you owe me a residual."

Truthiness

The Jacoby interview returns us to the idea of truthiness, the central concept of the show from which Colbert rarely strays far. "Truthiness" was the focus of "The Word" segment on Colbert's debut program in which he explains that the country is divided between "those who *think* with their heads and those who *know* with their heart." From the start, he insists which side he is on: "Anybody who knows me knows I'm no fan of dictionaries or reference books. They're elitist—constantly telling us what is or isn't true, or what did or didn't happen. Who's Britannica to tell me the Panama

Canal was finished in 1914? If I want to say it happened in 1941, that's my right. I don't trust books. They're all fact and no heart." Constructing a dichotomy between head and heart, fact and opinion, Colbert later brags to O'Reilly—that master of truthiness—that he doesn't "retain anything in books. They're just squiggly lines. They're full of facts. I'm more of an opinion man." Of course in the multilayered world of Colbert, in which his meaning rarely can be found in the literal interpretation of his words, the concept of truthiness functions not as celebration but as critical challenge to those who would disregard fact to preserve belief.

Colbert's nightly performance of truthiness, however, cuts deeper than simply highlighting the privileging of opinion over fact. Rather, the *Report* confronts the wider postmodern deconstruction of the very grammar of fact and the logic of objective inquiry—the "habit of disinterested realism" upon which journalism has long depended.[17] Colbert challenges PBS's Jim Lehrer, perhaps the last great exemplar of the high-modern approach to broadcast journalism, telling him he's "suspicious" of Lehrer because he never yells at his guests. When Colbert asks him if he has a liberal bias, Lehrer voices the high-modern insistence that a true journalist is unbiased and opinion-free, a neutral conduit for information. "But doesn't information itself have a liberal bias?" Colbert asks, rejecting the fundamental premise of journalism—and indeed scientific inquiry itself—that reality exists independent of human perception and can be objectively assessed. He invokes the postmodern argument that objective reality is unknowable and that facts themselves are social constructs, more the products of human institutions and cultural practices than reflective of any a priori reality.[18]

Colbert continues in this vein in his interview with Eli Pariser of the liberal group MoveOn. When Pariser cites opinion polls that find a majority of Americans have turned against the Iraq war, Colbert dismisses the argument. "I don't accept your statistics," he says. "Even if [they're] true, I don't accept them." He then questions the very ontological basis of fact. "A majority of Americans thought Hitler was a great guy," he insists. "That's a fact. I just made up that fact, but that doesn't keep it from being a fact." Colbert problematizes the definition of "fact" itself, rejecting any notion of fact as correspondence between statement and actuality and instead proposing that a fact simply is that which one proclaims it to be.

If Colbert's concept of truthiness intervenes in the cultural debate over the ontological possibility of fact, it more importantly focuses attention on the willful political manipulation of fact. It calls into relief the inherently cynical efforts by some to manufacture political spectacle, or what Jeffrey

Jones has referred to as "believable fictions," those narratives designed not to represent reality but to bolster a political agenda.[19] This is the clear critique in Colbert's response to White House Press Secretary Tony Snow's suggestion that the real problem with the apparently endless occupation of Iraq was that "so far, we have very few visuals that confirm what Americans *want to believe*." In response, Colbert's "Word" that night is simply a smiley face (..). Once again articulating the core critique of truthiness, he endorses Snow's suggestion that "what Americans want to believe is more important than what's actually happening." When a picture of a destroyed mosque appears on screen, he notes that "*this* is *not* what we want to believe." That picture is then replaced by a YouTube video of a kitten falling asleep, and Colbert exclaims, "*This* is." He continues, "How could kittens fall asleep in a world where Iraq is *not* on its way to becoming a democracy?" But Colbert recognizes, as does Tony Snow, that "visuals are not enough." He quotes from Snow again, this time suggesting that what supporters of the Iraq war need is "a surge of new facts," the kind of truthy "facts," Colbert concludes, "that confirm what America wants to believe."

Wikiality

At the core of Colbert's critique of truthiness lies a consistent concern for the politically motivated manufacturing of facts, or at least the perception thereof. As Lance Bennett and his colleagues have noted, for most of its time in power, the Bush administration enacted a "keenly postmodern epistemology" that saw reality as unfixed and malleable and power as a "prism through which facts are filtered and distorted to fit preferred versions of reality."[20] That point underlies truthiness and a second of Colbert's key terms: "wikiality"—the postmodern world in which "we can create a reality we can all agree on." Colbert's notion of wikiality stems from the popularity of the online, user-generated encyclopedia Wikipedia, which he lauds as "the encyclopedia where you can be an authority, even if you don't know what the hell you're talking about." As he says to Wikipedia's creator Jimmy Wales, "What I love about it is it brings democracy to information. For too long, the elite, who study things, got to say what is or isn't real."

Colbert here appears to celebrate the breakdown of a modernist epistemology and the decentering of its institutions of knowledge production. The theorist Michel Foucault reminds us that central to any social epoch, and any discursive formation, is the allocation of epistemic authority—the unequal right, "sanctioned by law or tradition, juridically defined or spontaneously accepted" to speak of what is.[21] In an age of wikiality, the epistemic authorities of modernity—the scientist, the scholar, the journalist—increasingly are objects of suspicion. Instead, as new media scholar Henry Jenkins has noted, epistemic credibility is being relocated among electronically networked kinds of collective intelligence, such as Wikipedia.[22] For Jenkins, this shift contains democratic potential. Jimmy Wales likewise in his interview endorses the web-enabled power of "the community" to transcend traditional top-down epistemic structures.

Jenkins, however, rightly notes that the diffused, horizontal power of any knowledge community is always in tension with the top-down and highly centralized influence exerted by corporations and governmental authorities.[23] For that reason, Colbert's wikiality is a deeply skeptical concept. In the Wales interview, for example, Colbert worries about the susceptibility of "group think" to control and manipulation. Likewise, in his original iteration of the term, he draws close connections to truthiness: "I'm no fan of reality (*It Has A Liberal Bias*), and I'm no fan of encyclopedias (*Just Fat-Ass Dictionaries*). I've said it before, who is Britannica to tell me that George Washington had slaves. If I want to say he didn't, that's my right. And now, thanks to Wikipedia, it's also a fact (*Wikipedia Can Tell A Lie*)." The immediate concern, which Colbert often voices, is the status of truth when statements, however absurd, are echoed with enough frequency and volume that they become accepted as fact. The deeper critique, though, lies with the potential for the willful manipulation of wikiality—the Bush administration's insistence that "we create our own reality."[24] He suggests that the administration was, in the summer of 2006, still on "the cutting edge of information management" and the leading practitioner of wikiality:

> While they've admitted that Saddam did not have weapons of mass destruction, they've also insinuated he did possess weapons of mass destruction (*Have No Yellowcake And Eat It Too*), insinuations that have been repeated over and over again on cable news for the past three and a half years (*24,000 Hour News Cycle*). And now, the result is, eighteen months ago only 36 percent of Americans believed it, but 50 percent of Americans believe it now.

Colbert concludes that "what we're doing is bringing democracy to knowledge (*Definitions Will Greet Us As Liberators*)." But that too is ironic critique—a warning that democracy demands knowledge, and both have become harder to find in an age of truthiness and wikiality.

Jacksquat

At its heart, then, *The Colbert Report* articulates a consistent concern for the vitality of democratic discourse in a postmodern age. The concepts of truthiness and wikiality provide modernist points of agitation against dominant political inclinations to reject objective inquiry and intellectual engagement in favor of hollow political spectacle. As Bennett and his coauthors point out, however, such efforts could never succeed without the media's "culture of compliance" in circulating the narratives of power.[25] That point underlies a third, although lesser known, key term from the Colbert lexicon—"Jacksquat," which he specifically uses to critique the right-wing media's complicity in the Iraq war and their avoidance of accountability as the war dragged on:

> I didn't get where I am today by thinking about anything *(Ignorance Accomplished)*. I got here by feeling about everything. And what I'm feeling about Iraq is angry. I've done everything I could to solve this Iraq problem *(Kept Shopping)*. I have tried saying there isn't a problem ... not reporting the news that could lead one to believe there might a problem ... saying there is a problem, but we've solved it *(The Lie-Fecta)*. Nothing seems to help.

Noting the eventual ineffectiveness of pro-war propaganda to mask reality, Colbert suggests that the next step is to find a scapegoat. "I blame the Iraqi people," he says, "all of them. Just like Papa Bear Bill O'Reilly said to uncle bear Geraldo Rivera ... " Here Colbert's monologue is intercut with a clip from the *Factor*, in which O'Reilly barks at Rivera: "The Iraqis have got to step up and at least try to fight for their democracy, instead of being this crazy country. Shia wants to kill Sunni.... [*throwing his hands up in a gesture of frustration*] I mean, I don't ever want to hear 'Shia' and 'Sunni' again!" Exposing O'Reilly's disinterest in reality and his unwillingness to acknowledge that which does not conform to the narrative, Colbert concludes insightfully: "Nothing I'm saying means anything. For it to mean something, I would have had to have thought about it. And I don't play that game *(Thinking Makes Terrorists Win)*. I and every pundit who have supported this war have the right to stop hearing about it. We've done all we can *(Jacksquat)* ... and that's 'The Word.'"

"Jacksquat" captures the essence of Colbert's critique of mediated political speech. Like the philosopher Harry Frankfurt's notion of "bullshit"—those statements that "avoid, elude, dissuade questions of accurate representation" and obscure the true intentions that lie behind them—so too is much media discourse empty, hollowed out of informational content, vacant of propositional weight. "Jacksquat" suggests that nothing seems to mean anything, that most public speech is simply hot air. All of these—hot air, bullshit, and Colbert's jacksquat—are effects of postmodernity. The "contemporary proliferation" of BS, Frankfurt argues, is inseparable from the "various forms of skepticism which deny that we can have any reliable access to an objective reality, and which therefore reject the possibility of knowing how things truly are. These 'antirealist' doctrines undermine confidence in the value of disinterested efforts to determine what is true and what is false, and even in the intelligibility of the notion of objective inquiry."[26] In the absence of any belief in a coherent or knowable reality, Frankfurt suggests—and Colbert would likely agree—bullshit becomes the primary form of public discourse, and the bullshitter too easily comes to dominate the halls of public power.

A New Kind of Political Art

The Colbert Report thus offers a nightly interrogation of truth and power in a postmodern world. Rich in information and steeped in critical commentary, it embodies the ideals of high-modernism and its belief in the press as a confrontation with power, a searchlight of public accountability. The program functions as a kind of public sphere—another of the ideals of modernity—a discursive arena in which a range of people come to discuss a variety of issues of social and political significance. But of course, the *Report* is by no means a modernist undertaking resembling the nightly news of old. Its democratic conversation, its recurrent concern for the governance of a nation, is always interwoven with a host of other discourses. Colbert is interchangeably silly and banal, gratuitously self-promotional, and at times distinctly surreal.

Shaped by a discursively integrated flow that moves fluidly and unpredictably among contradictory topics and tones, the *Report* has all the markers of postmodernity. Linking a jumble of apparently unrelated signifiers and continuously shifting voices, intonations, and intimations, it looks nothing like public affairs television as previously practiced. Obsessing in fragments and fractures, Colbert himself performs as a spectacle created for the televisual screen—a *simulacrum* or a copy for which no original exists. All too convincingly, he appears to be little more than a linguistic mask and is easily confused, to borrow from the theorist Fredric Jameson, with a kind of postmodern pastiche: superficial and depthless "speech in a dead language" that complicates the efforts to orient oneself in a political landscape in which the real and the imaginary, the true and the false, seem hopelessly conflated.[27]

Colbert flirts with pastiche, but ultimately he avoids the instability of postmodern irony and its debilitating cynicism that plunges us "into a sea of doubt and indeterminancy."[28] He does indeed borrow from what Jameson might call an "abnormal tongue," but that is a modernist discursive technique, one built upon the critical impulse, a faith in the constructive power of satire and the conviction that, despite appearances, some "healthy linguistic normality still exists."[29] Colbert's postmodernism thus is a stylistic play of surfaces, but one that rests on a consistent foundation or ethos. Indeed, his parody pierces the abnormal tongue of Bill O'Reilly and the mouthpieces of the right-wing media machine—those who so readily substitute truthiness for truth, wikiality for reality, and jacksquat for meaning. In contrast Colbert's parody continuously invokes a faith in fact, reason, and democratic accountability—a modernist belief that one *can* say what one means and that democracy ultimately depends on it.

The *Report* thus is deeply political—not just because it is an unlikely source of serious and indeed critical discussion of public affairs. More importantly, it is a critique of and intervention in political culture in a postmodern age. Jameson once wrote that the disorienting nature of postmodernity demanded a new kind of "political art," one that recognized the realities of postmodernism but at the same time could envision "some as yet unimaginable new mode" of representation. The hope was for a political art form that could help us "again begin to grasp our positioning as individual and collective subjects and regain a capacity to act and struggle."[30] If such an agenda once motivated the practice of journalism in the high-modern era, that "real" kind of news has long since melded into a postmodern reality TV. As we have seen, most mainstream media rarely encourage or assist in meaningful political action. Instead, *The Colbert Report*, with its hybrid blend of postmodern style and modernist ideals, sits at the vanguard in the reimagination of a democratically viable form of television.

8

♦ ♦ ♦

NETWORKED NEWS

STEWART, COLBERT, AND THE NEW PUBLIC SPHERE

In the midst of their lengthy run for the presidency, Barack Obama, Hillary Clinton, and the other Democratic presidential hopefuls gathered for yet another national debate. This one, however, provided a clear indication we had entered the post-network age. Broadcast by CNN—the cable news network that itself was once new media challenging the old guard—the questions came in the form of video clips ordinary citizens had uploaded onto the truly new and wildly popular website YouTube. The debate was an experiment in convergence, an attempt to blend the populist accessibility of the Internet with the institutional power of CNN. David Bohrman, CNN's executive producer, celebrated the debate. He said it was democratizing the national political conversation, giving the public "a seat at the table." The critics, though, lamented that many of the questions were silly and trivial, hardly the stuff of serous journalism, and ultimately demeaning, they said, to the national discourse. Even as he touted the debate's democratic potential, Bohrman himself acknowledged that the most popular questions, at least on YouTube, were the ones asking if Arnold Schwarzenegger really was a cyborg sent to save planet Earth and whether the candidates would convene a national meeting to discuss UFOs.[1]

That kind of apolitical banality seemed very much on display on YouTube a few months earlier, when one of the more popular clips was a "user-generated" music video entitled "Late Night Special," in which four young men ostensibly demonstrated their sexual technique by taking turns humping a piece of living-room furniture. The irony that YouTube could both circulate such videos and become a central site for presidential politics was not lost on *The Daily Show*, where John Oliver parodied the whole affair. "If YouTube *is* the future of political discourse," he suggested, "perhaps it's time to embrace it." That provided the lead-in to his own mock debate video, set in a living room identical to the one in the "Late Night Special" piece. There, Oliver and three other *Daily Show* correspondents, dressed in their usual suits and ties, also taking turns gyrating on top of an ottoman, while asking political questions. "Yo yo, this is your boy, Double J," proclaims Jason Jones, stepping into the frame. "Check it!" He dives onto the ottoman and, with his hips pumping, turns to the camera and says, "*Oooh*, do you think Barack Obama has enough foreign policy experience [for] the presidency?" Samantha Bee follows: "Yo yo, this is your girl Juicy Fruit. I'm about to get buck wild!" She too starts humping the ottoman and breathlessly asks, "If you are elected ... what will be your strategy for extricating us from Iraq?"

Oliver suggests that it might be time for mainstream political media to "embrace" YouTube, but his parody reflects the general sense that the shift of political discourse into the ungovernable realm of cyberspace was indeed demeaning the national political conversation, hopelessly blending the popular and the political, the trivial and the serious, the inane and the significant. That, of course, is itself ironic. As we've seen, *The Daily Show* has been at the forefront in melding news and entertainment and politics and comedy in ways that provide a much-needed corrective to the kind of political discourse on which the mainstream media usually insist. *The Daily Show*'s rise to political prominence itself has been enabled by the same broad transformations in communication technologies, media industries, and audience practices—what Henry Jenkins has called "convergence culture"—that also have allowed for the emergence of YouTube and its brief partnership with CNN.

The CNN-YouTube debate, Jenkins suggests, was one "attempt to work through the still unstable and 'untried' relations" between different media systems—old and new, professional and amateur—and the kinds of political discourses they produce.[2] So too can *The Daily Show* and *The Colbert Report* be understood as experiments in convergence. Exploring the borderlands between discursive domains, they also increasingly sit at the intersection of television and the Internet, accessible both on the TV screen and through Wi-Fi–enabled laptops, iPods, and cell phones. Migrating into an online environment, they are bridging the continuously decreasing divide between media technologies and forms. In so doing, they are challenging the ways we think about news content, its distribution patterns, and its relationship to its audience. In this chapter I explore that migration, following *The Daily Show* and *Colbert* into an emerging media landscape marked by the tension between the vertical dissemination of news, opinion, and entertainment and the horizontal production and circulation of information, argument, and what the theorist Manuel Castells has called "cultural code."[3]

Digital Content

At the least, a U.S. audience no longer even needs a television to watch *The Daily Show* and *The Colbert Report.* As the number of households equipped with broadband Internet continues to rise and the technological capabilities to host and stream high-resolution video continue to improve, traditional media companies are rushing to make more and more full-length programs accessible through the Internet. Thus Comedy Central streams full episodes of the two shows through its website and also has made them available at Hulu.com, a convergence partnership between old media giants NBC Universal and Rupert Murdoch's News Corp. For Comedy Central, the strategy is a kind of multiplexing—the near-simultaneous distribution of programming through a variety of media platforms intended to attract niche audiences and develop ancillary revenue streams.[4] One of the results is the shift toward on-demand viewing, the severing of the television program itself from previous institutional structures that long dictated what kinds of programs people could watch and when they could watch them.

There is, however, something more complex going on than the simple transferring of shows from one medium to another and the concomitant challenges that poses to an older concept of programming. Instead, as the television scholar John Caldwell has described, the program itself is being reconceptualized as content, no longer a linear, bounded artifact, but a divisible data stream of image, text, and sound. Caldwell argues that in the nonlinear environment of the Internet, with its proclivity toward cutting and pasting, television content is being repurposed—that is, segmented, abridged, appended, or otherwise reassembled into different distribution cont

Caldwell notes that television dramas and other forms of narrative-based fiction largely resist this kind of segmentation. The newscast, however, with its inherently segmented internal format and its emphasis on isolated sound bites and images, has readily lent itself to repurposing. Not coincidentally, NBC News helped pioneer the concept, repurposing its flagship *Nightly News* for twenty-four-hour cable (including MSNBC and CNBC) and the Internet (MSNBC.com). Thus NBC's Brian Williams appears on network television in a half-hour program each night, but around the Internet "bits and pieces" of him "now show up in the form of migratory texts customized and endlessly individuated as e-content."[5]

The Daily Show and *Colbert* likewise provide a convenient fit for the multiplatform strategy of repurposing. Like the news and opinion programs they mimic, both shows are comprised of individual content segments generally ranging in length from thirty seconds to seven minutes. At times various segments reference one another, but most are self-contained, able to retain their coherence apart from the program in which they originally appear. And all of these individual segments are available now through the shows' websites, where one can view any clip from the past week's shows, in any order. After that, every clip, past and present, is housed in a publicly accessible archive, searchable by date, interview guest, or any combination of name or keyword. The clip archive also is indexed by the site producers. Each segment is "tagged" with a number of keywords—clickable content categories that link to every other clip dealing with the same topic. Thus it was possible during Campaign 2008 to find every one of Jon Stewart's thirteen interviews with John McCain or to watch any of the hundreds of *Daily Show* clips discussing the war in Iraq. With that, the television show has morphed into an unlikely database of political humor, criticism, and conversation, a collection of rhetorical artifacts that extends and expands the show's discursive reach. Segments that in their initial context of daily television quickly would have faded from public view instead now remain continuously viewable and, in some instances, continually viewed.

Take, for example, Colbert's intriguing discussion of the U.S. government's terrorist watch list, broadcast in May 2008. There he reports on a *USA Today* story revealing that the list of people the government has deemed potential threats to national security had burgeoned to contain more than 750,000 names. Hoping that the list "will soon hit our goal of . . . *everybody*," Colbert notes that one of the people on the list is Nobel Peace Prize winner Nelson Mandela. Pointing out the inherent absurdity, Colbert explains that Mandela is on the list because his African National Congress had been labeled a terrorist group in the 1980s by the apartheid government of South Africa it was fighting against. From there, Colbert segues into a discussion of his "favorite suspected terrorist," the artist Hasan Elahi, a U.S. citizen born in Bangladesh who was wrongly detained by the FBI in 2002. Colbert explains that despite the fact that Elahi was innocent, the FBI still insisted he give them periodic updates of his whereabouts. In response, Elahi began continuously reporting on himself, creating a website containing a satellite map tracking his every move and thousands of photographs documenting the most mundane aspects of his daily life. Elahi, of course, then appears on set with Colbert, where he recounts his run-in with the government and discusses his web-based political project—an artistic form of technologically enabled cyberactivism.

The segment is a powerful moment of television, a critical interrogation of the threat the "war on terror" may pose to civil rights. It is also intellectual TV, with Elahi and Colbert engaging in an esoteric discussion of secrecy, surveillance, and national security. The contrast between this segment and most of what passes for contemporary public affairs television is remarkable. But like all moments of television, in its original form the Elahi interview is ephemeral, here and gone in seven minutes, with Elahi unlikely to appear on other public affairs shows. The transient nature of television ultimately limits its effectiveness as a means of political information and public debate. Online, however, the clip takes on a greater sense of permanence. Several months after its original airing, the clip had been viewed more than 53,000 times, a number that continues to increase with each passing month.

In comparison to the 1 million that watch Colbert on TV (or the 11 million that still watch Brian Williams each night), 53,000 seems a trivial number. But as the scholar Yochai Benkler argues, the driving engine in new media is not so much mass appeal, but rather deep engagement among a narrow and highly committed subset of people.[6] For them, the Elahi interview and Colbert's critique of the terrorist watch list remains relevant and worth attending to. Further, the interview is placed within a hypertextual context that facilitates linkages to wider networks of information and conversation. On the *Colbert* website, one could find the Elahi segment accompanied by a number of links, including ones to the original *USA Today* story that Colbert referenced, the African National Congress's homepage, the Wikipedia entry on the INS, and the homepage for the FBI's Terrorist Screening Data Base. Elahi's website, of course, also was linked, as was an article about him in *Wired* magazine and a blog posting that taps into an ongoing conversation about Elahi's project and the wider issue of "surveillance society." What begins on television, therefore, as a bit of critical comment and a moment of public exposure for Elahi becomes on the Internet a node within a wider network of information and discussion, one an interested audience can use as a launching point for deeper exploration.

Participatory Culture

Underlying this repurposing of content is a profound reconceptualization of the audience. The television business, in both its entertaining and its informational forms, has long seen the audience as passive receptors of content that itself is assumed to follow a unidirectional path, from a single sender to potentially infinite receivers. Perhaps no image better captures this dynamic than the closing shot the NBC *Nightly News* once used of anchor Tom Brokaw, his image projected onto the giant screen overlooking Manhattan's Times Square, while the voiceless masses toiled below. In the new media environment, however, the viewer has been transformed into the user, an active individual not only seeking out what he or she is interested in but treating the content more as a resource to be worked with than as a product to be passively consumed. Proponents of "active audience" theory such as John Fiske have long argued that audiences are never as passive as media producers traditionally have assumed. But the kind of activity Fiske and others have imagined has remained at the level of interpretation, the accepting or rejecting of a text's dominant meaning. By contrast, Benkler and others rightly argue that the web and digital media are truly enabling the emergence of the user as a "new category of relationship to information production and exchange."[7]

Central to that new relationship is a sense of active, and often public, engagement with media. Both *The Daily Show* and *The Colbert Report* cultivate a notion of active audience, demonstrated in part by the live studio audience that attends the taping of the television programs. There the audience plays a role in the program, often through laughter and applause but also in a more critical sense, through a range of vocal reactions that affirm or challenge the show's discursive content. Colbert in particular has opened unprecedented spaces for audience engagement, suggesting that he sees the audience as a central character in the "scene I'm playing." Regularly he calls on his audience, inviting them into the Colbert Nation, where he asks them not only to applaud on cue but to take action in the real world, altering Wikipedia entries, voting for him in various online contests, and spreading his "wriststrong" bracelets. The website ColbertNation in particular is built around the concept of audience participation. Alongside its professionally produced content is a great deal of user-posted material, ranging from discussions on the site's "Col-Board," to photographs taken or doctored by fans, to audience-submitted links to related media content. Here the audience functions not necessarily as a "nation" but certainly as an online community, one whose members see themselves as contributors to an ongoing media project. In their research on Colbert fandom, Catherine Burwell and Megan Boler note that fans regularly speak of a sense of "empowerment"—as one suggested, "other fandoms are just passively running alongside the limos of their objects of fanship; we're doing a tango with ours."[8]

At times, the Colbert audience also functions as cocreators of content. In 2006, for example, Colbert launched his first "greenscreen challenge," in which show producers posted video on the website, inviting the audience to download it and edit anything they chose into the background. All of the entries in that contest were posted online, and some were aired on the show. During Campaign '08, Colbert began a new, explicitly political greenscreen challenge in response to John McCain's less-than-inspiring speech the night Barack Obama claimed the Democratic presidential nomination. Seizing on the fact that McCain delivered the speech in front of an unflattering green background, the *Colbert* producers posted video of it online and invited the audience to "make McCain exciting." That inspired a wealth of audience creativity, including one video entitled "Mad McCain" that melded McCain's speech with the animated opening of the Emmy-winning television drama *Mad Men*. There McCain's speech is interwoven with images of an office breaking apart and a suit-clad body, now adorned with McCain's head, slowly falling from a skyscraper. While the show's somber theme music plays, McCain's voice rhythmically proclaims: "Job loss, failing schools, prohibitively expensive health care, pensions at risk, entitlement programs approaching bankruptcy, rising gas and food prices, to name a few. But your government often acts as if it is completely unaware of the changes and hardships in your lives. And when your government does take notice, often it only makes matters worse." As the heavy beats of the theme music fade out, the final shot cuts to an ironic image of a campaign sign: "McCain '08."

Colbert's "Project Make McCain Exciting" exemplifies the move toward a participatory culture, one in which audiences qua users continuously shift between postures of consumption and production. Technological development has democratized the video production process, which is no longer the sole province of a few capital-rich corporate players but a communicative form open to a great number of people. In such an environment, some people may remain in the passive position of spectator that the television industry has long carved for them, but increasing numbers of people are coming to see the realm of cultural production as open and accessible. In turn, media products, and especially those in the domain of opinion and information, are being reconceptualized less as finished goods and more as open-ended processes.

"Project Make McCain Exciting" likewise opens novel terrain for political engagement. It highlights a set of tactics that Henry Jenkins has described as "photoshop for democracy"—the manipulation and recirculation of popularly available images and video resources. Jenkins rightly suggests that in an age of convergence, such photo or video montages have become legitimate rhetorical resources, their construction and dissemination increasingly important means by which amateurs can inject "images and thoughts into the political process."[9] Jenkins argues that *The Daily Show* provides its audience with models of how to construct critical texts. More than just inspiration, however, in this instance *Colbert* facilitates the remixing of political imagery and enhances its circulation, further blurring the boundaries between the professional world of television production and the web-based domain of user-generated content.

Reappropriation

The audience equally has come to function as a key circuit in the distribution of show material. After several years of fighting unauthorized peer-to-peer sharing of its content, Comedy Central now encourages it, providing a variety of tools that allow users to easily e-mail clips, embed them on their own websites, or post them to social networking and content aggregation sites. By facilitating file sharing, *The Daily Show* and *Colbert* have become more fully integrated into a new media landscape marked by the horizontal, networked exchange of image, video, music, and text. Indeed, analysts have noted that peer-to-peer sharing comprises more than 50 percent of all Internet traffic worldwide, and more than 60 percent of the content being shared is video.[10] By the 2008 election, the sharing of videos had become interwoven with the political domain, with an increasing number of people engaging with politics through e-mail, social networking sites, and online videos.[11]

Comedy Central's support for peer-to-peer sharing is not without irony. Its parent company, Viacom, has been fighting Google, parent company of

YouTube, in federal court. Accusing YouTube of copyright infringement for allowing the posting of Viacom-owned content, the company has been demanding more than $1 billion in damages. Early in its lawsuit, Viacom executives specifically cited the uploading of *Daily Show* and *Colbert* clips as a major source of concern, insisting that at least in one instance—a Jon Stewart interview with Bill Gates—a single clip had been viewed on YouTube as many as 500,000 times. Viacom executives admit they get a certain amount of promotional value from their material appearing on YouTube but claim they are losing millions of dollars in potential revenue.[12]

The real significance of sharing, however, lies deeper than questions of corporate revenue streams. At the heart of convergence culture is the restructuring of the relationship between media and their audience. The one-way flow of content from centralized media producers to isolated receivers is being complicated by more complex processes of production and exchange from corporate media but also among users empowered by Photoshop, video-editing software, and the social-networking infrastructure of the Internet. To increasing numbers of people, corporate media products are resources to be reappropriated: reedited, recontextualized, and recirculated among an emergent public sphere. For scholars such as Yochai Benkler, the Internet enables "citizens to participate in public conversations continuously and pervasively," not as passive recipients of closed content but as active participants in an ongoing process of social and political exploration.[13]

New media scholar Clay Shirky makes a similar point in an interview on *The Colbert Report*, arguing that the Internet gives voice to people who long lacked access to a public platform. Ever the narcissist, Colbert agrees with Shirky even as he seems to miss the point. Celebrating the power of new media, Colbert proclaims that *he* has given the people a platform—"*I* have given them a voice," he proclaims, "in the form of my voice." Colbert's joke, obviously made tongue-in-cheek, does however capture one of the central elements of convergence culture. He may not exactly speak for "the nation," but his voice—and Jon Stewart's—have become discursive resources, raw materials to be reappropriated in a new kind of public sphere.

To explore this phenomenon in greater depth, in the rest of this chapter I work through a case study of one segment from *The Daily Show*—an interview with CBS News reporter Lara Logan—and the ways it rippled around the Internet, recirculated and reappropriated by a range of organizations and individuals. Logan appeared on the show on June 17, 2008, an interview that at first seemed as if it would unfold like many of Stewart's conversations with TV news personalities: jocular and good-natured, but only lightly touching on substantive matters. "You remind me of a young Ted Koppel," Stewart tells her, highlighting the obvious differences between Koppel and the blonde native of South Africa who worked as a swimsuit model before becoming CBS's primary war correspondent. "That's what Dan Rather always told me," Logan jokes in response.

Underlying the humor, however, is a serious comparison between Logan and the high-modern journalism that, for Jon Stewart at least, Koppel still represents. And it is in that posture—as the journalist committed to public information—that Logan speaks for the rest of the interview. She offers a remarkably critical take on her network, and indeed her profession, arguing in no uncertain terms that the U.S. news media have left the American people largely ignorant of the realities of the wars in Iraq and Afghanistan. Explaining that she has to fight with her own editors to get informative stories on the air, she bemoans the quality of U.S. news, suggesting that if she herself had "to watch the news that you hear in the United States, I would just blow my brains out because it would drive me nuts." To that, the audience bursts into applause, loudly endorsing Logan's criticism of the media. Noting that that very day fifty-one Iraqis had died in a car bombing but that the story got little coverage in the United States, Stewart then asks her, "Are we numb? Have we lost our humanity with this entire situation?" In a voice thick with sorrow, Logan answers:

> Yeah, we have. I was asked once, "Do you feel responsible for the American public having a bad view, a negative view of the war in Iraq?" and I looked at the reporter, and I said, "Tell me the last time you saw the body of a dead American solider. What does that look like? Who in America knows what that looks like?" Because I know what that looks like, and I feel responsible for the fact that no one else does. That's what I feel responsible for, because no one really understands. And the soldiers do feel forgotten—they do. No doubt, from Afghanistan to Iraq, they absolutely do.

Offering a scalding critique of American journalism, the Logan interview stands in marked contrast to the kind of light-on-issues celebrity gabfest that NBC anchor Brian Williams indulges in when he visits the show. And unlike Williams's benign self-promotional chit-chat, the Logan interview reverberated online. At the time of this writing, the interview had been viewed nearly 75,000 times on *The Daily Show*'s website. That number, however, does not take into account the circulation of the Logan interview across hundreds of other websites. A Google search for the terms

"Lara Logan" and "*The Daily Show*" conducted a few weeks after the original airing of the program returned more than 3,000 results, a vast range of websites that re-presented, recontextualized, and even reedited the Logan interview in pursuit of a variety of agendas.

Mainstream Press

One website that made no mention of Lara Logan's interview was, not surprisingly, cbsnews.com. There her criticisms undoubtedly hit too close to home. One could, however, read all about it on the *New York Times* website. The *Times* used the interview as a launching point for a wider examination of Logan's charge that network newscasts were no longer interested in stories about war. Accompanied by a photograph of Logan and Stewart on the set of *The Daily Show,* the June 23 article "Reporters Say Networks Put Wars on Back Burner" quotes heavily from Logan's appearance. The piece then provides empirical data tracking the decline in airtime the networks devoted to war stories, and interviews with news personnel who largely support Logan's contentions. Among those is a second interview with Logan, which the reporter labels as a "follow-up"—follow-up, that is, from her *Daily Show* interview. In a remarkable inversion from the age in which the *Times* served as the central gatekeeper managing the flow of information into the public arena, the *Times* in this case draws its inspiration from *The Daily Show*—the "fake news" has become a primary source of newsworthy material. In turn, the *Times* amplifies and elaborates on *Daily Show* content, an indication of the complexity of contemporary pubic discourse, of the overlapping flow of voices among which *The Daily Show*'s has become increasingly salient.

If for the *Times* the Logan interview provides the impetus for investigation, for that other New York newspaper—Rupert Murdoch's *New York Post*—it amounts to a political threat, a challenge to the corporate media's refusal to interrogate the status quo. On its website, the *Post* provides its readers with a link to the interview, but, notably, the accompanying article has nothing to do with coverage of the war—or Logan's interview. Instead, under the headline "News Babe's 'Iraqi Tryst': In-Bedded Reporter 'Took My Hubby,'" the piece attacks Logan, placing her at the center of a months-old sex scandal. "Sexy CBS siren Lara Logan spent her days covering the heat of the Iraq war," reads the lead sentence, "but that was nothing compared to the heat of her nights." Shifting focus away from her accusations to her sexuality, the *Post* then provides a link to a gallery of photographs of Logan, including ones of her in cleavage-bearing evening wear, as well as to an online poll where readers could "vote for the hottest news babe." The *Post*'s sexually saturated response to Logan amounts to a barely disguised political counterpunch, one intended to impugn her credibility and implicitly undermine her criticism. At least one reader comment added to the *Post* site suggests the effort was successful. "This chick must have been trained at the NY Times," it reads. "Go back to bathing suit modeling Lara.... The only tough question you'll get then is 'Saline or silicone?'"

Activist Media

For both the *Times* and the *Post*, *The Daily Show* functions as political terrain, a discursive locale that demands monitoring and, at times, response. For a host of activist organizations, however, the Logan interview provided a resource to advance their explicit political agendas. Several media activist groups, for example, seized on the interview to further their goal of countering the corporate media. Like the *Times*, the satellite channel Link TV used it as the launching point for examining war coverage on U.S. television. As part of its web-based segment "Global Pulse," which compares and contrasts news coverage from around the world, Link edited segments of Logan's appearance into an original four-and-a-half-minute video entitled "War Isn't News Anymore." The piece interweaves sound bites from Logan's interview with a summary of the *Times* article and a sampling of the wider "whirlwind" of media reaction to the interview. Like *The Daily Show* itself, Link TV can be understood as a kind of "second-tier media," an alternative source of information and commentary whose purpose largely is to critique and correct the "first tier" of mainstream news.[14]

In this case, Link reworks existent media content to produce an original statement, one that recycles and repositions Logan's criticisms of network news. One sees something similar from the web-based alternative journalism project called "The Real News Network." Developed by a former Canadian Broadcasting Corporation journalist, Real News produces what it describes as "independent and uncompromising" video news and documentary—real news, it suggests, in comparison to so much of the fake news available on corporate TV. The group's efforts are informed by an extensive international advisory committee that includes, among many others, former CBS reporter Tom Fenton, who like Logan has appeared on *The Daily Show* bemoaning the quality of network news; Amy Goodman, whose program *Democracy*

Now! airs on Link TV and whose interview on *The Colbert Report* we considered in chapter 7; and John Nichols, the journalist and activist who helped create the media reform organization Free Press. Like Link TV, Real News edited segments from the Logan interview into a video commentary narrated by Brazilian journalist Pepe Escobar entitled "Iraq Story Buried by U.S. Networks." Using the powerful sound bite from Logan in which she worries that the networks were ignoring American casualties, Escobar elaborates on other blind spots of mainstream war coverage, such as the number of Iraqis killed or driven from their homes. He then concludes that Lara Logan "got it right," a claim immediately followed by the clip of her saying that if she had to watch U.S. news, she would "blow my brains out, because it would drive me crazy."

Both Link TV and Real News function similarly to what new media scholar Jodi Dean and her colleagues have referred to as "dot.orgs"—nongovernmental and often global organizations that are using the web to engage in a new kind of "civil society politics."[15] Another of these is the Free Press, spearheaded in part by Nichols and critical media scholar Robert McChesney. Fighting for public-information journalism and against the consolidation of media ownership, Free Press utilized the Logan interview in a variety of ways. On its website, it produced a multimedia report on the interview posted under the headline "*Daily Show* Slams Big Media's Version of Journalism." Arguing that Logan "highlighted the seriousness of the problems with American news coverage," Free Press draws connections between Logan's comments and the recent revelation that the Pentagon had employed retired generals to seed news media with pro-war propaganda. The full clip of the Logan interview is embedded on the page, and, along with it, one finds links both to the original *New York Times* reporting on the Pentagon scandal and to Free Press's extended discussion of the matter. Here the Logan interview is recontextualized, no longer simply one reporter's frustration but evidence of the much larger problem of the manipulation of public information. The piece then concludes with a call to action. "We can make a difference to stop the media from spreading misinformation, rumors and government and corporate propaganda," it reads, directing viewers to a page through which they can send a letter to Congress demanding an investigation into the "selling of the war." That is accompanied by a link to another Free Press video about the Pentagon's propaganda campaign, which also incorporates clips from *The Daily Show*. All of this is housed on the Free Press website under the category "Get Involved."

YouTube

Weaving the Logan interview into a grassroots political action campaign, Free Press also used it as a vehicle to increase its own exposure, editing a brief highlight video of Logan's comments and posting the clip on YouTube. Titling the piece "CBS News Correspondent: 'I'd Blow My Brains Out,'" the segment includes both that quote and her longer statement of regret that few people have seen "the body of a dead American soldier." At the time of this writing, the Free Press video had been viewed on YouTube more than 240,000 times. There, the clip also comes with a link directing viewers to Free Press's YouTube "channel," a page where one can find information about the organization, a link to its homepage, and dozens of other Free Press videos. Both Real News and Link TV also maintain channels on YouTube, where the Real News piece had been viewed nearly 30,000 times and the Global Pulse segment some 1,200.

Despite Viacom's efforts to keep its content off YouTube, bits and pieces of *The Daily Show* thus appear in multiple places, incorporated into alternative forms of public information and commentary. This reflects not only the utility of *Daily Show* content but also the increasing viability of YouTube as a platform for political discourse. Despite the common assumption that YouTube largely is a location for banal amusement and distraction—for videos of young men humping furniture—researchers find that a great deal of traffic on the site revolves around politics and current events. Videos offering information and opinion make up nearly a quarter of the most-viewed clips on YouTube and together comprise the second largest category of videos listed as "most favorite" by so-called YouTubers.[16]

More than just an alternative content distribution network, YouTube also functions as an extended online community, a virtual location for social networking, conversation, and political debate.[17] Users can post comments in response to videos and to one another. The Free Press video, for example, generated more than 1,200 comments, an exchange that continued to build months after the video was first posted. Much of that, unfortunately, is the kind of uncivil right versus left ranting that is all too common online, and several of the comments offer either anti-Semitic dismissals of *The Daily Show* or crudely juvenile commentary on Logan's sexual attractiveness. A number of them, however, engage in thoughtful arguments about the Iraq war and the nature of U.S. news media. One strand discusses whether Logan's comments violate her responsibility to remain objective, while others echo her central point that television news is failing to offer an accurate picture of the two wars. Says one user, "The news we watch in the US is what is called 'nationalistic.' We tend to always make the US look good while making other countries look bad. That's what happens when we have multi-billion dollar news corporations running our media. Also, our primary source for news from 'official sources' are always from government officials. There is too much room allowed for news to be manipulated unfortunately." Another responds that the interview was "excellent": "Jon Stewart's 'fake news' is so much more interesting than the endless cable pundit babble on who's up or down in the polls, and, unfortunately, it's often more informative than the network news, which dumbs down, oversimplifies, and underreports stories in order to have more time to sell prescription drugs and laxatives." A third simply concludes that "Its [*sic*] a sad testament to our society that a spoof talk show is the venue for real discussion of Iraq."

If the Logan interview, or more specifically the various YouTube videos covering it, provokes a wide-ranging discussion about politics, war, and media, it also inspires several people to respond by posting their own videos. The Real News segment, for example, received seven video responses. Those include a clip from an interview with Noam Chomsky about the historical significance of 9/11 and a lengthy video of a young man talking about allegations of government corruption involving Halliburton subsidiary KBR's work in Iraq. That piece was posted by a twenty-year-old user named Kyle, who calls his channel "seculartalk" and describes it as "refreshingly real liberal talk and news commentary." There, one finds several videos of Kyle discussing politics and current events, along with a number of clips he draws from various mainstream media sources. His response to the Real News video illustrates the convergence of consumption and production—the emergence of the "prosumer" or what new media scholar Axel Bruns calls the "produser," the "netizen" who is simultaneously audience for and cocontributor to the digitally networked sphere of news and public affairs media.[18]

Collaborative News

In following the Logan interview, what begins to come into focus is a multileveled network of information, conversation, and advocacy, a new kind of public sphere characterized by a markedly different shape than the mass media–dominated one of a slightly earlier era. Yochai Benkler has described an ongoing shift away from the unidirectional "hub-and-spoke architecture" of the mass media and toward a "distributed architecture with multidirectional connections among all its nodes," an alternative arena of information and cultural production based on "emergent patterns of cooperation and sharing" as well as "simple coordinate coexistence" of an immense variety of content producers. Benkler argues that within the potentially chaotic topology of the Internet, a number of high-visibility nodes provide relatively centralized points of access and "generate a common set of themes, concerns, and public knowledge" around which a coherent public sphere can take shape.[19]

The Huffington Post, for example, which the blog aggregator Technorati ranks as the most "linked-to" political blog on the Internet, plays a central role in the circulation of the Logan interview. Less than twenty-four hours after its original broadcast, the interview appeared there, the full clip embedded on a page entitled "CBS's Lara Logan Slams American Coverage of Iraq War." In addition to calling particular attention to Logan's "body of a dead American soldier" comment, the Huffington Post provides space for user comments, which within a few days had totaled more than three hundred. The Huffington Post itself is interwoven with a wide range of other sources of information and argument. The Free Press, for example, links directly to the Huffington Post page about the Logan interview. The following week, the Huffington Post covers the *New York Times* article, linking both to the *Times* website and to other related blog posts. Link TV's Global Pulse video quotes from that Huffington Post page, while the *Times* returns the favor, directing its readers to the Huffington Post through a link entitled "reactions from around the web." If the Huffington Post's content ripples outward, it is important to note that the flow is multidirectional—the site first picked up the Logan story from Think Progress, the blog produced by the Center for American Progress. Think Progress posted the clip of the Logan interview at ten AM following its original airing, linking it to articles from both the *New York Times* and the *Washington Post* detailing the government's efforts to prevent media coverage of U.S. military fatalities.

Together, sites such as Huffington Post and Think Progress perform a complex process of "observing, analyzing, and creating political salience for matters of public interest"—the kind of discursive work that used to be the sole province of the mainstream and capital-rich media.[20] In the new, networked public sphere, this process is increasingly decentralized. Although the superstar sites do play an inordinate role in shaping the contours of public discussion, many of them allow otherwise unaffiliated people to post their own material. Such was the case with the high-profile progressive blog DailyKos, where site users can maintain "diaries" through which they can circulate almost anything of importance to them. The Logan interview in particular was posted by a user operating under the pseudonym "Omar Little." Titling his diary entry "*The Daily Show*: The BEST Interview in Ages," Little writes that Logan's "candor and commitment to substantive journalism is simply amazing and I found myself nodding my head in agreement and saying 'amen' to much of what she said." He then invites his readers to watch the embedded clip and "chime in with thoughts/opinions." Here DailyKos engages in what Axel Bruns has called collaborative news production—not necessarily generating original reporting, but promoting items and issues that a multitude of contributors feel demand wider consideration.[21]

Small Blogs

In addition to appearing on the high-visibility sites, the Logan interview circulated around the web through dozens of scattered individual blogs, many of which are the work of single people. Internet scholars have for some time noted that the vast majority of blogs are small—little more than contemporary versions of individual home pages, appealing at most to highly localized clusters of readers. On this most horizontal, decentralized of levels, the reappropriation of the Logan interview serves a rather different function than it does on the big-group political blogs. If those aim to raise widespread public awareness and influence national politics, for the small blogs the Logan interview becomes more a means of self-expression and, in turn, personal empowerment.

Buckley McCann, for example, a twenty-nine-year-old from Indiana, writes a blog he calls "Swinging on Birches." There he explains that his blog is a "place for me to post my writings—creative, essays, reviews, and other personal stuff." That "personal stuff" includes photographs of him and his mother from their visit to local gardens and the Logan interview, which he posted the day after it aired. Blending the personal and the public, the affective and the rational, McCann embeds the full clip and offers brief commentary. "She's got integrity, grit," he writes, "and she's fighting for truth in reporting on the wars in Iraq and Afghanistan." He then encourages his readers to "watch and enjoy. Good stuff."

The sense that the Logan interview is "good stuff" equally appears to motivate a thirty-eight-year-old woman from Pennsylvania, who works under the username "cruzich" and writes a blog she calls "Dilletante's Dilemma." Along with her blog, she also maintains pages on a variety of social networking sites. On Flicker, one can find pictures of her house and family, on Last FM her favorite songs, on YouTube her favorite videos, and on her blog a detailed description of her latest career move, as well as her thoughts about the Logan interview. She posts the full clip and explains that she has become "a member of the cult of Lara Logan" since Logan's appearance on *The Daily Show.* She continues: "Candor from a MSM correspondent, anger, and a desire to get the real story out to the American people, with a feeling that if she doesn't she's failing us. Pretty damned impressive. I would also be remiss if I didn't mention her hotness." There is a clear sense of play here. For Cruzich, Logan is both impressive and "hot" (a sentiment that runs throughout the comments on most blogs), and circulating the interview is an expression of personal taste. Here personal affect is not necessarily distinct from public politics—in an age of discursive integration, the lines between fandom and citizenship become increasingly difficult to distinguish.

For other writers of small blogs, reappropriating the Logan interview becomes an attempt at citizen action on the most local of levels. A South Carolina woman named Vickie Whitaker, for example, posts a link to the Logan interview on her blog "Life with Ruffles." She then writes a powerfully emotional response to Logan's concern that the troops have been forgotten. She frames the issue in explicitly personal terms, explaining that she and her family deeply care about the troops. "I care. Bill cares. Kenna cares. Riley cares," she writes. "*We do care. We care* that you are coming home to a broken country when you thought you would save us. *We care* that you are coming home to substandard medical care. *We care* that you have witnessed horrors that you will never be able to speak of because we cannot understand. *We care* that you are in a war that was started for a lie." Interweaving the personal and the emotional with the public and political, she then explains that she hopes that her calling attention to the Logan interview, and indeed her blog more broadly, might help make a difference in a situation she fears is hopeless:

> *We have tried* to make ourselves heard. The bubble that surrounds the current administration has effectively rendered any of our protests mute. I live in South Carolina, a staunch Republican state. Though people in this state are now as disgusted with Bush and our government as I am, they are determined to protect the status quo—even if it means another four years of Bush-like government. I have exhausted every avenue that is open to me to no avail. One of the primary reasons I started a journal was because I was in danger of imploding from frustration with our current government.... *I care*, but our government doesn't.

For Vickie Whitaker, the ability to post this one clip from *The Daily Show* for the few people who might read her blog is an explicit act of rhetorical citizenship, an effort to make herself heard in a political environment that would otherwise render her mute. She illustrates the potential of a convergent media landscape that affords unprecedented methods and opportunities for political voice. That brings us back to Stephen Colbert's suggestion that he has given people voice—in the form of *his* voice. For Vickie Whitaker, that is no joke. Empowered by media technologies that allow her to produce and not simply consume media texts, she is able to harness *The Daily Show* and turn it into a rhetorical resource—a discursive tool that she can use to create a new form of public voice.

Putting the "Public" in Public Affairs

Jon Stewart's interview with Lara Logan exemplifies the remarkable contribution *The Daily Show* and *The Colbert Report* are making to television news—their critical interrogation of public communication and their regular airing of alternative voices and views. Unfortunately, there is little evidence that Logan's appearance did much to change the way the mainstream media report on war. In fact, shortly after the interview Logan was pulled out of the Middle East and reassigned to Washington, ostensibly a promotion to "chief foreign affairs correspondent." That may have been some form of retribution for her harsh words, or it could have been symptomatic of the news media's increasing disinterest in Iraq and Afghanistan. Online, however, the interview produced a far different result. There it rapidly spread through a complex network of information and exchange, fueling an integrated, multilayered discourse about real news, fake news, war, and politics that continued to develop for months afterwards.

As *The Daily Show* and *The Colbert Report* migrate into a networked environment, they are able to take advantage of an alternative distribution system through which their content spreads in more organic and longer-lasting ways than it could through commercial television. At the same time, they are intertwining with an emerging ecosystem of news and informational media, one in which enthusiastic, technologically enabled audiences are both circulating and reappropriating professionally produced public affairs media. The result is the creation of new and hybrid forms of public voice—professional and amateur, consumer and activist, corporate and citizen—that speak on behalf of a far wider variety of personal, organizational, and institutional agendas that one could find in the corporate media. In this new media environment, *The Daily Show* and *Colbert* no longer are simply alternative sources of information and commentary but also have become discursive resources to be used, not simply consumed, by increasingly active audiences. As such, the two shows are aligned with an emerging cultural milieu defined by the increasing proclivity toward participation in content production and a more acute critical consciousness—an age, Benkler writes, in which people are becoming "less susceptible to manipulation by others than they were in the mass-media culture."[23]

This emergent media culture stands in contrast to the CNN-YouTube debate with which this chapter began, and its distinctly mass-mediated approach to convergence. There YouTube gave exposure to the kind of voices long denied a public platform, but for CNN the point was to farm those voices for the raw materials that could enrich the corporate product. In this form of vertical convergence, public speech is reduced to a resource to be exploited by the same centralized, capital-intensive institutions that dominated public discourse in an earlier era. It becomes a marketing device constructed for consumer appeal and not a meaningful form of public engagement. In the more horizontal model of convergence we have seen here, however, the dynamic is inverted, and the corporate product rightly becomes a resource for the citizenry. In such an environment, the vitality of news and public affairs media lies not simply in the information they contain—although the need for accurate information may be greater now than ever—nor with the people they allow to speak, but also in their ability to stimulate engagement, reaction, and response. In short, the true measure of public affairs media, be it CNN, *The Daily Show,* or the nightly news, lies increasingly in their public nature, the extent to which they resonate and integrate with an expanding public sphere.

9

♦ ♦ ♦

REAL NEWS, FAKE NEWS, AND THE CONVERSATION OF DEMOCRACY

> We have standards. Anybody with the kind of journalism experience and professionalism that you have displayed over these years cannot work for my program.
>
> —Jon Stewart, speaking to Bill Moyers

It was little surprise that when the public affairs journalist Bill Moyers returned to PBS in the spring of 2007, he did so with a piercing documentary investigating the mass media's complicity in the misconceived invasion of Iraq. As he explained prior to the debut of *Buying the War,* Moyers—who had begun his national career as Lyndon Johnson's press secretary—was troubled by the increased "symbiotic relationship between the political elites and media elites." That relationship, he suggested, had made it nearly impossible for those in the mainstream media to fulfill their obligation to hold national power brokers accountable for their actions. The problem was magnified, he continued, by the fact that the for-profit media were now entirely owned by megamedia corporations holding "vested interests in Washington policy" and more committed to seeking "favors from the government" than informing the public or demanding democratic accountability. Moyers himself was no stranger to the hurdles facing journalists who still believed their purpose was to challenge the power structure. He had resigned from his previous job at PBS—as anchor for the public affairs program *Now*—following the 2004 election and not long after learning that the Bush-appointed head of the Corporation for Public Broadcasting had secretly hired a consultant to monitor *Now* for "anti-Bush" and "anti-business" bias.[1]

What may have been a bit more surprising, though, was that two days after airing *Buying the War,* Moyers began the first regular episode of the new *Bill Moyers Journal* with an interview with Jon Stewart, where the two continued the conversation about journalism, politics, and war.[2] They share their frustration with the mainstream news media, with the "kind of wink-wink questioning" that has come to characterize the relationship between press and politics—the "failure of the quote 'professional' journalists," as Moyers puts it, to ask serious questions and demand honest answers. Suggesting, perhaps, that the Washington press corps is no longer in the business of real news, Moyers contrasts the dominant form of political news on television with *The Daily Show,* which he rightly notes has become a serious source of political journalism in a rapidly changing media environment.

In particular, Moyers calls attention to Stewart's recent interview with presidential candidate John McCain, the thirteenth time McCain appeared on *The Daily Show.* For McCain, thirteen was indeed an unlucky number. Stewart challenged him and his position on the Iraq war, refusing to back down as McCain grew increasingly testy. He asked McCain to explain the government's treatment of the troops—including extending their tours of duty, calling them back into service after the end of their official tour, and failing to provide adequate medical care at the Walter Reed veterans' hospital. Put on the spot, McCain instead tried to deflect Stewart's serious question, arguing that the troops were "fighting for freedom" and that their parents were "proud of the services of their sons and daughters." "Very unfair way to deal with this issue," Stewart snapped in response, chastising McCain for resorting to emotionally evocative spin in place of a reasoned answer. As Stewart explains on *Bill Moyers Journal,* when faced with a critical challenge, McCain "stopped connecting and just looked at my chest and decided, 'I'm just gonna continue to talk about honor and duty and the families should be proud'—all the things that are cudgels emotionally to keep us from the conversation, but things that weren't relevant to what we were talking about."

For his part, Stewart says his goal for the interview was to confront those "emotional cudgels"—to "deconstruct" the talking points about Iraq and ask, "Is this really the conversation that we're having about something

as significant as this war?" Throughout his discussion with M
expresses his concern for the vitality of "the conversation," th
exchange through which citizens and politicians alike shoul
their policy preferences. In that, one can hear traces of Moye
long career at both PBS and CBS—where he was the last
commentators on the *Evening News*—has strived to bring wh
"conversation of democracy" to television.[3] Perhaps for that reason, Moyers insists that despite Stewart's adamant denials, *The Daily Show* is a powerful kind of journalism. "So many people seem to want just what you did," he says, "somebody to cut through the talking points, and get our politicians to talk candidly and frankly." In the McCain interview in particular, Moyers tells Stewart, "your persistence and his inability to answer without the talking points did get to the truth"—a truth the mainstream media were largely refusing to consider. For his part, Stewart continues to deny that *The Daily Show* or *The Colbert Report* could be a new kind of journalism. "If we do anything in a positive sense for the world," he says, it is to "provide one little bit of context," to help people see a "larger picture" than they might otherwise. That, he concludes, "is how we fight back."

Three Paradigms

The exchange between Moyers and Stewart contains strands of all three paradigms of journalism—the residual, the dominant, and the emergent—that take us along the path from Cronkite to Colbert. Moyers, who worked with Walter Cronkite at CBS News, embodies the high-modern paradigm and its deep abiding faith in journalism as the Fourth Estate, that public searchlight of truth and accountability. By contrast, the mainstream news media and the Washington press corps that Moyers and Stewart criticize are largely engaged in the postmodern approach to news, the for-profit corporate product that is all too often complicit in the selling of political ideologies and agendas. Finally, Stewart and Colbert, whose *Report*, Stewart notes, is "made of the same genetic material as our show," are at the vanguard of the neo-modern paradigm. Functioning "very much outside any parameters of the media or the government," as Stewart stressed to Moyers, *The Daily Show* and *The Colbert Report* offer a new kind of democratic activism, a hybrid form of truth telling and public dialogue beholden to none of the paradigmatic conventions that limit the effectiveness of much contemporary journalism.

There is a growing body of evidence that regular viewers of *The Daily Show* and *Colbert* know more about politics and current events than do those who watch network, cable, or local TV news.[4] However, if, as Robert Park suggested many years ago, news is a form, and not just a source, of knowledge—a means by which a society orients itself and knows where it stands—the implications of the paradigm shift from Cronkite to Colbert eclipse a measure of what people know.[5] Rather, the fundamental question becomes *how* we know—the ways in which we talk of and think about politics, and act in political ways. That is, the question becomes one of political culture, of the contributions that different discourses of news make to our values and dispositions, our assumptions and orientations, and the very conceptual frames through and with which we are able to make sense of journalism, the political system, and our place within it.

Residual

When Moyers jokes that he was turned down for a job on *The Daily Show*, Stewart explains that it was because Moyers has too much "journalism experience and professionalism" to work in fake news. For his part, Moyers similarly criticizes many in the Washington press corps for being just "*quote* 'professionals,'" and thus not really journalists at all. Both Moyers and Stewart here invoke the ideals of the high-modern paradigm, ideals that still shape our assumptions about what exactly "real news" is or should be. For them, journalism is a profession, its practitioners committed to the public good. As we saw during Watergate, the age when Walter Cronkite was said to be the most trusted man in America, broadcast news was assumed to be an agent of democracy, an unofficial branch of government that held the actions of the powerful up to the "hot light" of public scrutiny. The journalists themselves were supposed to be informational experts—credentialed and authoritative—able to bracket their subjectivity and separate fact from opinion in the pseudoscientific pursuit of what Walter Lippmann once called "the habit of disinterested realism." In turn, the goal of the nightly news was to produce objective summaries of the day's evidence and argument, the reliable record of "the way it is." Finally, the audience was assumed to be comprised of rational citizens who tuned in each night for help in their efforts to form reasonable opinions about matters of public significance.

Moyers and Stewart are not alone in advocating this understanding of real news. The Society of Professional Journalists, for example, admirably continues to assert that "public enlightenment is the forerunner of justice and the foundation of democracy," and that "*the duty of the journalist* is to further those ends by seeking truth and providing a fair and comprehensive account of events and issues."[6] As the path from Cronkite to Colbert reveals, however, the high-modern paradigm was a product of a particular moment in history, one that scholars date roughly to the sixty years between World War II and the end of the twentieth century. It was a legacy of the network age, the rise of the truly mass media, and the consolidation of national power. So too was it inseparable from the wider social framework of modernity, that project of rationalization in which the political-normative—the serious realm of elections and governance—was assumed to be distinct from the aesthetic-expressive—the realm of pleasure and play.

As we have seen, high-modern news drew sharp, although arbitrary, boundaries between the informative and the entertaining, between the kind of news citizens would need to know and the sort of stories they would rather hear. Bolstered by both the economic stability provided by the network's lucrative entertainment programming and the belief that network news was essential for the conduct of democracy, CBS's Richard Salant and his colleagues could celebrate the point, insisting they would never pander to the audience by using techniques that would titillate rather than inform. Salant recognized that such an approach might make his newscast "a little less interesting to some," but that, he said, was a price the networks must pay "for dealing with fact and truth."[7]

Insisting on that clear line between journalism and entertainment, high-modern news thus depended on a wider culture of citizenship, the presumption that individuals recognized their democratic responsibility to "follow the news." That, however, may never have been an accurate explanation of why people watched the nightly news. Although as many as one out of four Americans tuned in to Walter Cronkite or the other network anchors each night, researchers suggest that may have had as much to do with the lack of viewing choices during the "dinner hour" as it did with the audience's desire to be informed. Markus Prior's work, for example, confirms the intuitive expectation that many people—but by no means all—would rather watch entertainment than news and, when given the choice, they do so. But he also finds that if the choice is, as it was in the network age, between watching news or watching no television at all, the majority of people would chose news over nothing. Prior's conclusion is that in an age when the average American home received only a few channels and all of them showed news at the same time, the audience was captive, at least to the extent that people wanted to watch television in the early evening, forced to watch news as much by institutional convention as by a sense of democratic duty.[8]

If it appealed only to the audience's sense of citizenship, the discourse of high-modern news paradoxically closed off potential avenues for political engagement. A product of a historical moment marked by centralization and the presumption of cultural homogeneity, the high-modern paradigm imposed a unitary language on the political domain, presenting itself as the only legitimate way to talk about and to understand politics. In its idealization of the "the reasonable and prudent man," it was a patriarchal discourse that drew sharp lines between dispassionate inquiry and passionate engagement, between rational argument and moral understanding, and ultimately between fact and value. As such, it narrowed the boundaries of political discussion, eliding most voices while demanding that individuals conform to its topics, tone, and mode of reasoning if they wished to become participants in the public sphere. At the same time, though, it relegated the audience to the margins of that public sphere, substituting itself for the public conversation. It justified itself in the public's name—news was something, Salant insisted, that CBS "owed to the public"[9]—but it offered no role for the public to play save that of passive audience, whose requirements for citizenship could be fulfilled simply by watching TV. High-modern news thus encouraged a kind of thin citizenship, one that James Carey argues confirmed the public's "psychological incompetence" to participate in the "culture of democratic publicity."[10]

Dominant

In the years following Watergate, a number of transformations—technological, economic, and cultural—would shatter the existing hegemony, loosening both the network's dominance of the airwaves and the unquestioned acceptance of the high-modern paradigm's methods and modalities. As the network age morphed into the multichannel era, audiences increasingly turned away from network news, with some seeking alternative sources of information and others opting for no news at all. Competing now for audiences, and particularly profitable market segments, high-modern news evolved into something distinctly more postmodern.

The lines that once seemed obvious—between news and entertainment, journalism and show business, media and marketing—all but dissolved as newsrooms were absorbed into larger corporate structures, which in turn were integrated into massive conglomerate portfolios. In such a corporate landscape, broadcasters became more committed to capital accumulation and shareholder value than to any theoretical concept of the public good. In turn, news was recrafted as infotainment, a fusion of genres engineered in the commercial pursuit of audiences now assumed to be consumers, not citizens. On a deeper level, the reworking of news as infotainment was part and parcel of the wider breakdown of modernity's project of social rationalization, an effacing of discursive boundaries at once liberating compared to the narrow forms of political speech considered legitimate in a high-modern paradigm but, as we've seen, too often incoherent, scattered, and disorienting.

For broadcast news, this meant not just the embracing of the techniques and topics of entertainment, but also the privileging of story over actuality, of narrative over the real. This was in part a result of the commercial mandate to attract audiences, but it also was an outgrowth of an increasing "antirealist" skepticism, the postmodern belief that any attempt to represent reality in words or pictures is at best incomplete and at worst devious, a play of power and a tactic of sociocultural dominance. Fueled by the unspoken assumption that the high-modern claim to be a "window to the world" was indeed, as the critical scholar Stuart Hall once argued, a "naturalistic illusion,"[11] objectivity itself was reconceptualized. No longer claiming to be the dispassionate effort to accurately describe what is, a postmodern paradigm instead promised to provide "fair and balanced" coverage of "both sides"—a recounting of competing sets of reality claims, absent any serious effort to determine the veracity or reasonableness of any of them.

It was this kind of fake news that enabled the Bush administration's aggressive efforts to manipulate the news media and public information. Staging spectacles designed for the screen and seeding public discourse with carefully scripted sound bites and spin, the administration enacted a keenly postmodern epistemology, the belief that reality is isomorphic with perception and the latter can be generated through the exercise of power. In the darkest years, between the terrorist attacks of September 11, 2001, and the Bush reelection of 2004, the postmodern news functioned as little more than a tool for the machinations of presidential power, each night coconstructing the chosen narrative through the circulation of spectacle and the amplification of spin. Broadcast news thus became complicit in imposing an instrumental rationality on the public sphere, a culture of democratic publicity reworked into an arena for strategic speech. A "government of fact and law," to borrow from the theorist Herbert Marcuse, transformed into "the rule of force and opinion,"[12] and the audience qua consumer was again reconceptualized, now as a test subject to be manipulated, an object upon which to generate an effect.

Aware of this dynamic, but either unwilling or unable to challenge it, the postmodern broadcast journalists countered their own complicity—in what we saw reporter Jim Axelrod once refer to as the "war of messages and messengers"—with a debilitating cynicism, a pervasive distrust of public speech. Interested less in truth than in motive, the guiding assumption becomes that anyone who would speak in public is engaged in a ruse and that politics is a "dastardly business," irreparably divorced from problem solving or community building.[13] Undermining both a belief in the possibility of positive political actions and the very credibility of the news—that effort to explain each day what is—such cynicism becomes part of the fiber of postmodern life, the "spontaneous philosophy," as Foucault put it, "of those who do not philosophize."[14]

It is little surprise, then, that during the ascendancy of a postmodern paradigm, people retreat from formal politics, turning their attention toward civic activism and lifestyle issues and away from elections and legislation. So too do they understandably tune out from a news media that strayed so far from the ideals of the Fourth Estate. It is also in such a time that critics bemoan the collapse of modernist ideals, warning of crises—of politics, of public communication, of a democracy without citizens. Finally, it is in such times that rather than call for a return to an older status quo or an idealized past, the more imaginative begin to think of new alternatives. As we have seen, the theorist Fredric Jameson, among others, held out hope not for a more serious kind of news, but for a new kind of political art, an "as yet unimaginable" mode of representation that could overcome "our social confusion" and help restore our "capacity to act and struggle."[15]

Emergent

Such a perspective sheds revealing light on Jon Stewart's suggestion that *The Daily Show* and *The Colbert Report* are their way of "fighting back." For even as George Bush could insist that the mission was actually accomplished or that Brownie really was doing a "heckuva job," the wider conditions of media and public discourse were undergoing profound transformations, changes that we are still watching take shape. The multichannel era has given way to the truly post-network age—a landscape shaped by the drastic and ongoing multiplication of media channels and platforms, the democratization of the technologies of video production, and the convergence of all forms of media, old and new, top-down and bottom-up, professional and amateur.

In turn, the postmodern approach to broadcast news, although still dominant, is itself giving way to an emergent paradigm, of which *The Daily Show* and *The Colbert Report* stand in the vanguard. They illustrate what I have described as the flip side of infotainment, in part the injection of politics into previously nonpolitical spaces, but more importantly the harnessing of the power of entertainment in pursuit of high-modern ideals. A reaction to the breakdown of "real" news and the ascendancy of the postmodern, *The Daily Show* and *Colbert* have been at the leading edge of the effort to reinvent public affairs television and reconfigure the conversation of democracy.

On their surface, they appear to be something quite different, perhaps two more examples of postmodern media marked by a border-effacing slippage between the serious and the silly. They seem all too indulgent in the postmodern obsession with fragments, the play of surfaces, and the celebration of irony as the primary mode of public speech. Underneath the laughter, however—or more precisely, *through* it—one finds a quite modernist agenda, motivated by the critical impulse. Unlike the real postmodernists, they display a continuous faith in fact and accountability and the belief that words can, and should, mean something. Standing outside, perhaps necessarily, of that symbiotic relationship of media and government, they pierce the bubble of spectacle and spin and challenge the mutual embrace of press and politics. Deconstructing the talking points, they offer a daily dose of rhetorical criticism and a much-needed effort, as Bill Moyers celebrated, to get at the truth. Thus they provide the kind of critical inquiry—that hot light of public exposure—that political theorists have long insisted a democracy demands.

In place of the talking points—the emotional cudgels—they reinvigorate the practice of reasoned discourse, both demanding and enacting the ideals of deliberative democracy, the concept that open, honest, and rational conversation is the only legitimate means of determining political preferences and reaching policy decisions. They provide a platform for public discussion that is at once more open than that allowed by high-modern media, which limit public voice to the established agents of power, and more serious and erudite than the postmodern media, which pander to those who simply perform well on camera. In turn, this televisual discussion is linked to a wider network of discourse; it functions as a high-visibility location where a diverse array of advocates and activists converge and extend the public argument they advance elsewhere. For proponents of deliberative democracy, this kind of informal discursive network becomes the essence of democratic communication in a fundamentally pluralistic and multimediated age. Contemporary democracy, they suggest, demands not a vertically oriented mass media that controls the circulation of public argument, but rather a horizontal public sphere comprised of "mutually interlocking" networks of "deliberation, contestation, and argumentation" that together function to identify problems, contemplate solutions, produce "good reasons," and invalidate others.[16]

Such a concept recognizes that in a post-network and convergent age, the public sphere is a collaborative venture, *between* public affairs media of all types and, more importantly, *among* citizens themselves. In a neo-modern paradigm, the audience transcends its position as simply audience for or consumer of media, and instead moves toward being an active participant, a coconstructor of the conversation of democracy. Henry Jenkins rightly suggests that *The Daily Show* (and by extension, *Colbert*) offers a nightly primer in the construction of critical texts, a do-it-yourself guide to crafting "user-generated" forms of political argument.[17] So too are they increasingly facilitating this kind of public engagement, providing the discursive resources that active audiences can reappropriate in the production of their own versions of hybrid public affairs media.

Critical Reawakenings

In the waning days of the Bush presidency, the outgoing president—whose 24 percent approval rating not only was one of the lowest in American history, but also more than 40 percent below where it stood when he donned a flight suit to declare "mission accomplished"[18]—took to the podium for one last go-round with the Washington press corps. He remained—as many would have expected—defiant, insisting that history would vindicate his willingness to "make the hard decisions." He did, though, finally admit to making some "mistakes"—naming in particular the premature "mission accomplished" announcement. He refused, though, to suggest that the poorly planned invasion of Iraq, the Abu Ghraib torture scandal, or his government's failed response to Hurricane Katrina were "mistakes," instead characterizing them as "disappointments." On *The Daily Show,* Jon Stewart offered his usual terse summary and critical insight. "Do you see what the president is doing here?" he asked, guiding the audience through their daily dose of rhetorical criticism. "He's using the word 'disappointment.'

Disappointment is what you feel when *others* make mistakes." Ill-conceived wars and torture were not "disappointments," Stewart insisted. "When the prize under the cap of your Diet Coke is for more Diet Coke, *that's* a disappointment."

The mistakes the president was willing to take responsibility for, however, were tellingly all matters of strategy and spectacle. Declaring "mission accomplished" was a mistake, he explained, because it "sent the wrong message." Of Katrina, though, he insisted that the only real issue was whether he should have flown over the area (as he did) or landed Air Force One (which he did not), but *not*, as Jon Stewart noted, telling "the head of FEMA what a great job he was doing," nor, more importantly, having "*that* guy *as* the head of FEMA." Refusing to acknowledge the failure of his government to function adequately, Bush was concerned only with appearance and effect, regretting those decisions that "sent the wrong message," not those that had disastrous consequences.

Bush's final press conference was in keeping with his administration's strategy of privileging public relations over public service. In tandem with its lapdogs of the postmodern press, that approach to governance had provided years of easy material for *The Daily Show* and *The Colbert Report*, which, according to Stewart, see themselves as being in the business of writing "jokes about the absurdity that we see in government."[19] For his part, though, Stewart may have preferred otherwise. On the eve of the 2004 election he told his audience that if the more reasonable John Kerry were to win the presidency, his job would be harder. "Please," he implored, "make my job harder." In 2004, of course, that was not to happen. George Bush may indeed have been, as his campaign chair Marc Racicot said on *The Daily Show* that year, "a man for our times"—a man for postmodern times, that is: a leader for a cynical age when image trumps substance and truthiness is so much more readily circulated than truth.

It also was in 2004, though, that former Labor Secretary Robert Reich would insist to Jon Stewart and the cheers of the audience that "irrationality rules the day, but reason is in the wings." Indeed, since then, the neo-modern watchdogs of late-night comedy have provided a continual stream of critical inquiry—interrogating spectacle, critiquing rhetoric, and deconstructing talking points offered by those who imagined they could create reality by manipulating public perception. And in the few years since then, Stewart and Colbert's popularity has continued to climb, while that of George Bush and his fellow practitioners of postmodern politics has plummeted. So too has citizen engagement with the political sphere increased dramatically, both cause and effect of Barack Obama's remarkable 2008 campaign for the presidency.

These changing times were well on display the day prior to Bush's final press conference, when Obama held one of his own, one of his many meetings with reporters to discuss his economic stimulus plan. As we saw on *The Daily Show* that night, Obama struck a far different tone than Bush ever had, insisting he was open to all good ideas—"Democrat or Republican"—and answering questions candidly, because to do otherwise, he said, "would be disingenuous." "That is *not* how a newly elected president sounds," Stewart bemoaned, offering a bit of postmodern wisdom he had learned during the Bush years. "You're *supposed* to be disingenuous!" Comparing Obama, who addressed each reporter in the room by full name and institutional affiliation, to Bush, who largely treated reporters as "Sweat Hogs in Mr. Kotter's classroom," Stewart lectured the new president. "You've got to diminish the Fourth Estate," he explained. "You must seek to belittle and demean" them. "What are they," he asked, "professionals?"

With that, we come to the pressing question that stands at the end of the path from Cronkite to Colbert. As the seeds of a critical reawakening continue to germinate, what role will broadcast journalism and the mainstream news media play in a post-network democracy? It seems both unlikely and undesirable that they revert to an older posture of professionalism, that top-down paradigm of dispassionate informational expertise that could so unreflexively insist that it alone knew "the way it is." But neither is it a viable option to cling to the postmodern approach that has gutted the democratic vitality of the nightly news and undermined its own credibility. Rather, in a continuing age of discursive integration—of technological convergence and conceptual hybridity—if television news, and perhaps journalism itself, is to remain relevant, its practitioners must follow the path of its leading innovators, drawing on multiple paradigmatic traditions and generic forms to reinvent the Fourth Estate and reinvigorate the conversation of democracy.

♦ ♦ ♦

NOTES

Notes for Chapter 1

1. Throughout this book, all quotations from broadcast programs come from the author's own transcriptions, unless otherwise noted.

2. Pew Research Center for the People and the Press, "Audience Segments in a Changing News Environment," 2008, http://people-press.org/reports/pdf/444.pdf.

3. E.g., Daya Kisan Thussu, *News as Entertainment: The Rise of Global Infotainment* (Thousand Oaks, CA: Sage, 2007).

4. Bill Kovach and Tom Rosenstiel, *The Elements of Journalism: What Newspeople Should Know and the Public Should Expect* (New York: Crown, 2001), 17.

5. Edward J. Epstein, *News from Nowhere: Television and the News* (New York: Random House, 1973).

6. W. Lance Bennett, Lynne A. Gressett, and William Haltom, "Repairing the News: A Case Study of the News Paradigm," *Journal of Communication* 35 (1985): 50–68.

7. Richard M. Cohen, "The Corporate Takeover of News: Blunting the Sword," in *Conglomerates and the Media*, ed. Erik Barnouw (New York: New Press, 1997), 31–59; James Fallows, *Breaking the News: How the Media Undermine American Democracy* (New York: Vintage, 1997).

8. Jürgen Habermas, *The Structural Transformation of the Public Sphere* (Cambridge, MA: MIT Press, 1989).

9. Neil Postman, *Amusing Ourselves to Death: Public Discourse in the Age of Show Business* (New York: Penguin Books, 1986); Thussu, *News as Entertainment*.

10. Pew Research Center for the People and the Press, "Social Networking and Online Videos Take Off: Internet's Broader Role in Campaign 2008," 2008, http://people-press.org/reports/pdf/384.pdf.

11. Michiko Kakutani, "The Most Trusted Man in America?" *New York Times*, August 17, 2008.

12. Pew Research Center for the People and the Press, "Audience Segments"; National Annenberg Election Survey, "*Daily Show* Viewers Knowledgeable about Presidential Campaign," 2004, http://www.annenbergpublicpolicycenter.org/Downloads/Political_Communication/naes/2004_03_late-night-knowledge-2_9-21_pr.pdf.

13. James H. Fowler, "The Colbert Bump in Campaign Donations: More Truthful than Truthy," *PS: Political Science and Politics* 41 (2008): 533–39.

14. Maureen Dowd, "Stewart and Colbert: America's Anchors," *Rolling Stone*, November 2006.

15. Michael X. Delli Carpini and Bruce A. Williams, "Let Us Infotain You: Politics in the New Media Environment," in *Mediated Politics: Communication in the Future of Democracy*, ed. W. Lance Bennett and Robert M. Entman (New York: Cambridge University Press, 2001), 160–81.

16. Michel Foucault, *The Archaeology of Knowledge* (New York: Pantheon Books, 1972).

17. Mikhail M. Bakhtin, *The Dialogic Imagination* (Austin: University of Texas Press, 1981).

18. Brian S. Brooks, George Kennedy, Daryl R. Moen, and Don Ranly, *Telling the Story: The Convergence of Print, Broadcast and Online Media* (New York: Bedford/St. Martin's, 2004), 11.

19. Quoted in Dean Alger, *Megamedia: How Giant Corporations Dominate Mass Media, Distort Competition, and Endanger Democracy* (New York: Rowman & Littlefield, 1998), 4.

20. John Nichols and Robert W. McChesney, *Tragedy and Farce: How the American Media Sell Wars, Spin Elections, and Destroy Democracy* (New York: New Press, 2006).

21. Robert E. Park, "News as Form of Knowledge: A Chapter in the Sociologic of Knowledge," in *News: A Reader*, ed. Howard Tumber (New York: Oxford University Press, 1999), 13, 15. Emphasis added.

22. James W. Carey, *Communication as Culture: Essays on Media and Society* (New York: Routledge, 1988).

23. John Corner and Dick Pels, "Introduction: The Re-Styling of Politics," in *Media and the Restyling of Politics*, ed. John Corner and Dick Pels (Thousand Oaks, CA: Sage, 2003), 3.

24. Foucault, *Archaeology*, 136.

25. Reuven Frank, *Out of Thin Air: The Brief Wonderful Life of Network News* (New York: Simon & Schuster, 1991).

26. Amanda D. Lotz, *The Television Will Be Revolutionized* (New York: New York University Press, 2007).

27. James W. Carey, "The Mass Media and Democracy: Between the Modern and the Postmodern," *Journal of International Affairs* 47 (1993): 1–21.

28. Epstein, *News from Nowhere*; Les Brown, *Television: The Business Behind the Box* (New York: Harcourt Brace Jovanovich, 1971).

29. Carey, "Mass Media and Democracy," 10.

30. Epstein, *News from Nowhere*, 4; Bruce A. Williams and Michael X. Delli Carpini, *The End of Broadcast News: Media Regimes and the New Information Environment* (unpublished manuscript, 2008).

31. Edward Bliss Jr., *Now the News: The Story of Broadcast Journalism* (New York: Columbia University Press, 1991).

32. Robert B. Horwitz, *The Irony of Regulatory Reform: The Deregulation of American Telecommunications* (New York: Oxford University Press, 1989).

33. Epstein, *News from Nowhere*, 48.

34. Markus Prior, *Post-Broadcast Democracy: How Media Choice Increases Inequality in Political Involvement and Polarizes Elections* (New York: Cambridge University Press, 2007), 72.

35. Quoted in Ken Auletta, *Three Blind Mice: How the TV Networks Lost Their Way* (New York: Random House, 1991), 285.

36. Frank Stanton, "The Critical Necessity for an Informed Public," *Journal of Broadcasting* 3 (1958): 204.

37. Cohen, "The Corporate Takeover of News," 31.

38. Daniel C. Hallin, "The Passing of the 'High Modernism' of American Journalism," *Journal of Communication* 42 (1992): 14–25; Carey, "Mass Media and Democracy."

39. Quoted in Mark Gunther, *The House that Roone Built: The Inside Story of ABC News* (New York: Little, Brown, 1994), 51. Emphasis added.

40. Richard J. Schaefer, "The Development of the CBS News Guidelines During the Salant Years," *Journal of Broadcasting and Electronic Media* 42 (1998): 8.

41. Jürgen Habermas, "Modernity—An Incomplete Project," in *The Anti-Aesthetic: Essays on Postmodern Culture*, ed. Hal Foster (Seattle: Bay Press, 1983), 3–15.

42. Schaefer, "CBS News Guidelines," 8.

43. Carey, "Mass Media and Democracy."

44. Bakhtin, *Dialogic Imagination*.

45. Alger, *Megamedia*; Patricia Aufderheide, *Communication Policy and the Public Interest: The Telecommunications Act of 1996* (New York: Guilford Press, 1999); Horwitz, *Irony of Regulatory Reform*.

46. Quoted in J. F. MacDonald, *One Nation Under Television: The Rise and Decline of Network TV* (Chicago: Nelson-Hall, 1990), 228.

47. Auletta, *Three Blind Mice*, 475.

48. Quoted in Williams and Delli Carpini, *The End of Broadcast News*.

49. Frank Rich, "The NASCAR Nightly News: Anchorman Get Your Gun," *New York Times*, December 5, 2004.

50. Peter Johnson, "Zooming in on Brian Williams," *USA Today*, November 10, 2004.

51. Pew Research Center for the People and the Press, "Audience Segments."

52. Lotz, *The Television Will Be Revolutionized*, 5.

53. John Caldwell, "Convergence Television: Aggregating Form and Repurposing Content in the Culture of Conglomeration," in *Television After TV: Essays on a Medium in Transition*, ed. Lynn Spiegel and Jan Olsson (Durham, NC: Duke University Press, 2004), 41–74.

54. Pew Research Center for the People and the Press, "Audience Segments."

55. Brian McNair, *Journalism and Democracy: An Evaluation of the Political Public Sphere* (New York: Routledge, 2000), 40.

56. Henry Jenkins, *Convergence Culture: Where Old and New Media Collide* (New York: New York University Press, 2006), 243.

57. Jeffrey P. Jones, *Entertaining Politics: New Political Television and Civic Culture* (New York: Rowman & Littlefield, 2005).

58. Delli Carpini and Williams, "Let Us Infotain You."

59. Bakhtin, *Dialogic Imagination*, 370. Emphasis in the original.

60. Bakhtin, *Dialogic Imagination*, 262–63.

61. Center for Media and Public Affairs at George Mason University, "Late-Nite [*sic*] Talk Shows Were Road to White House: Study Finds Candidates Appeared Over 100 Times," 2008, http://www.cmpa.com/media_room_comedy_12_29_08.htm.

62. CBSnews.com, "Couric Wins Walter Cronkite Award," 2009, http://www.cbsnews .com/blogs/2009/03/10/couricandco/entry4856848.shtml.

63. Dannagal G. Young, *Recreatin' Sarah Palin: Journalists, Tina Fey and the Construction of a Political Persona* (unpublished manuscript, 2009).

64. Jeffrey P. Jones, "Pop Goes the Campaign: The Repopularization of Politics in Election 2008," in *The 2008 Presidential Campaign: A Communication Perspective*, ed. Robert E. Denton Jr. (Lanham, MD: Rowman & Littlefield, 2009).

65. Gary Levin, "All Is Forgiven: Letterman, McCain Are Pals Again," *USA Today*, October 17, 2008.

Notes for Chapter 2

Portions of this chapter first appeared as "Packaging Reality: Structures of Form in U.S. Network Coverage of Watergate and the Clinton Impeachment," *Journalism* 5 (2004): 279–99. The author gratefully acknowledges Sage Publications for permission to adapt and reprint.

1. Comedy Central, *The Daily Show*, http://www.thedailyshow.com/about.html (accessed October 22, 2007).

2. Michael Schudson, *The Power of News* (Cambridge, MA: Harvard University Press, 1995).

3. Daniel C. Hallin, "The Passing of the 'High Modernism' of American Journalism," *Journal of Communication* 42 (1992): 14–25.

4. Barbie Zelizer, "CNN, the Gulf War, and Journalistic Practice," *Journal of Communication* 42 (1992): 66–81.

5. E.g., Richard J. Schaefer, "Editing Strategies in Television News Documentaries," *Journal of Communication* 47 (1997): 69–88; Kevin G. Barnhurst and Catherine A. Steele, "Image-Bite News: The Visual Coverage of Elections on US Television, 1968–1992," *Press/Politics* 2 (1997): 40–58; Catherine A. Steele and Kevin G. Barnhurst, "The Journalism of Opinion: Network News Coverage of US Presidential Campaigns, 1968–1988," *Critical Studies in Mass Communication* 13 (1996): 187–209; Daniel C. Hallin, "Sound Bite News: Television Coverage of Elections, 1968–1988," *Journal of Communication* 42 (1992): 5–24; Michael Griffin, "Looking at TV News: Strategies for Research," *Communication* 13 (1992): 121–41.

6. Kevin G. Barnhurst and John Nerone, *The Form of News: A History* (New York: Guilford Press, 2001); Schudson, *Power of News*.

7. Videotapes were obtained from the Vanderbilt Television News Archives.

8. Bill Nichols, *Representing Reality: Issues and Concepts in Documentary* (Bloomington: Indiana University Press, 1991), 113.

9. Richard J. Schaefer, "The Development of the CBS News Guidelines During the Salant Years," *Journal of Broadcasting and Electronic Media* 42 (1998): 8.

10. Neil Postman, *Amusing Ourselves to Death: Public Discourse in the Age of Show Business* (New York: Penguin Books, 1986).

11. Edward J. Epstein, *News from Nowhere: Television and the News* (New York: Random House, 1973).

12. Schaefer, "Editing Strategies."

13. Schaefer, "CBS News Guidelines," 8.

14. Walter Lippmann, *Public Opinion* (New York: Free Press, 1922), 229.

15. Nichols, *Representing Reality*, 189.

16. Daniel C. Hallin, "Commercialism and Professionalism in American News Media," in *Mass Media and Society*, 3rd ed., ed. James Curran and Michael Gurevitch (New York: Oxford University Press, 2000), 218–37.

17. Barnhurst and Nerone, *The Form of News*, 188.

18. Schaefer, "CBS News Guidelines," 11.

19. Schaefer, "CBS News Guidelines," 3.

20. Quoted in Lawrence Grossberg, Ellen Wartella, and D. Charles Whitney, *MediaMaking: Mass Media in a Popular Culture* (Thousand Oaks, CA: Sage, 1998), 383.

21. Schaefer, "CBS News Guidelines," 3.

22. Hallin, "Sound Bite News," 10.

23. Barnhurst and Steele, "Image-Bite News."

24. Bela Balazs, "The Close-Up," in *Film Theory and Criticism*, ed. Gerald Mast, Marshall Cohen, and Leo Braudy (New York: Oxford University Press, 1992), 261.

25. Quoted in Siegfried Kracauer, "The Establishment of Physical Existence," in *Film Theory and Criticism*, ed. Gerald Mast, Marshall Cohen, and Leo Braudy (New York: Oxford University Press, 1992), 253.

26. Schaefer, "Editing Strategies."

27. Thomas E. Patterson, *Out of Order* (New York: Alfred A. Knopf, 1993); Barnhurst and Steele, "Image-Bite News."

28. Richard M. Cohen, "The Corporate Takeover of News: Blunting the Sword," in *Conglomerates and the Media*, ed. Erik Barnouw (New York: New Press, 1997), 31–59.

29. Nichols, *Representing Reality*, 179.

30. Walter Benjamin, "Art in the Age of Mechanical Reproduction," in *Film Theory and Criticism*, ed. Gerald Mast, Marshall Cohen, and Leo Braudy (New York: Oxford University Press, 1992), 675.

Notes for Chapter 3

Portions of this chapter originally appeared in "Strategies of Illumination: U.S. Network

News, Watergate, and the Clinton Affair," *Rhetoric & Public Affairs 6 (2003): 633–56, published by Michigan State University Press. The author gratefully acknowledges permission to adapt and reprint.*

1. Walter Lippmann, *Public Opinion* (New York: Free Press, 1922), 229.

2. Bruce Baum, "Freedom, Power and Public Opinion: J. S. Mill on the Public Sphere," *History of Political Thought* 22 (2001): 507.

3. Slavko Splichal, "The Principle of Publicity, Public Use of Reason and Social Control," *Media, Culture, and Society* 24 (2002): 5–26.

4. Simone Chambers, "A Culture of Publicity," in *Deliberation, Democracy, and the Media*, ed. Simone Chambers and Anne Costain (New York: Rowman & Littlefield, 2000), 193.

5. Jürgen Habermas, *The Structural Transformation of the Public Sphere: An Inquiry into a Category of Bourgeois Society* (Cambridge, MA: MIT Press, 1989).

6. James W. Carey, "The Mass Media and Democracy: Between the Modern and the Postmodern," *Journal of International Affairs* 47 (1993): 14.

7. George Lakoff, "The Contemporary Theory of Metaphor," in *Metaphor and Thought*, ed. Andrew Ortony, 2nd ed. (New York: Cambridge University Press, 1993), 202–51; Andrew Ortony, "Metaphor, Language, and Thought," in Ortony, *Metaphor and Thought*, 1–18.

8. Edward Jay Epstein, *News from Nowhere: Television and the News* (New York: Random House, 1973), 252.

9. Gaye Tuchman, *Making News: A Study in the Construction of Reality* (New York: Free Press, 1978).

10. George E. Marcus, W. Russell Neuman, and Michael Mackuen, *Affective Intelligence and Political Judgment* (Chicago: University of Chicago Press, 2000).

11. See Splichal, "Principle of Publicity."

12. James Bohman, "Citizenship and Norms of Publicity: Wide Public Reason in Cosmopolitan Societies," *Political Theory* 27 (1999): 176–202; Geoff Eley, "Nations, Public, and Political Cultures: Placing Habermas in the Nineteenth Century," in *Habermas and the Public Sphere*, ed. Craig Calhoun (Cambridge, MA: MIT Press, 1992), 289–339; Nancy Fraser, "Rethinking the Public Sphere: A Contribution to the Critique of Actually Existing Democracy," in Calhoun, *Habermas and the Public Sphere*, 109–42.

13. Fraser, "Rethinking the Public Sphere," 126.

14. Alison M. Jaggar, "Love and Knowledge: Emotion in Feminist Epistemology," in *Gender/Body/Knowledge: Feminist Reconstructions of Being and Knowing*, ed. Alison M. Jaggar and Susan R. Bordo (New Brunswick, NJ: Rutgers University Press, 1989), 145–71.

15. Michael X. Delli Carpini and Bruce A. Williams, "Let Us Infotain You: Politics in the New Media Environment," in *Mediated Politics: Communication in the Future of Democracy*, ed. W. Lance Bennett and Robert M. Entman (New York: Cambridge University Press, 2001), 168.

16. Paul Lucey, *Story Sense: Writing Story and Script for Feature Films and Television* (New York: McGraw-Hill, 1996).

17. Joshua Meyrowitz, *No Sense of Place: The Impact of Electronic Media on Social Behavior* (New York: Oxford University Press, 1985).

18. Sonja K. Foss and Karen A. Foss, "The Construction of Feminine Spectatorship in Garrison Keillor's Radio Monologues," in *Readings in Rhetorical Criticism*, ed. Carl R. Burgchardt (State College, PA: Strata, 2000), 526–43; Sandra Harding, *Whose Science? Whose Knowledge? Thinking from Women's Lives* (Ithaca: Cornell University Press, 1991); Iris Marion Young, *Inclusion and Democracy* (New York: Oxford University Press, 2000).

19. John Durham Peters, "Historical Tensions in the Concept of Public Opinion," in *Public Opinion and the Communication of Consent*, ed. Theodore L. Glasser and Charles T. Salmon (New York: Guilford Press, 1995), 3–32.

20. Bohman, "Citizenship and Norms of Publicity," 182.

Notes for Chapter 4

1. Ken Auletta, "Sign-Off: The Long and Complicated Career of Dan Rather," *New Yorker*, March 7, 2005.

2. John Hutcheson, David Domke, Andre Billeaudeaux, and Phillip Garland, "U.S. National Identity, Political Elites, and a Patriotic Press Following September 11," *Political Communication* 21 (2004): 27–51.

3. W. Lance Bennett, Regina G. Lawrence, and Steven Livingston, *When the Press Fails: Political Power and the News Media from Iraq to Katrina* (Chicago: University of Chicago Press, 2007), 17.

4. Michael Pfau, J. Brian Houston, and Shane M. Semmler, *Mediating the Vote: The Changing Media Landscape in U.S. Presidential Campaigns* (New York: Rowman & Littlefield, 2007); Jeffrey P. Jones, "The Shadow Campaign in Popular Culture," in *The 2004 Presidential Campaign: A Communication Perspective*, ed. Robert E. Denton (New York: Rowman & Littlefield, 2005), 195–216.

5. Pew Research Center for the People and the Press, "Cable and Internet Loom Large in Fragmented Political News Universe," 2004, http://people-press.org/reports/pdf/200.pdf.

6. Pew Research Center for the People and the Press, "Online News Audience Larger, More Diverse: News Audiences Increasingly Politicized," 2004, http://people-press.org/reports/pdf/215.pdf.

7. Amanda D. Lotz, *The Television Will Be Revolutionized* (New York: New York University Press, 2007).

8. Bennett et al., *When the Press Fails*, 55–59.

9. Thomas E. Patterson, *Out of Order* (New York: Alfred A. Knopf, 1993).

10. Stephen J. Farnsworth and S. Robert Lichter, *The Nightly News Nightmare: Network Television's Coverage of U.S. Presidential Elections, 1988–2000* (New York: Rowman & Littlefield, 2003).

11. Kate Kenski and Natalie J. Stroud, "Who Watches Presidential Debates? A Comparative Analysis of Presidential Debate Viewing in 2000 and 2004," *American Behavioral Scientist* 49 (2005): 213–28.

12. Patterson, *Out of Order*.

13. Patterson, *Out of Order*, 73.

14. Farnsworth and Lichter, *Nightly News Nightmare*, 51; Elizabeth A. Skewes, *Message*

Control: How News Is Made on the Presidential Campaign Trail (New York: Rowman & Littlefield, 2007), 52.

15. Patterson, *Out of Order,* 89.

16. Skewes, *Message Control,* 52.

17. Herbert Marcuse, "Some Social Implications of Modern Technology," in *The Essential Frankfurt School Reader,* ed. Andrew Arato and Eike Gebhardt (New York: Continuum, 2003), 138–62.

18. Bennett et al., *When the Press Fails,* 3.

19. Quoted in Kathleen Hall Jamieson, *Electing the President 2004: The Insiders' View* (Philadelphia: University of Pennsylvania Press, 2006), 151.

20. Quoted in Jamieson, *Electing the President,* 156.

21. Murray Edelman, *Constructing the Political Spectacle* (Chicago: University of Chicago Press, 1988), 96.

22. Edelman, *Political Spectacle.*

23. W. Lance Bennett, "News as Reality TV: Election Coverage and the Democratization of Truth," *Critical Studies in Media Communication* 22 (2005): 171–77.

24. Quoted in Jamieson, *Electing the President*: 158, see also Skewes, *Message Control.*

25. Skewes, *Message Control*: 80.

26. Stuart Hall, Charles Crichter, Tony Jefferson, John Clarke, and Brian Roberts, *Policing the Crisis: Mugging, the State, and Law and Order* (London: MacMillan Press, 1978).

27. Bennett et al., *When the Press Fails,* 47.

28. Quoted in Jamieson, *Electing the President,* 141.

29. Roderick P. Hart, *Seducing America: How Television Charms the Modern Voter* (Thousand Oaks, CA: Sage, 1999), 77–100.

30. Hayden White, *Metahistory: The Historical Imagination in Nineteenth-Century Europe* (Baltimore: Johns Hopkins University Press, 1973), 38.

31. Bennett et al., *When the Press Fails,* 42.

32. For an overview of the story and its fallout, see Corey Pein, "Blog-Gate: Yes, CBS Screwed Up Badly in 'Memogate'—But So Did Those Who Covered the Affair," *Columbia Journalism Review* 43 (2005): 30–35.

33. Pein, "Blog-Gate," 31.

34. Quoted in Jamieson, *Electing the President,* 148.

Notes for Chapter 5

A portion of this chapter first appeared as "Emerging Models of Journalistic Authority in MTV's Coverage of the 2004 U.S. Presidential Election," *Journalism Studies* 8 (2007): 382–96. The author gratefully acknowledges the Taylor & Francis Group for permission to adapt and reprint.

1. Corey Pein, "Blog-Gate: Yes, CBS Screwed Up Badly in 'Memogate'—But So Did Those Who Covered the Affair," *Columbia Journalism Review* 43 (2005): 30.

2. Jan Wieten and Mervi Pantti, "Obsessed with the Audience: Breakfast TV Revisited," *Media, Culture & Society* 27 (2005): 21–39.

3. Wieten and Pantti, "Breakfast TV Revisited," 34.

4. W. Lance Bennett, Regina G. Lawrence, and Steven Livingston, *When the Press Fails: Political Power and the News Media from Iraq to Katrina* (Chicago: University of Chicago Press, 2007), 56.

5. Liesbet van Zoonen, *Entertaining the Citizen: When Politics and Popular Culture Converge* (New York: Rowman & Littlefield, 2005), 3.

6. Steven Clayman and John Heritage, *The News Interview: Journalists and Public Figures on the Air* (New York: Cambridge University Press, 2002).

7. Van Zoonen, *Entertaining the Citizen*, 20–33.

8. Fredric Jameson, *Postmodernism, or, the Cultural Logic of Late Capitalism* (Durham, NC: Duke University Press, 1991), 26.

9. E.g., Pew Research Center for the People and the Press, "Audience Segments in a Changing News Environment," 2008, http://people-press.org/reports/pdf/444.pdf.

10. Beretta E. Smith-Shomade, *Pimpin' Ain't Easy: Selling Black Entertainment Television* (New York: Routledge, 2008), xiv.

11. Roland E. Wolseley, *The Black Press, U.S.A.*, 2nd ed. (Ames: Iowa State University Press, 1990), 5. See also Patrick S. Washburn, *The African American Newspaper: Voice of Freedom* (Evanston, IL: Northwestern University Press, 2006).

12. Robert M. Entman, *Democracy Without Citizens: Media and the Decay of American Politics* (New York: Oxford University Press, 1990).

13. Catherine Squires, "The Black Press and the State: Attracting Unwanted (?) Attention," in *Counterpublics and the State*, ed. Robert Asen and Daniel C. Brouwer (Albany: State University of New York Press, 2001), 113.

14. Smith-Shomade, *Pimpin' Ain't Easy*, 48–49.

15. BET covered Barack Obama's presidential campaign through sporadic news reports and special programs scattered within its entertainment lineup. It did, though, offer saturation coverage of the Obama inauguration.

16. Allison Romano, "Cable: The Numbers Game," *Broadcasting and Cable*, 134, no. 28 (2004): 18.

17. Susan Sherr and Meredith Staples, "News for a New Generation Report One: Content Analysis, Interviews, and Focus Groups," The Center for Civic Learning and Engagement, 2004, http://www.civicyouth.org/PopUps/WorkingPapers/WP16Sherr.pdf.

18. Mikhail M. Bakhtin, *The Dialogic Imagination* (Austin: University of Texas Press, 1981), 342.

19. Bakhtin, *Dialogic Imagination*, 342.

20. Sherr and Staples, "News for a New Generation."

21. P. David Marshall, *Celebrity and Power: Fame in Contemporary Culture* (Minneapolis: University of Minnesota Press, 1997), 19. See also John Corner and Dick Pels, eds., *Media and the Restyling of Politics: Consumerism, Celebrity and Cynicism* (Thousand Oaks, CA: Sage, 2003).

22. Dick Pels, "Aesthetic Representation and Political Style: Re-Balancing Identity and Difference in Media Democracy," in Corner and Pels, *Media and the Restyling of Politics*, 58.

23. Marshall, *Celebrity and Power*, 190.

24. Marshall, *Celebrity and Power*, 187.

25. Marshall, *Celebrity and Power*, 196, 141.

26. Doris A. Graber, "Adapting Political News to the Needs of Twenty-first Century Americans," in *Mediated Politics: Communication in the Future of Democracy*, ed. W. Lance Bennett and Robert M. Entman (New York: Cambridge University Press, 2001), 445–46.

27. James W. Carey, "The Press, Public Opinion, and Public Discourse," in *Public Opinion and the Communication of Consent*, ed. Theodore L. Glasser and Charles T. Salmon (New York: Guilford Press, 1995), 390–91.

28. Gerald Hauser, *Vernacular Voices: The Rhetoric of Publics and Public Spheres* (Columbia: University of South Carolina Press, 1999), 78.

Notes for Chapter 6

Portions of this chapter first appeared as "The Daily Show: Discursive Integration and the Reinvention of Political Journalism," *Political Communication* 22 (2005): 259–76; and "Crafting New Communicative Models in the Televisual Sphere: Political Interviews on The Daily Show," *Communication Review* 10 (2007): 93–115. The author gratefully acknowledges the Taylor & Francis Group for permission to adapt and reprint.

1. Verne Gay, "Not Necessarily the News: Meet the Players Who Will Influence Coverage of the 2004 Campaign," *Newsday*, January 19, 2004; PBS, *NOW with Bill Moyers*, 2003, http://www.pbs.org/now/transcript/transcript_stewart.html.

2. Amanda D. Lotz, *The Television Will Be Revolutionized* (New York: New York University Press, 2007).

3. For the Salant quote, see Richard J. Schaefer, "The Development of the CBS News Guidelines During the Salant Years," *Journal of Broadcasting and Electronic Media* 42 (1998): 8. For an overview of Pierre Bourdieu's concept of fields, see Rodney Benson and Erik Neveu, *Bourdieu and the Journalistic Field* (Cambridge: Polity Press, 2005).

4. David S. Niven, S. Robert Lichter, and Daniel Amundson, "The Political Content of Late Night Comedy," *Harvard International Journal of Press/Politics* 8 (2003): 118–33.

5. David L. Paletz, *The Media in American Politics: Contents and Consequences*, 2nd ed. (New York: Longman, 2002), 13.

6. Project for Excellence in Journalism, "Journalism, Satire or Just Laughs?" 2008, http://www.journalism.org/files/Daily%20Show%20PDF_3.pdf.

7. W. Lance Bennett, Regina G. Lawrence, and Steven Livingston, *When the Press Fails: Political Power and the News Media from Iraq to Katrina* (Chicago: University of Chicago Press, 2007).

8. Susan Douglas, "*Daily Show* Does Bush," *Nation*, May 5, 2003, http://www.thenation.com/doc/20030505/douglas.

9. John Street, *Mass Media, Politics, and Democracy* (London: Palgrave, 2001), 69.

10. Dustin Griffin, *Satire: A Critical Reintroduction* (Lexington: University Press of Kentucky, 1994).

11. Paletz, *The Media in American Politics*, 13.

12. Griffin, *Satire*, 42.

13. Eric Schlosser, "The Kids Are Alright," *Columbia Journalism Review* 41 (2003): 27–30.

14. Griffin, *Satire,* 139.

15. Quoted in Frank Rich, *The Greatest Story Ever Sold: The Decline and Fall of Truth from 9/11 to Katrina* (New York: Penguin Press, 2006), 30.

16. Simon Dentith, *Parody,* The New Critical Idiom (New York: Routledge, 2000).

17. Project for Excellence in Journalism, "Journalism, Satire or Just Laughs?"

18. Ann Marie Kerwin, "The Oprah of the Beltway Set," *Advertising Age,* November 21, 2005, http://www.adage.com/news.cms?newsId=46772.

19. Harry G. Frankfurt, *On Bullshit* (Princeton, NJ: Princeton University Press, 2005), 43–44.

20. Thomas McCarthy, *The Critical Theory of Jürgen Habermas* (Cambridge, MA: MIT Press, 1978).

21. James Bohman and William Rehg, *Deliberative Democracy: Essays on Reason and Politics* (Cambridge, MA: MIT Press, 1997).

22. Bohman and Rehg, *Deliberative Democracy,* xiv.

23. Roderick P. Hart and Johanna Hartelius, "The Political Sins of Jon Stewart," *Critical Studies in Media Communication* 24 (2007): 263.

24. Robert Hariman, "In Defense of Jon Stewart," *Critical Studies in Media Communication* 24 (2007): 276.

Notes for Chapter 7

Portions of this chapter first appeared as "Stephen Colbert's Parody of the Postmodern," in *Satire TV: Politics and Comedy in the Post-Network Era,* ed. Jonathan Gray, Jeffrey Jones, and Ethan Thompson (New York: New York University Press, 2009), 124–44. The author gratefully acknowledges New York University Press for permission to adapt and reprint.

1. "Colbert Roasts President Bush," 2006 White House Correspondents' Association Dinner, April 29, 2006, http://video.google.com/videoplay?docid=-869183917758574879.

2. David Carr, "Carson-Era Humor, Post-Colbert," *New York Times,* April 23, 2007.

3. Richard Cohen, "So Not Funny," *Washington Post,* May 4, 2006.

4. David L. Paletz, *The Media in American Politics: Contents and Consequences,* 2nd ed. (New York: Longman, 2002).

5. E.g. Fredric Jameson, *Postmodernism: Or, the Cultural Logic of Late Capitalism* (Durham, NC: Duke University Press, 1991).

6. Mike Conway, Maria Elizabeth Grabe, and Kevin Grieves, "Villains, Victims and the Virtuous in Bill O'Reilly's 'No-Spin Zone': Revisiting World War Propaganda Techniques," *Journalism Studies* 8 (2007): 197–223.

7. Murray Edelman, *Constructing the Political Spectacle* (Chicago: University of Chicago Press, 1988); see also Dick Pels, "Aesthetic Representation and Political Style: Re-Balancing Identity and Difference in Media Democracy," in *Media and the Restyling of Politics,* ed. John Corner and Dick Pels (Thousand Oaks, CA: Sage, 2003), 41–66.

8. See Geoffrey Baym, "Representation and the Politics of Play: Stephen Colbert's *Better Know a District,*" *Political Communication* 24 (2007): 370–71.

9. Simon Dentith, *Parody,* The New Critical Idiom (New York: Routledge, 2000), 16.

10. Douglas C. Muecke, *The Compass of Irony* (London: Methuen, 1969), 23.

11. Megan Boler, *Digital Media and Democracy: Tactics in Hard Times* (Cambridge, MA: MIT Press, 2008), 23.

12. Jürgen Habermas, *The Structural Transformation of the Public Sphere: An Inquiry into a Category of Bourgeois Society* (Cambridge, MA: MIT Press, 1989).

13. See Baym, "Representation and the Politics of Play," 370.

14. Boler, *Digital Media and Democracy,* 208–9.

15. See Claire Colebrook, *Irony* (New York: Routledge, 2004).

16. Harvard's Institute of Politics, "A Conversation with Stephen Colbert," http://video.google.com/videoplay?docid=5550134133036374310.

17. Walter Lippmann, *Public Opinion* (New York: Free Press, 1922), 229.

18. E.g. Richard Rorty, *Philosophy and the Mirror of Nature* (Princeton, NJ: Princeton University Press, 1979); Mary Poovey, *A History of the Modern Fact: Problems of Knowledge in the Sciences of Wealth and Society* (Chicago: University of Chicago Press, 1998).

19. Edelman, *Constructing the Political Spectacle*; Jeffrey P. Jones, "Believable Fictions: Redactional Culture and the Will to Truthiness," in *The Changing Faces of Journalism: Tradition, Tabloidization, Technology and Truthiness,* ed. Barbie Zelizer (New York: Routledge, 2009).

20. W. Lance Bennett, Regina G. Lawrence, and Steven Livingston, *When the Press Fails: Political Power and the News Media from Iraq to Katrina* (Chicago: University of Chicago Press, 2007), 139.

21. Michel Foucault, *The Archaeology of Knowledge* (New York: Pantheon Books, 1972), 50.

22. Henry Jenkins, *Convergence Culture: Where Old and New Media Collide* (New York: New York University Press, 2006), 254; see also Peter Walsh, "That Withered Paradigm: The Web, the Expert and the Information Hegemony," in *Democracy and New Media,* ed. Henry Jenkins and David Thorburn (Cambridge, MA: MIT Press, 2004), 365–72.

23. Jenkins, *Convergence Culture,* 245.

24. Quoted in Bennett et al., *When the Press Fails,* 138.

25. Bennett et al., *When the Press Fails,* 138.

26. Harry G. Frankfurt, *On Bullshit* (Princeton, NJ: Princeton University Press, 2005), 33–34, 64–65.

27. Jameson, *Postmodernism,* 17.

28. Dustin Griffin, *Satire: A Critical Reintroduction* (Lexington: University Press of Kentucky, 1994), 65.

29. Jameson, *Postmodernism,* 17.

30. Jameson, *Postmodernism,* 54.

Notes for Chapter 8

1. Henry Jenkins, "Why Mitt Romney Won't Debate a Snowman," in *Satire TV: Politics and Comedy in the Post-Network Era,* ed. Jonathan Gray, Jeffrey Jones, and Ethan Thompson (New York: New York University Press, 2009), 187–209.

2. Jenkins, "Why Mitt Romney Won't Debate a Snowman"; see also Henry Jenkins,

Convergence Culture: Where Old and New Media Collide (New York: New York University Press, 2006).

3. Manuel Castells, *The Rise of the Network Society*, 2nd ed. (Malden, MA: Blackwell, 2000).

4. John Caldwell, "Convergence Television: Aggregating Form and Repurposing Content in the Culture of Conglomeration," in *Television after TV: Essays on a Medium in Transition*, ed. Lynn Spiegel and Jan Olsson (Durham, NC: Duke University Press, 2004), 48–49.

5. Caldwell, "Convergence Television," 48–49.

6. Yochai Benkler, *The Wealth of Networks: How Social Production Transforms Markets and Freedom* (New Haven: Yale University Press, 2006), 13.

7. Benkler, *Wealth of Networks*, 138.

8. Catherine Burwell and Megan Boler, "Calling on the Colbert Nation: Fandom, Politics and Parody in an Age of Media Convergence," *Electronic Journal of Communication* 18 (2008).

9. Jenkins, *Convergence Culture*, 2.

10. Morley Winograd and Michael D. Hais, *Millennial Makeover: MySpace, YouTube and the Future of American Politics* (New Brunswick, NJ: Rutgers University Press, 2008), 150.

11. Aaron Smith and Lee Rainie, "The Internet and the 2008 Election," Pew Internet & American Life Project, 2008, http://www.pewInternet.org/PPF/r/252/report_display.asp.

12. Abbey Klaassen and Claire Atkinson, "Viacom Gives YouTube the Napster Treatment," *Advertising Age*, February 5, 2007.

13. Benkler, *Wealth of Networks*, 130.

14. Axel Bruns, *Gatewatching: Collaborative Online News Production* (New York: Peter Lang, 2005).

15. Jodi Dean, Don W. Anderson, and Geert Lovink, "Introduction: The Post-democratic Governmentality of Networked Societies," in *Reformatting Politics: Information Technology and Global Civil Society* (New York: Routledge, 2006), xvi.

16. Jean Burgess and Joshua Green, "The Uses of YouTube," paper presented at the annual meeting of the International Communication Association, Montreal, May 2008.

17. Patricia G. Lange, "Publicly Private and Privately Public: Social Networking on YouTube," *Journal of Computer-Mediated Communication* 13 (2008): 361–80.

18. Bruns, *Gatewatching*.

19. Benkler, *Wealth of Networks*, 212, 256.

20. Benkler, *Wealth of Networks*, 0.

21. Bruns, *Gatewatching*, 31.

22. Benkler, *Wealth of Networks*.

23. Benkler, *Wealth of Networks*, 130.

Notes for Chapter 9

1. Peter Johnson, "Moyers Hammers the Media for 'Buying the War' in Iraq," *USA*

Today, April 23, 2007; Steve Goldstein, "Political Turmoil at PBS, NPR," *Philadelphia Inquirer*, June 5, 2005.

2. PBS, *Bill Moyers Journal*, 2007, http://www.pbs.org/moyers/journal/04272007/transcript1.html.

3. Bernard M. Timberg, *Television Talk: A History of the TV Talk Show* (Austin: University of Texas Press, 2002), 96.

4. Pew Research Center for the People and the Press, "Audience Segments in a Changing News Environment," 2008, http://people-press.org/reports/pdf/444.pdf; National Annenberg Election Survey, "*Daily Show* Viewers Knowledgeable about Presidential Campaign," 2004, http://www.annenbergpublicpolicycenter.org/Downloads/Political_Communication/naes/2004_03_late-night-knowledge-2_9-21_pr.pdf.

5. Robert E. Park, "News as Form of Knowledge: A Chapter in the Sociologic of Knowledge," in *News: A Reader*, ed. Howard Tumber (New York: Oxford University Press, 1999), 13.

6. Society of Professional Journalists, Code of Ethics, http://www.spj.org/ethicscode.asp. Emphasis added.

7. Richard J. Schaefer, "The Development of the CBS News Guidelines During the Salant Years," *Journal of Broadcasting and Electronic Media* 42 (1998): 8.

8. Markus Prior, *Post-Broadcast Democracy: How Media Choice Increases Inequality in Political Involvement and Polarizes Elections* (New York: Cambridge University Press, 2007), 72.

9. Quoted in Ken Auletta, *Three Blind Mice: How the TV Networks Lost Their Way* (New York: Random House, 1991), 285.

10. James W. Carey, "The Press, Public Opinion, and Public Discourse," in *Public Opinion and the Communication of Consent*, ed. Theodore L. Glasser and Charles T. Salmon (New York: Guilford Press, 1995), 390–91.

11. Stuart Hall, "The Rediscovery of 'Ideology': Return of the Repressed in Media Studies," in *Culture, Society and the Media*, ed. Michael Gurevitch, Tony Bennett, James Curran, and Janet Woollacott (London: Methuen, 1982), 76.

12. Herbert Marcuse, "Some Social Implications of Modern Technology," in *The Essential Frankfurt School Reader*, ed. Andrew Arato and Eike Gebhardt (New York: Continuum, 2003), 146.

13. Roderick P. Hart, *Seducing America: How Television Charms the Modern Voter* (Thousand Oaks, CA: Sage, 1999).

14. Michel Foucault, *The Archaeology of Knowledge* (New York: Pantheon Books, 1972), 136.

15. Fredric Jameson, *Postmodernism: Or, the Cultural Logic of Late Capitalism* (Durham, NC: Duke University Press, 1991), 54.

16. Seyla Benhabib, "Toward a Deliberative Model of Democratic Legitimacy," in *Democracy and Difference: Contesting the Boundaries of the Political*, ed. Seyla Benhabib (Princeton, NJ: Princeton University Press, 1996), 74; see also Jürgen Habermas, "Popular Sovereignty as Procedure," in *Deliberative Democracy: Essays on Reason and Politics*, ed. James Bohman and William Rehg (Cambridge, MA: MIT Press, 1997), 35–65.

17. Henry Jenkins, *Convergence Culture: Where Old and New Media Collide* (New York: New York University Press, 2006), 224.